AF488694

Fine China

Cheryl J. McCullough

Copyright © 2024 by Cheryl J. McCullough

All rights reserved. This is a work of fiction. The publisher prohibits reproduction, distribution, or transmission of this publication in any form or by any means, including photocopying, recording, or other electronic or mechanical methods, without prior written permission. However, copyright law permits brief quotations embodied in critical reviews and certain other noncommercial uses.

For permission requests, write to the publisher, addressed "Attention: Permissions Coordinator," at the address below.

Burkwood Publishing Services
P O Box 1772
Albemarle, NC 28001-5704
www.burkwoodmedia.com

Printed in the United States of America

ISBN: 979-8-218-35410-7

Acknowledgement

A special thank you to my amazing team;

Barbara, Chris, Debra, Kendra, Kimberly,

Kristen, Nina and Sherry.

You each did your part to make this project a reality.

 Dedication

To Gianna and Hunter.

Honey loves you more than anything!

PROLOGUE

"Thank you, Sir, God bless you."

"And you. Take care of your family," he said as they shook hands.

He picked up the boxes, and his wife picked up the one bag with everything of value to them. She smiled and nodded. He looked at her, and they walked away, both their hearts beating rapidly. As six had done before them, they walked into freedom via making a delivery for Mr. Augustus Fine and the Fine China Company.

He knocked at the back door of the gift shop. A young woman opened the door, smiling.

"Yes, may I help you?"

"Yes, madam. I have a delivery from the Fine China Company."

"This way, please. We are expecting the delivery."

CHAPTER 1

Charlotte, North Carolina

Augustus Fine was the proprietor and buyer of the Fine China Company, a specialty mercantile. He sold china and fine gift items. His clientele were people like him, well to do. Those who could afford to be served their afternoon tea from a genuine sterling silver tea service and eat their meals on china.

The Fine fortune had been acquired through farming and the slave trade. Augustus' father and his uncle had bought and sold slaves for profit. Although they regarded the slaves as property, the Fine brothers treated them better than most slave owners. Their philosophy was to keep them healthy and garner more resources in the sale. In many instances, slaves were bought for the expressed purpose of making money on the subsequent sale.

While in school with a few students who were members of the "Religious Society of Friends," Augustus found he ascribed to many of their beliefs, and eventually formally became a member of the Society. He met Susannah through the meetings.

But much unlike his clientele, Augustus and his wife Susannah were abolitionists. As Quakers, they were opposed to slavery, and Augustus spoke out against the practice of owning slaves. While they had "help" on their plantation, they provided for their field hands and domestics.

Augustus made a trip to Europe annually to purchase china and the like to sell in his shop. Because the trip was expensive and the travel tedious, he seldom took his wife, but he was always accompanied by a staff of people, and his son Cornelius starting when he was thirteen. Because the Fine family's servants were taught to read, and some taught mathematics, the ones who made the trip with him were assets.

For this year's trip, Mr. Fine prepared two slaves to travel with him to Vienna, Austria. But a few days before they were scheduled to leave, he became very ill. Susannah Fine wanted him to cancel the trip. She knew Jacob and Bessie would be disappointed, but understandably, was more concerned about her husband. Augustus wanted to take them, but he was more concerned about his inventory and about the money he had already spent to prepare for the trip. He knew the ship's captain wouldn't refund his deposit. The best he could hope for was to postpone the trip for a few days.

"Sir, may I speak with you?"

"Sure, son. What's on your mind?"

"I can make the trip. I'm prepared. I know the ins and outs of the process, all the processes."

Augustus Fine looked at his son.

Cornelius Baldwin Fine, named for his maternal grandfather, was the older of the two Fine children. Hannah, his sister, was eighteen months younger. Cornelius was engaged to marry Beatrice Kenward. The Kenward family lived on a plantation twenty miles away. Augustus didn't particularly care for her father but agreed to the marriage because of the business contacts they could provide.

Cornelius was learning the business, and his father had taken him on trips. "I presume it's time," Augustus said with a chuckle. He coughed. When he could finally talk, he asked for time to consider his son's request.

Augustus and Susannah discussed what Cornelius asked. Susannah was reluctant but understood the financial ramifications of canceling the trip. Considering this would be Cornelius' first trip, Augustus was less concerned about the importing of the products than he was about exporting Jacob and Bessie. If anything went wrong with the transaction, it could mean disaster on many fronts. Perhaps even criminal prosecution for Augustus Fine. The sale and purchase of slaves was big business and the way Augustus and the network of Abolitionists were granting freedom to many was unprecedented. Slaves from the United States were being freed into Canada, Austria, Italy, Great Britain, and France.

Down to the wire, Augustus and Cornelius had a lengthy discussion and Augustus agreed to let Cornelius make the trip with one caveat: Tapper, Augustus' right-hand man, would accompany them as well. Tapper usually stayed behind to keep things running smoothly on the plantation when Augustus was away. But this time Augustus needed Tapper to handle things on the trip. He had to move quickly to secure travel documents for Tapper. The trip was delayed by only one day.

Augustus and Tapper had grown up together. Tapper's mother had served the Fine family when Augustus was a boy. Tapper learned to read and write and do mathematics just as Augustus had. Being an only child, Augustus was like a brother to him. Tapper married Mary, and they lived in the basement of the Fine's main house. Their daughter Grace was Hannah Fine's companion. The talk among the slaves was the first Master Fine was Tapper's father too, even though Tapper had a dark complexion and favored his mother. Tapper's mother had never married, and none of the slave community could say they knew her to "take up" with a man. Their further evidence, Master Fine, had been particularly fond of Tapper.

Tapper and Mary were the only servants who knew what the Fines, and their friends, did. They talked many late nights about being freed, but they knew there wasn't much chance that Augustus would let that happen. And the truth was, they didn't really want to leave. They had a decent life as it was, on the Fine Plantation. They agreed, though, that Grace needed to leave. She was smart and deserved what freedom could offer her.

It was 1824, and Quakers would purchase slaves and set them free. Augustus had done that a few times. His practice of releasing slaves to the network through his deliveries worked well. As the years passed, his son Cornelius Fine assumed the responsibility of buying for the Fine China Company and the responsibility of releasing slaves. When they didn't return, it was assumed they were sold. The story worked so well; the Fine family didn't say any different.

Cornelius and Beatrice were married and expecting their first child shortly after Cornelius made his second solo trip. At his father's request, Cornelius didn't tell Beatrice about the Quaker's network. Augustus didn't want her to tell her father. She didn't pay much attention to the slaves anyway, and wouldn't notice anybody being gone.

In the Spring of 1830, Augustus Fine decided Cornelius would make his last trip. The trips were not cost effective anymore. Passenger ships with cargo areas were now available and purchasing cabins on one of those vessels and paying to ship his cargo would save him substantial money.

Augustus and Cornelius discussed it one evening after dinner. Tapper listened as he fixed them a nightcap. Later that night, he told Mary about the discussion.

"You know what that means, Mae."

"I know, but she so young, jus' 20 years old," Mary replied.

"This be our only chance. Her only opportunity to be free." Tapper said to Mary, trying to convince himself this was the right thing to do. Tears were in Mary's eyes. Tapper pulled her into his arms.

"We might never see her again." Mary whispered as the tears rolled down her cheeks.

"Hush Mae. Ain't no use in cryin.' Grace deserves this."

Before Mary could really cry, Grace came in. "Mama, Miss Beatrice need you! The baby comin,'" Mary wiped her face and followed Grace upstairs.

It was a long labor and a hard delivery, but Cornelius and Beatrice's first child, a boy, was born very early the next morning. They named him Adam Cornelius Fine.

CHAPTER 2

Charlotte, North Carolina

The alarm sounded at 5:00, and he hit the snooze. At nine past five, the second alarm sounded. He stretched and got up. At twenty past five, he was in his home gym. Toward the end of his workout, he was on the treadmill, where he checked his overnight email messages and watched the news. Good news from the European markets overnight always got his day off to a good start.

The housekeeper would be in at 7:00 and have breakfast on the table by 7:30. He liked breakfast, and she obliged him Monday through Friday when he was in town. This morning there was a vegetable omelet, hash brown potatoes and French toast. At 6'6" it took a lot to fill him up.

At 8:30, he would arrive at the office. His executive assistant would already be there. "Mornin,'" he said to Robin, with a hug and a quick peck on the cheek

"Good morning yourself."

A few minutes later, they were in his office talking and going over his schedule for the week.

"Will hit two home runs last night!"

"Are you serious? I'm glad he's doing well, but man, I really wanted him to be a basketball player." They laughed. He shook his head.

"You obviously haven't talked to Rita."

"No, why?"

"Joy had a double-double at her game."

"Finally!" He stretched his arms wide and looked toward the sky. "Somebody is following in my footsteps." Their laughter was interrupted by a tap at the door.

"Yes," Robin said. Knowing it would be their administrative assistant who smiled, spoke and gave Robin the mail. Robin flipped through it quickly, handed a couple pieces to him, laid one on her lap and gave the others back to the assistant, who left the office, and closed the door.

"Last thing; you have a lunch meeting with Natalie and Natasha Joyner."

"Miss Nina's not joining us?" He asked, lifting one eyebrow and smiling a crooked smile.

Robin laughed. "That girl is too young for you!"

"Can't blame a brother for trying!"

Wilson Peters, Jr., was the middle and only male child of five. He was a standout college basketball player and played a few seasons in Europe before giving it up to run the "family" business. Fine Enterprises was the parent company for Fine Imports and Gifts, Fine Wines and Fine China.

The Peters family inherited what was originally Fine China. Wilson Peters, Sr., added Fine Wines and Tobacco. Wilson Jr. added imports and gifts because of living in Europe and moved tobacco to the import side. He didn't particularly care for the tobacco and it wasn't consistently profitable, but his father had been a cigar and pipe smoker, and worked hard to acquire the best products. Outside of the Fine Companies, Wilson owned a fleet of trucks, a courier service, a limousine service and two dry cleaners, one with a laundry mat.

His baby sister Robin was his best friend, confidant and basically ran the Fine Companies. His sister Rita oversaw the operations of the other companies. Both their older sisters, Judith and Jeanette, were teachers, as their mother had been.

None of the sisters were fans of Wilson's longtime girlfriend, Paris Motley. Paris and Robin didn't like each other at all. Rita tried to explain to Paris that Robin was the other woman in Wilson's life and they would never be happy until she accepted that. Paris chose to fight, and Robin obliged her. It made her happy when Wilson mentioned other women.

Natasha and Natalie Joyner were planning their strategy for meeting with Wilson Peters. They always had a game plan, but didn't really need to. He always made sure they had what they needed. He was chairman of their board of directors, and a major benefactor to their clinic. He gave them the building that now housed the Midtown Family Medical Clinic. Natalie, the youngest of the three sisters, was the CEO. It was her dream to open the clinic. She earned a Masters in Health Care Management, went to work in a hospital clinic and learned as much as possible. Natalie talked Natasha into working at the clinic on her days off from the hospital. Eventually, Natasha left the hospital and came to the clinic full time as Nurse Practitioner, and the clinic's nursing supervisor.

The middle sister Nina was a CPA and Natalie wanted her as the CFO of the clinic, but she had minimal interest in what was going on there. Nina was a dancer, owned a dance studio, and performed with several dance companies on the east coast. Nothing made her happier than being called to New York to perform. Dancing was her passion. She earned the accounting degree at her father's insistence. He said dancing was "not a real college major."

Nina made sure the clinic's finances were in order, but seldom showed up for meetings or had any involvement in the day-to-day operation. She took it upon herself to employ an intern, a college student usually, to handle the accounts payables, receivables, and payroll, to keep from having to do it. Nina loved her sisters and supported their dreams. They just weren't hers.

CHAPTER 3

Charlotte, North Carolina

With all the excitement of the new baby in the Fine household and plans for the christening, nobody seemed to notice that Beatrice wasn't taking to the baby, having basically handed him over to Grace, which was not the plan. Susannah Fine had chosen another slave to be his wet nurse. Hannah wanted Grace away from the baby, too. Not only for herself, but to protect her brother from himself. She knew and suspected Beatrice did, that Cornelius was in love with Grace.

When they were young, teens even, he showed an affinity towards her. Grace had confided in Hannah that they kissed on his sixteenth birthday on the back porch after dinner, while she and her mother were cleaning up. Hannah didn't care for Beatrice, but knew Cornelius couldn't consort with Grace, at least not openly, and God forbid he got caught. It seemed Beatrice's rationale was to keep an eye on Grace and take up a lot of her time by having her care for Adam.

On the day of Adam's christening, Beatrice seemed a little better. Her family was coming, and knew Cornelius would be on his best behavior. Her suspicions had been confirmed the night before. Cornelius went out for a smoke. The baby was fussy and when Beatrice sent for Grace, another slave came to see about him and told her Grace was attending to Hannah. Beatrice left the baby with the wet nurse and went to find Hannah, who was out for the evening. Beatrice was relieved until she walked onto the porch for some air and could smell cigar smoke. Walking across the grounds to find

Cornelius and meeting him coming back to the house, out of the corner of her eye, there was Grace heading to the basement entrance.

CHAPTER 4

Charlotte, North Carolina

"Are you crazy?" Hannah asked Cornelius. Her voice was a forceful whisper.

"No, Father made the decision that it's time for Grace to go. This is the last trip."

"And you're taking her, knowing you are in love with her and may never see her again."

"Hannah, never speak of this again." Cornelius left his sister's room without responding directly to her comment.

Hannah didn't want Grace to go, for her own purposes. Grace was her best friend; they were like sisters. In theory, Hannah understood the need for Grace to be free, but wished there was another way to make it happen.

Grace was around during all the christening activities. She helped her mother serve and attend to the details. Hannah observed her actions and body language around Cornelius, and his around her. There wasn't anything suspect about it. He was totally attentive to Beatrice. When it was time for Adam to be put down for a nap, his mother sent for another servant. All was well. After their guests left, Cornelius and Augustus had a cigar and nightcap on the veranda, and then Cornelius went in to Beatrice.

When the house was quiet and Tapper, Mary, and Grace were in their quarter's downstairs, they had cake and coffee and talked.

Tapper paced back and forth across the small room. Mary and Grace cried. The inevitable was here. They had one week left together.

Mrs. Fine had given Mary some dresses that belonged to Hannah to mend and alter for Grace. She also gave her a pair of shoes, a coat and hat.

All the other slaves Augustus Fine released were couples. This was the first time for a single. Discussing that fact with his father, Cornelius thought it was in their best interest to have a slightly different plan. He would accompany Grace to make the delivery. Augustus didn't like that plan. He thought it was too risky. But thought of an alternative. He would have the receiving family come to the ship to get Grace. The sale of a slave would not be questioned. Cornelius agreed with his father's plan, but he didn't like it. He wanted time with Grace. His sister was right. He loved her and would probably never see her again.

On the morning they left, Mary and Tapper prayed for Grace, put on a brave face and watched her wave goodbye. Both their hearts were breaking. The pain they felt was rivaled only by the pain in Grace's heart. Her only solace was to make her parents proud. She hadn't ever asked Cornelius for anything, but would ask him to allow a message to her parents through the network from time to time. He wouldn't say no unless it was absolutely dangerous.

Each day, as they sailed, Grace attended to Cornelius and the others, cooking, cleaning and serving them. But each night, after they were all asleep, he came to her small room at the bottom of the boat to see her. They talked. He told her things about business and money, specifically the Fine China Company. He agreed she could send a message now and then, and promised to let her know if anything happened to her parents.

On their last night together, as she lay naked in his arms, Cornelius told her he loved her. Before leaving her room, he gave her money. A lot of money. "Don't tell anyone you have this. Be careful how you use it. But when you can, make a good life for yourself."

"I will, thank you. I love you too."

On a sunny Sunday morning, Elizabeth and Samuel Hickson came to the shipyard where Cornelius Fine docked his ship, to retrieve the goods they ordered from the Fine China Company. Because Elizabeth was expecting their third child, she required the assistance of one of the servants on the ship to help her prepare the silver and china for her dinner party the following evening.

"This is Grace, who will be glad to assist you," Cornelius said.

Without looking back, Grace picked up the bag her mother packed for her, the money Cornelius gave her sewn in the hem of a dress, and put it on her shoulder, picked up a box of teacups and saucers and followed Elizabeth Hickson to a waiting carriage. Grace was somewhat relieved to see the driver. He was colored like herself. He climbed down, helped Elizabeth climb up, waited for Samuel who climbed up on his own, and then he helped Grace with her bag, took the box and placed it in the back of the carriage and then helped Grace into the back as well. In the back of a horse-drawn carriage, Grace Fine rode into freedom in Ontario, Canada.

CHAPTER 5

"The full board will need to see the proposed budget, but I'll support the new numbers, so we shouldn't have a problem getting it approved," Wilson said, looking at the papers in front of him.

Natalie wanted to hire another nurse, part time at least, and make their part time admin full time. The clinic was busy, and it was important to maintain their level of patient service. Volunteer doctors staffed the clinic, and she didn't want them to get frustrated because the support staff was insufficient.

Nina was at the meeting because the budget was under discussion. Wilson asked her to lunch. She accepted; without being asked twice. They didn't let her sisters know they were going.

"Why did you invite me to lunch, Wilson?"

"Why did you come, Nina?"

"Don't answer a question with a question."

"Because we need to talk about the other night."

Nina laughed. "No, we don't! Why would we talk about a kiss that meant nothing? Why would we talk about you wanting to go home with me when we both know Paris was at your house?"

He didn't respond, so she kept talking.

"Because otherwise you would have taken me to your house and made mad, passionate love to me all night. We wouldn't have left the house for 48 hours, showered together, and ate grilled cheese sandwiches in bed. You would send me roses the next day, then not see each other again for months, until we show up at the same event somewhere."

"Sweetie, that kiss didn't mean nothing. I kissed you because I wanted to. You didn't stop me because you didn't want me to stop." He let out a deep sign. My situation with Paris is…

"Complicated," they said in unison.

She laughed. He didn't. "It's been complicated for years, Wilson. I really don't want to hear all that."

"May I have the mixed green salad and add shrimp?" her attention turned to the waitress.

"Nina!" He said as the waitress walked away.

"Let it go, please."

On the drive back to the studio, Nina replayed the conversation with Wilson, proud of herself for not being on defense with him. They had been on and off for years, never establishing an actual relationship. He always initiated any time they spent together. Early on, Nina thought it was the ten years' difference in their age. They met when he hired her as a college intern one summer. She initially connected her sisters with him. And eventually surmised that his complicated situation with Paris was societal pressure. They were viewed as "the power couple." A well-known, well-respected businessman and a well-known, well-respected attorney. Paris and her brother inherited their father's very successful law firm when he was elected judge.

Most people disliked Paris initially. Her personality was demanding, assertive, and entitled. The truth was, she didn't care.

Paris had only one or two friends, didn't do girls' night out or weekend getaways. Nina was told her mother was the same way. But Wilson liked her. He called her sweet, said they had a good time together and had good conversations. His sisters agreed it was the sex.

The real story, unlike some of the women Wilson knew and had known, Paris didn't need anything from him. She had her own money, businesses, and interests. Her life did not revolve around him, and he liked that. He wanted a wife and children, so Paris Motley wasn't necessarily the right woman for him. Paris didn't want a husband or children, so Wilson Peters wasn't the right man for her. In comparison, Nina Joyner didn't need anything from him, either. She had her own money, business, and interests. Her life did not revolve around him. But Nina wanted a husband and children, and because he wanted that too, she was right for him.

CHAPTER 6

Ontario, Canada

Grace realized she was pregnant shortly after moving in with the Hicksons but waited until it couldn't be hidden anymore before talking to Elizabeth about it. One afternoon, as they were preparing to move her daughter to another room and rearrange the smaller room for the new baby, Grace confided in her.

Elizabeth didn't say much at first, but actually wasn't surprised having noticed the interaction between Grace and Cornelius. He hugged her as they were leaving the ship. They didn't know anyone saw them. Tragically it happened, but she thought differently of Cornelius Fine. Who would have thought him to be a "master" who would take advantage of his slaves? Thinking again of how they looked at each other. This was different. But it was still sensitive.

The only man Grace had been with was Cornelius Fine. He was back in North Carolina on the plantation with his wife, his family, and her parents. There wasn't anybody to tell him or her parents about the baby. The only way they would know is if Elizabeth or Samuel told the Fines. Even then, there was no guarantee Cornelius would tell her parents. Grace wasn't sure she wanted them to know. They wanted freedom for her to have a better life, not to have a baby out of wedlock.

Everyday Grace prayed for her parents, for her new life and now for her baby. Praying for a brown baby, so no one would know his or her daddy was white. Cornelius had black hair and brown eyes. If the baby had some of his features, maybe it wouldn't be obvious.

The plan of the Quaker system was for the freed slaves to move twice the first year and then to settle permanently. Because Grace was pregnant, it wasn't recommended that she move. The trouble with that, the Hicksons, were supposed to receive another freed slave. Elizabeth and Samuel discussed in detail what to do, and decided not to move Grace until after the baby came, and they decided not to tell the Fines about Grace's baby. They would let them think she moved on through the system.

A few months later, a brown baby boy was born. Grace named him James Tapper Fine. When James was six months old, the Hicksons thought it was time for Grace to move on. With hand-me-down things for her baby, Grace packed one bag and left the life she knew in Ontario and moved to New Amsterdam, New York, settling into the home of Margaret Muncy.

Margaret and Grace hit it off immediately. Grace found her very easy to talk to. Margaret was a big woman who cooked and ate big meals. She owned a dress shop, making and selling dresses to the elite of the area. Because Grace was a beautiful seamstress, the business grew, and Margaret gave her more and more responsibility. From time-to-time Grace would experience opposition from some customers. They didn't want "the colored girl" to serve them, not understanding "the colored girl" made the dress.

All was well. James was growing, and Margaret was doting toward him. He was a curious child and Margaret allowed him to be. She showed him flowers and birds and other outside creatures. The shop was closed half a day on Wednesday and under the auspice of doing errands, Grace, Margaret, and James would see their town, and the surrounding towns.

Over the years, nine or ten other people came through the home of Margaret Muncy, slaves who were freed through the Quakers network, but Grace and James never left.

CHAPTER 7

Charlotte, North Carolina

The evening of the day that Tapper Fine passed was the first time in a long time that Cornelius allowed himself to think of Grace. She deserved to know, needed to know. Mary came to him directly and asked if he could get a message to her. "I will try, Mary. I promise I will. But even if I do, it may not be safe for her to come."

"I understand," Mary said, with tears in her eyes.

It took several days, and Tapper was already buried, but Cornelius found out Grace was in New York. Now what to do? He decided he would not send a telegram; he would deliver the news in person. A business trip to New York would not be hard to explain to his wife or his mother. He confided only in Mary and his father the true reason for his trip. She cried, ever so thankful to know Grace was okay, and to know he would tell her she was missed and loved.

CHAPTER 8

Charlotte, North Carolina

Nina, Natalie, and Natasha met monthly on a Sunday for brunch. It was always the Sunday their parents went to Wilmington to visit their maternal grandparents. The girls would go now and then. Otherwise, Sunday brunch, after the early church service, with their parents. They took turns hosting. Natalie cooked, Natasha and her family cooked, and their parents cooked. Nina would take the family out for brunch.

Today was a very comfortable seventy-two degrees in Charlotte, with no humidity. They decided to sit outside. Nina loved this area of town. There were all kinds of "characters" in the neighborhood. A lot of the dancers who Nina worked with in her studio lived in the area. As they were seated, ordered mimosas and looked at the menu, a family rode by on bicycles, all four wearing helmets. Natalie and Nina laughed. They constantly teased Natasha because her family wore helmets and went on family bike rides.

The waiter walked over and thanked the threesome and wished them a good Sunday. "Thank you, but we didn't get our check," Nina said with a smile.

"No check, Ms. Joyner, it's been taken care of."

Nina dropped her head, smiled, and looked up at her sisters.

"Excuse me for a minute."

She went inside the restaurant. He wasn't there. It was his M.O. The flowers would come the next day. He just needed to stop.

Back in the studio office, Nina worked on her next two performances. The first rehearsal for the Queen Charlotte Ballet Company was slated for the next day. She was the choreographer for this one, but was dancing in the other with the North Carolina Classical Dance Ensemble. It would be hard to juggle two rehearsal schedules, but since the state ensemble was rehearsing in Charlotte this time, it would work.

With the paperwork done, Nina walked into the studio and turned-on part of the lights. She used the remote to turn on the music, not knowing what was even in the deck, stretched a few minutes and then danced a simple ballet routine. Very elementary, adding a Pirouette, and then another. Then a Pas de Valse and Glissade finishing with an Arabesque. Nina called this routine a stress reliever. These were steps she did and taught every day and performed mindlessly, but it caused her to concentrate on her body, and not things or people around her, or her life.

At home, Nina sat in the middle of her new king-sized bed, eating a bowl of cereal and laughing at her dog Oreo, a three-year-old black German shepherd with one white ring around his neck. When Oreo turned over and stood, Nina knew he heard something. The doorbell rang. Instinctively, looking at the clock, it was 9:49. "Who could that be? He wouldn't," she thought. Oreo walked swiftly toward the door, barking. Nina looked down at her clothes; leggings, T-shirt, and nothing else. Looking out of the peephole, her shoulders relaxed. He didn't. It was her neighbor.

CHAPTER 9

New Amsterdam, New York

Margaret opened the door to see a gentleman there with a kind face, sure he was lost and looking for directions or selling something. When he introduced himself, she gasped.

Inviting him in and offering him a cup of tea, Cornelius explained to Margaret the reason for his visit. She understood why he couldn't alert her he was coming.

As they talked, a little boy walked into the room. A brown child with curly hair and large, light brown eyes. He looked to be about seven years old. "Where's my mother?" he asked. Cornelius realized he was staring at the child. Margaret lifted her substantial girth out of the chair. "Sweetheart, can you introduce yourself to my guest?"

"My name is James Tapper Fine," he responded confidently. Cornelius cleared his throat before he could say anything.

"It's nice to meet you, James." Margaret met Cornelius' eyes. She reached for James' hand and led him to the kitchen for some milk. Cornelius had to gather his thoughts. He knew James was his boy, but he didn't know what to do about it. He heard Margaret tell James his mother would be home soon.

He had come to New York to tell Grace of her father's passing, not to deal with a son he knew nothing about and couldn't claim. For a couple of minutes, Cornelius turned his attention to Margaret and James. He could hear him reciting the books of the Bible. "Ezra, Nehemiah, Esther, Job…" He wouldn't believe it if he hadn't heard it with his own ears. James was a year younger than his son, Adam, but more advanced intellectually. That was thanks to Margaret and, of course, Grace.

Margaret came back to the dining room to freshen Cornelius' tea and brought him a piece of cake as they chatted about life in the South and on the Fine Plantation. Cornelius noticed James had a book. He frowned. "I am teaching him to read." Margaret had disdain for Cornelius Fine, for all white men who took advantage of the adored women in servitude to their families, especially for those who professed to abhor slavery. She wanted his father to know he would be okay without him. Margaret told Cornelius about the other families who had come and gone. He told her about the families who remained on the plantation as sharecroppers. They both agreed that the need for their Quaker network was done, and they were glad.

Cornelius thought momentarily about how intelligent Grace was growing up, grasping the things she was taught immediately. For a split second, he remembered the things they talked about when they were alone. He discussed things with her he shouldn't have discussed with any woman, certainly not a colored woman and a slave woman at that. No matter how much he loved her. He literally shook his head so as not to continue the thought.

Catching a glimpse of something pass the side window of the house, his heart pounded. Cornelius knew it was Grace. He heard the door open, heard her voice and then James' voice and then heard her call "Miss Margaret."

"In the parlor," Margaret replied. Grace came in, James hiding behind her skirt. She gasped at the sight of him, and her hand flew to her mouth. Their eyes held for a long moment.

"Hello," she said, composing herself, but didn't move.

"Good day," he said, standing.

Margaret stood as well, taking James by the hand. "We're going to the garden."

Hearing the door close, he reached to hug her, but she offered both of her hands. They sat with an awkward silence between them. Finally, Grace spoke.

"If you came here without telling Miss Margaret, something must be wrong."

"I do have something to tell you, but I think you have something to tell me, too."

Removing her hands from his and clasping them in her lap. Grace asked quietly, "how are my parents?"

"Your mother is fine and sends her love. Your father…" His voice cracked. He cleared his throat and continued, "Tapper has passed on." Grace immediately cried. He reached to comfort her, but she didn't allow him to. Amid her tears, asking, "was he sick?"

"No, thankfully he was not. He went in his sleep."

"I'm sure my mother is heartbroken."

"Yes, that's true, but Mary knows the Lord, and knows Tapper is in Heaven." Grace only nodded, and reached into her pocket, took out a handkerchief, and wiped her face. Cornelius looked at her. She hadn't aged, and was still beautiful. Her hair was pulled into a thick bun, but he recalled how beautiful it was down on her shoulders.

"How is your father? He and my daddy were like brothers."

"He is heartbroken as well. Very sad."

Grace cried again, but quieted when Margaret and James came in.

"Mommy, I brought you something!" James came into the parlor. He showed his mother a tomato. It was more green than red.

"It's your favorite Mommy!" She hugged James and held him tight.

"Thank you, son."

Margaret, Grace, and Cornelius talked a few more minutes and then Margaret asked Cornelius to leave, but invited him to lunch the following day. Cornelius wasn't accustomed to being told what to do, especially by a woman, but it was her home, and this was New York, not North Carolina. He wanted to ask Grace about James, but it would have to wait another day.

During their conversation, Cornelius told Grace about Hannah getting engaged and about the other people she remembered who were still on the plantation. He didn't mention his wife directly, but did mention he now has a daughter as well.

When Cornelius was gone, and James was in bed, Margaret approached Grace about her conversation with Cornelius. Grace cried a bit more while telling Margaret what Cornelius said about her father's passing. Margaret suggested she write her mother a letter and send it to her by Cornelius. Grace agreed that was a good idea.

Late into the night, Grace wrote the letter to her mother. There was a lot to tell, starting with the sadness about her father passing, and how much she wanted to be home with her. Over and over, writing, "I love you. I miss you."

"I know you sent Cornelius to tell me, and I thank you. There has not been a day that passed since I left that I have not thought of you both and not a moment that passed when you were not in my heart."

Grace wrote about the long journey to Canada, about some people she met, and told her mother about the Hickson family and about Margaret Muncy. She wrote about her job in the dress shop, thanking her mother for teaching her to sew.

Back in his room at the hotel, Cornelius lay in the bed thinking of Grace. He was aroused at the thought of seeing her. He was ashamed. He didn't feel the same way toward his wife. He had a series of thoughts as he laid there; get up, pack his things, and head back to North Carolina, or get up, get dressed, and go back to Margaret Muncy's home. Rising to his feet, he stood there for a minute. There was no need to do either. Margaret would not let him in, and the train didn't leave until the next evening. Either way, he would not get to see Grace and ask her about James.

As Grace continued to write, she was overcome with emotion. Margaret could hear her crying from the other room, but decided to let her cry. Once it was all out, Grace returned to the desk to finish the letter.

"Mother, one last thing to say before I close, as it is very late, and I must work tomorrow. You have a grandson. He is seven years old. His name is James Tapper Fine. James for your father and Tapper for my father. He is a fine boy. You would love him so much, and father would have too. He is learning to read and write already. Miss Margaret is teaching him many things. His birth was easy. The midwife the Hicksons had was satisfactory, but I so wanted you.

Cornelius arrived for lunch the next day with flowers for Margaret, a puzzle for James, and a China trinket box for Grace. "Thank you, sir," James said, without being prompted as he sat on the parlor floor to explore the package. Margaret went to the kitchen to put the flowers in water. Grace thanked Cornelius for her gift and lifted the lid. There was a small velvet pouch inside the box. She pulled the ribbon to open it. There was money inside. A lot of money. Grace drew the string to close the bag and put the pouch in the pocket of her skirt so Margaret wouldn't see it. A pin in the shape of a tulip lay on the velvet lining. It was gold. She knew because Hannah had one just like it. Grace looked at Cornelius and frowned slightly. He nodded yes and looked at James.

During the meal, Margaret asked Cornelius when he was leaving town.

"I'll leave this evening."

"I expect that you and Grace need to talk…"

He nodded.

Margaret continued, "I'll trust Mr. Fine, that the things you learn in my home will never be spoken of again; for the protection of everyone involved."

He agreed.

Grace and Cornelius walked into the parlor as Margaret and James went to the garden. She sat and nervously smoothed the folds in her skirt. He spoke first.

"I am quite surprised to learn about James. Did you know about the baby before you left?" "No."

"Have you known another man, Grace?"

She looked at him hard and didn't immediately answer.

"I don't mean to offend you." His voice was even.

Again, a one-word answer. "No."

"So, he is my son?"

Grace gathered her strength. He was not her master; she was not his servant. She was free and could say what needed to be said. "I mean no disrespect, Cornelius. Thank you for coming all the way here to tell me about my father. That was your only mission. As Miss Margaret told you anything else, you now know you mustn't speak of ever again. James is my son. We have a good life here."

"Yes Grace, you do. Please don't misunderstand my intent. When I return to North Carolina, I will tell your mother you are well. That's my only report. James is a fine boy. I am proud of him and will carry him in my heart. There is nothing to gain for me or you by revealing this information."

"There is nothing for James to gain, either."

"You speak truth," he nodded. "My family would not understand."

Cornelius thought of the conversation he and Hannah had all those years ago. Cornelius took Grace's hand and pulled her to her feet. He put his arm around her, and they held each other for a full minute.

"I love you, Grace."

She didn't respond.

"If this were another time and place, you would be my wife."

Grace still didn't respond. Just as they broke their embrace. Margaret and James came in. Grace walked out of the parlor and came back with a package.

"Please deliver this to my mother."

"I am glad to."

Along with the letter, Grace had quickly made her mother a cape and matching hat. Also in the package were handkerchiefs that Grace often made from leftover fabric. As they said their farewell, Grace knew she would never see Cornelius Fine again; and also knew James would never know his father. She knew in her heart, no matter how much Cornelius may think he loved her, he was going back to his life. He wasn't going to do anything about any of this.

CHAPTER 10

New Amsterdam, New York

On the return trip to North Carolina, Cornelius thought of Grace and James, and he thought of Beatrice and their children, Adam, and Rebekah. He was fond of Beatrice. He loved his son and daughter, but he genuinely loved Grace. He had since he was sixteen years old. He remembered their first kiss on the back porch after his birthday dinner, and he remembered their first intimate encounter on the ground by the pond near the blackberry vines. He closed his eyes and forced the thoughts from his mind. He looked down to see the package Grace was sending to her mother. He assumed it was something she made. Margaret mentioned Grace was a superb seamstress. He was very glad she was doing well and glad for James, too. Closing his eyes again, he vowed to himself to dismiss the thought of Grace and James. Not only would he never speak of what he found out at Margaret Muncy's home, he would never think of it again either.

Grace stood on the porch, thinking over the last two days. She never expected to see Cornelius again when he left her in Ontario, almost eight years before. Now she had, and he knew about their son. Tears swelled in her eyes thinking about her father, having missed him so much over these years. Now he was gone, and her mother was alone. As the tear streamed down her face, Grace decided to figure out a way of getting her mother out of North Carolina and move her to New York. She had money. Cornelius gave her money on his visit, not knowing she still had the money he gave her in Ontario, and the wages Margaret paid her for working in the shop. The cost would not be the issue. Grace just had to figure out how to make it work, and the timing was critical.

"Miss Margaret will help me."

CHAPTER 11

Mary was in the kitchen cleaning up after breakfast and heard the children laughing. Then she heard Cornelius' voice. Immediately, tears stung the back of her eyes. Drying her hands on the apron and walking into the foyer, they made eye contact, and he smiled. After a minute or two with the children, he came to the kitchen.

"Mary, may I have a cup of tea?" She fixed the tea, sat it before him and stood there, not moving an inch, waiting for him to tell her about Grace.

"Have a seat, please Mary. Grace is fine, very sad to learn of her father's passing, and sends her love. She lives with a very nice woman. Margaret is her name. Grace sews in her dress shop." Cornelius' voice was just above a whisper. He got up from the table and went to the porch. He came back with the bundle wrapped in brown paper and tied with string.

"Grace sent you this."

Mary slowly reached for the package. Her hands trembled. Finally, taking it from Cornelius and holding it to her heart, Mary let the tears flow. She was so overcome with emotion, Cornelius took her hands and led her to the porch, out the back door and down the steps to the basement entrance. By this time, her whole body was shaking. "Why don't you go to your room for a while," he said. Mary just nodded. Once in her room, Mary sat in the rocking chair, still clutching the package. The paper was stiff and made a noise as she lowered her chin to rest on top of it. Closing her eyes and rocking slowly, she inhaled, trying to capture her daughter's scent. After a few minutes, Mary finally laid it in her lap and slowly untied the string, and just as slowly opened the folds of the paper. First, seeing the handkerchiefs, one pink, one white with lace trim, one purple with satin trim and a floral one. That one was her favorite immediately. Glancing over at her bedspread, it was flowers too. Tapper hadn't liked it, but he indulged her. The same for the curtains. She had made them herself after Grace left, to pass the time. Under the handkerchiefs was the letter, several pages and folded in half. Mary held the paper to her heart and then tried to get her daughter's scent again. She moved the letter just for a moment to see what else was in there and saw the black cape and hat. It was stunning. Velvet on one side and satin on the other. The hat was satin with a velvet bow. Mary looked closely at the stitches. "This is well done. Grace must have a new sewing machine," noticing the quality of the fabric. Cornelius told her Grace sewed in a dress shop, so Mary knew the women she sewed for were well off, like Mrs. Fine, Hannah, and Beatrice. Standing, Mary placed the hat carefully on her head and then wrapped the cape around her arms, loving the way it felt. Then there it was, a whiff of her daughter's scent. The soap Hannah used to give her. "I guess Miss Margaret is giving it to her now," Mary said out loud, taking the cape and hat off, folding the cape, and laid it on the bed. Reaching for the letter, one of the other housekeepers called her name. "Be right there," she replied, and folded the letter and laid it under the cape.

CHAPTER 12

It had been a busy day, very busy, in fact, at the clinic. Natasha was cleaning up in the lab area when Natalie came in to tell her there was an emergency, a child who appeared to be having an asthma attack. Natasha glanced at her sister, snatched off her gloves, threw them in the trash can, and stomped out of the room. Natalie felt bad knowing Natasha was overworked, but the clinic was there to serve the community. But Natalie also knew they couldn't keep this up. She had to figure out how to get more staff, free staff, or, like she preferred to say, "volunteer staff," or the clinic was going to lose Natasha.

Of the three of them, Natasha was the most settled. She and her husband Jeff were high school sweethearts and married right out of college. They did everything together. They had two children and a dog. Nina told Natasha all they were missing was the white picket fence.

Jeff was a complete geek. He had a business setting up and maintaining electronic management systems for businesses. He designed and installed the clinic's system and assigned a technician to make sure it ran properly. He believed in what the clinic was there for. But amid all the information technology, his real passion was football. He was a college football referee and flew all over the country during the season to officiate games.

Natasha needed to get the asthma attack situation under control and get home. She and Jeff needed to talk. Their son Clark brought home a permission slip to attend spring work outs for football. He would be eligible to play in the next season when he entered seventh grade. Jeff was completely fine with him playing. Natasha was not and was prepared to give him the medical argument; concussions to Osgood—Schlatter disease to broken bones. The interesting thing was, their daughter Camryn was a gymnast, with some of the same risks. Except for the hits on the head and the concussions possibility, and Natasha was fine with that.

Natasha finished cleaning up the lab and walked up front to see flashing lights. It was the paramedics. The little boy needed to go to the hospital. If there was a doctor there, a trip to the ER wouldn't have been necessary.

CHAPTER 13

"Miss Margaret, can I get you a cup of tea?" Grace asked.

"No, thank you dear, but come in and tell me what's on your mind."

Grace came in with her tea and sat across from Margaret. "Can you get a message to Cornelius?"

"He was just here. What do you need him to know?"

Grace sighed before answering. "My mother is alone. I would like for her to come here, to live with us." Grace realized she had not asked Margaret if it would be okay for Mary to come. But if the answer was no, Grace would get a place for herself, her mother, and James.

"If it's alright with you, Miss Margaret, I don't mean any disrespect or to assume anything." Margaret looked at Grace seriously, not saying anything for a few moments. Grace sipped her tea.

"I should check on James." Grace went into the other room. Margaret leaned back in the chair. Closing her eyes for a few seconds, thinking about what Grace said. There was plenty of space. That wasn't an issue, but could it, would it work? She didn't want to get Grace's hopes up and not be able to accomplish it.

"Grace…"

"Ma'am," she answered and walked back toward the sitting room.

"Do you think your mother would want to leave the Fines, having been in servitude to them for a long time?"

"All her life… She was born on the plantation," Grace whispered. "I don't know, but I want her to. My mama should know James and meet you. We are very happy here, thanks to you. Miss Margaret, you have been a mother to me and a grandmother to James. I want her to know a better life, too."

As Margaret listened to Grace talk, the love in her eyes was clear, but also the innocence. She didn't clearly understand the ramification of her request. There could be consequences for the Fine family and for her if things went wrong. There was no way to know, even after all these years, if they may get caught. The Quakers believed what they did was right. They believed slavery was inhumane, and freeing slaves was their mission, but they also knew there were many who did not agree with their philosophy.

"Please give me a day or two to think this over," Margaret said to Grace with a smile.

"Yes ma'am. Thank you."

The following day, while James practiced writing his letters, and Grace worked in the back room of the dress shop, Margaret sat at the desk in the front and penned a letter to Cornelius Fine.

CHAPTER 14

After dinner and making sure everything was quiet and everybody was settled for the evening, Mary went back to her room, lit the lantern, and sat it on the table. Taking the letter from under the cape, sitting down, adjusting her glasses, and, taking a deep breath, started to read.

Page after page, Mary read, laughing and crying. The paragraph revealing the knowledge of James and especially his parentage caught her completely off guard. She re-read that portion of the letter. "Lord have mercy," Mary said and laid the letter down. Sitting for a few minutes, to digest having a grandson, and him being the son of Cornelius Fine.

"Please forgive me for not doing what you taught me. I know you are disappointed that I knew a man that I was not married to. Be assured he did not force me. We loved each other even when we were teens. I became aware that I would have a baby after I was living with the Hickson family. Cornelius met James on this visit. He had no idea. Miss Margaret told him never to speak of what he knows. I trust he won't."

For the first time since Tapper passed, Mary was glad he wasn't there to witness this. She had no doubt James was a fine boy and loved him immediately upon learning of him, but Tapper would be furious to know Grace had laid with Cornelius. Whether or not he forced Grace, it was a terrible situation. It would have been even worse if the baby was on the plantation. In her letter, Grace said he was a brown boy. Mary was thankful.

Grace's letter ended by telling her mother not to worry about her or James.

We are well. Miss Margaret says this is our home. We can live here as long as we want. James can go to school here, there is a school for colored children. I am not working for free; I am paid wages, and I put away the money. Miss Margaret just doesn't want the white customers to know. I know everything about the business, and I practically run the shop. It was a hard decision for you and Daddy to let me leave, but what you wanted for me, I have. I love you. I miss you. Somehow, someway, I will see you again. Please take care of yourself. God bless you.

Your daughter, Grace

CHAPTER 15

Charlotte, North Carolina

Hannah was on the porch, sitting in the swing. Cornelius walked up behind her and pulled her hair.

"Stop! What do you want?"

"Go for a walk with me," her big brother said seriously. She looked back, and seeing his face, climbed down and followed him off the porch.

They made small talk about the Fall foliage and such as they walked. When they were close to the lake, Cornelius slowed his steps. Hannah knew the routine; this is where they came over the years to talk about things they couldn't allow anyone to overhear. Their seats, two tree stumps. He brushed off one for her, but not immediately one for himself. He looked away, squinting at the sun. Hannah waited for him to share what was on his mind. A couple of minutes passed, and he sat. Looking at the ground and moving a rock back and forth with the toe of his boots, he started talking.

"My trip to New York was not all business. The main reason I went was to tell Grace about Tapper passing."

"You saw Grace?" Hannah whispered.

"Yes," he said and paused.

"Oh Lord," Hannah responded. "Grace lives in New York? How is she? Where is she? What is she doing?"

Cornelius held up his hand to slow her from asking questions. "Fine. Really well. She lives and works in the community of New Amsterdam, residing in the home of Mrs. Margaret Muncy. Her job is sewing in Mrs. Muncy's dress shop." He paused again and took a deep breath, blowing it out slowly.

"I can only imagine how heart sick Grace must be to know of her dear father's passing," Hannah said.

"Very much so." Cornelius told Hannah about his visit with Grace and Margaret.

"She is pleased to know you will marry in a few months."

"I miss her so much. Did you tell Mary you saw her?" Hannah whispered again.

"Yes, I did. Mary asked if I could get a message to Grace, and when I could locate her, I delivered the message in person."

"You still love her, don't you?" Hannah asked seriously.

"That is not important now. There is more to tell. The reason I brought you out here…" He looked up at his sister with sadness in his eyes. "Grace has a son, a seven-year-old boy; James." Hannah looked at him like she had seen a ghost. Cornelius continued to talk. "Hannah, he is a fine boy; bright, good looking, strong. Tapper would be so proud of him." Before Hannah could ask, Cornelius interrupted her, "he is my son."

CHAPTER 16

Margaret's letter to Cornelius Fine was carefully worded. It began as a thank you note for his personal delivery of the cake plate and matching serving utensils, and an inquiry if there were matching accessories, such as plates, teacups, and saucers. "These items are of great interest to me, and I desire to set a lovely table for the holidays." The truth, there was no cake plate. The letter began that way to camouflage the rest of the information.

Margaret did not mention Grace by name in the letter, only referred to her as "she" and referred to Mary as Mother.

"She wants Mother to join us for the holidays and perhaps stay for an extended visit. I hope you will accommodate her, as she has been sad since the change in the family."

That was an understatement. Grace was more quiet than usual since Cornelius' visit, but not necessarily sad. Margaret was not sure if the change was because of the news of her father's death or the surprise of seeing Cornelius and him now knowing about James. Margaret ended her letter by saying,

Please post to me soon to acknowledge the order, and include the cost.

Very truly yours, MM

Mary re-read Grace's full letter. Partly because there were her daughter's words and partly out of disbelief. She stood, laid the folded pages on the table, and paced the room for a few minutes, not really thinking, just being. Finally, Mary got down on her knees beside her bed and prayed. As always for Grace, but tonight, for James and for Margaret, and then for herself, asking God for peace, guidance, and to bridle her tongue. How would she look Cornelius in the face, knowing he had fathered her grandson? How was she going to look at Adam and Rebekah with all their birthrights and think of James being their brother? But Mary knew two things; Grace would take good care of James and it was best under the circumstances he was not growing up on the Fine Plantation.

The next day was tough on Mary. When Cornelius, Adam, or Rebekah were around, she thought of her beloved Grace and James. It brought tears to her eyes when Adam hugged her tightly around the legs, told her the stew they had for lunch was delicious, and that he loved her. Cornelius came into the kitchen to get the list for the market. He was as nice to Mary as ever. It was business as usual for him. He made no mention of Grace or the package. Mary was angry and wanted him to say something. When he left, she sat for a minute to gather her thoughts. He didn't know she knew. Grace said in her letter that he promised not to speak of it, and he wouldn't. He didn't realize Grace put the letter in the package. That meant there was no way of asking him to send a letter back to Grace for her. Mary was sad again. She wanted to respond to her precious daughter.

CHAPTER 17

Hannah was speechless. Of all the conversations she had with her brother, this was undoubtedly the most surprising. Of all the thoughts running through her head, none could be verbalized. Finally, Hannah said, "start at the beginning."

Cornelius told Hannah that he and Grace had been hiding out to spend time together since shortly after the kiss on his 16th birthday.

"We used to just walk out here by the lake and talk. Sometimes I helped her wash the linens or pick blackberries. Then one day we were over there, he pointed across the water, kissing, and I put my hand under her skirt. One thing led to another and we…"

"I know."

"Then whenever we could, we did, but not too often. Mostly, I would just look at her." Cornelius sounded sad. "Until we were adults."

"So, she was your first?" Hannah asked.

"Yes, and when I was courting Beatrice, I stayed away from Grace. But I wanted to be around her. When I knew we were getting married, I told Grace we had to stop. She agreed, but then when I came to know Beatrice, I desired Grace even more."

"Because you truly loved Grace and not Beatrice."

He nodded, and after a moment he said, "I love Beatrice, but it's a different feeling."

"Brother, I told you marrying Beatrice was a convenience for you and father."

"That is true, but I couldn't marry Grace!"

"No, you couldn't, but if you had courted someone else, not who father wanted for you, Grace wouldn't be a casualty."

"That is unfair sister, Grace is not a casualty."

"She most certainly is and now there is a child too!" Hannah raised her voice. Cornelius turned his back to her. Hannah sat patiently. This was not an unusual level of exchange for them. They continued to talk, and Cornelius shared more than he thought he would, or intended to. The truth, though, he was glad to get it off his chest.

"It may have happened the night of Adam's baptism or on the ship…"

"On the way to Canada?"

"Yes…"

"So that's why you wanted to take her," she interrupted him.

"Not completely. I knew I would never see her again, and I wanted to make sure she was released safely and into a good situation, and there was some business to conduct."

"But you also managed to bed her."

"Oh, Hannah…" Cornelius signed heavily.

They went back and forth over and over. He told her about the instant James walked into the room, and he knew in his heart that was his son. "I promised Mrs. Muncy to never speak of this information again."

"I will not betray you, brother, you know that, but you must promise to never return to New York. Grace must stay in your past," Hannah said, reaching for her brother's hand.

"Your words are true, my sister, and I promise."

CHAPTER 18

Robin called Wilson. "Natalie Joyner is on the line for you."

"Tell her I will call back in a few minutes from the car."

Natalie told Wilson about the asthma attack incident. "I need a doctor, or at least a P.A.," she said. "I know we can't hire full time and I appreciate the volunteers we have, but I need more regularity."

"Let me see what I can do, Natalie. I don't have an immediate thought of how to make this happen," Wilson told her.

As he drove, he thought about the desperation in Natalie's voice. She worked so hard, and he knew asking him meant all other options had been exhausted. Natalie also knew he would do his best for her. He had a thought. As he engaged the phone, he figured Natalie had already talked to her, but this gave him an excuse to call.

Nina was reading a text, and a call came in. It was Wilson. She finished reading the text and listened to the voicemail message Wilson left before returning the call.

"Nina, Wilson, please call me regarding the clinic." He sounded very business-like. She quickly ran through her head if anything had been forgotten. Nothing came to mind immediately. She called back.

"Hey beautiful!"

"Hey handsome!" She gave him a dose of his own medicine.

He smiled to himself but didn't say anything. "How are you?" He asked.

"I'm good and you?"

"All is well." There were a couple seconds of silence.

"Have you given any thought to the clinic needing a P.A.? I know we don't have the money in the budget, but Natalie sounded desperate."

Nina shrugged. "I'm not sure what you're talking about."

"Oh, forgive me. I was sure she had discussed the situation with you and Natasha."

"Probably with Tasha, but not with me." He quickly told her about his conversation with Natalie.

"I don't know how I can help."

"Are any of your rich friends' doctors?" He chuckled.

Nina laughed too. "Which rich friends are you referring to?"

"Your rich ballet benefactors."

"Wow! Um, let me think a minute."

She thought of one person and Wilson asked her to send him the name and he would do the vetting and set up a meeting.

"I will need you to be in the meeting," Wilson said seriously.

"Of course, I will."

Nina went to her desk to retrieve the information. While looking in her database, she thought to make sure Wilson knew the dance company couldn't afford to lose any funding.

True to his word, Wilson set up a meeting with Dr. Kasper Rasmus and his wife Alla. Mrs. Rasmus insisted they come to their residence for brunch. Wilson insisted on picking Nina up. Not wanting him to come to her house, she told him to meet her at the office. She barely made it before he showed up. When he came in, they didn't linger. As they drove, they discussed strategy, and Nina made sure he knew her priority was the dance company and would not be agreeable to giving up Dr. Rasmus' donations.

"Sweetie, I don't want his dollars. Natalie needs his time. The clinic needs more hours with doctors. You know that."

"What I know is, this is Natalie's dream, but it's becoming a nightmare for the rest of us." She ignored the "sweetie," comment.

Shocked at her comment, Wilson didn't really know how to respond, and didn't for a few moments. Finally, he said, "I didn't know you felt that way."

"I do. This whole clinic thing takes too much of my time. Natasha is overworked and underpaid, but Natalie is steady asking for more." Wilson had the feeling that what Nina was fussing about wasn't what she was mad about, so he pressed her.

"Well, I'm glad you shared that. I will make the board aware to look for your replacement. If your heart isn't in it, you shouldn't be involved. Midtown and its work are important." He was looking straight ahead.

Nina looked over at him. "Don't say anything to the board. I need to tell Nat and Tasha myself, and I need to be diplomatic about it, because as soon as she tells my parents, my dad is going to flip." Again, he wasn't sure how to take her comments. He didn't know if she was serious or playing him. It would have to wait. They were approaching the Rasmus' residence.

Wilson vetted the Rasmus family. Kaspar and Alla Rasmus came to the United States from Estonia when he finished medical school and was invited to join a classmate's practice. Their son Erik and daughter Aldona were born in the United States. Kaspar was an Internal Medicine doctor, and Erik was an ER physician. Aldona was a pediatrician. Alla was a music teacher. Their family dynamics would work perfectly for the clinic if Wilson could convince them to help and to top it all off, they had plenty of money. His concern right then was Nina's attitude. If she went in and wasn't supportive, there was no actual need to be here.

He opened the door and helped her out of his SUV and held her hand briefly.

"You okay? Nina, it's pointless for us to be here if we don't agree on why."

"I'm good," she said, and let his hand go.

The food was great, as was the atmosphere and the company. Nina and Alla talked about music and dance. Alla confided she wanted to dance professionally, but her dad opposed the notion. With teary eyes, Nina shared her story. "My dad told me dance wasn't a real major; thus, the accounting degree." Alla reached over to squeeze her hands. Wilson took this opportunity to move the conversation along.

He explained their dilemma, the structure and culture of the clinic, and went directly to what he wanted. "We need more hours per week with a doctor in the clinic." Nina spoke up and listed the paid staff and reinforced what Wilson said about the budget. He relaxed a little when she backed him up.

"You all are great supporters of the dance company, and we need you to stretch a little further," Nina said, and smiled. Mrs. Rasmus smiled too.

They talked for a few minutes and the door alarm beeped. Alla patted her husband's hand and left the table, returning to the dining room with a beautiful young lady. As she leaned over to kiss her dad, Alla introduced her as Aldona, their daughter. They shook hands and Aldona sat quietly for a few minutes before becoming involved in the conversation. After a few questions, Aldona simply said, "I'm in, and so is Erik." Dr. Rasmus laughed.

"You shouldn't commit your brother's time without his permission," her mother said.

"Of course I should. He doesn't have a life, and he owes me money."

Dr. Rasmus explained, "Erik and Aldona are twins. She is twelve minutes older, and has always been the more assertive of the two."

"And I sold him my car, but he hasn't paid me, so he can work off the debt!"

"Oh, Aldona, he has worked off that debt a dozen times!" Alla said. They all laughed.

At the end of the conversation, Dr. Rasmus and Aldona agreed to give the clinic some hours, and she assured them Erik would too. Back in the car, they talked about the food, particularly a pastry Alla served. "I will have to dance for hours to get that off my hips."

"Girl, leave those hips alone. I like what I see," Wilson looked over at her. He reached for her hand and rubbed his thumb across her thumb. She didn't take her hand out of his, but wouldn't look at him. Just as he started to say something, the phone rang through Bluetooth. On the display; PARIS. She held her breath to see if he would answer. Wilson pressed the button. Nina took her hand from his and looked out the window.

CHAPTER 19

Charlotte, North Carolina

A few days after Hannah and Cornelius' talk, a letter arrived for him. It appeared to be personal, and Augustus held on to it, until he could give it to Cornelius himself. He didn't want to risk Hannah, Beatrice, or Susannah finding it. After dinner that evening, Augustus asked Cornelius to join him in the yard for a cigar. As they walked along the grounds, Augustus remarked that these times caused him to miss Tapper. "He would have accompanied us, shared his wit and wisdom."

"You speak truth, Father."

As they walked, Augustus asked Cornelius about his trip to New York and took the letter from his jacket.

Cornelius told his father about the business side of the trip, and when they were a good way away from the house, told him about delivering the news to Grace that Tapper had passed on. Cornelius told Augustus how sad Grace was. He told him about Margaret Muncy and that Grace sent Mary a package, "probably something she made," he said as he explained her job in Mrs. Muncy's dress shop.

"I am well pleased that Grace is getting along so famously," Augustus remarked.

"I am also," was Cornelius' response. As they walked back toward the house, Cornelius read the letter from Margaret Muncy. He had to tell his father it was business.

"Mrs. Muncy wants to place an order for a cake plate and matching serving plates," he explained. We discussed it during my visit.

"Ah, good news. Please ship it right away, as she can use it for the holidays." Augustus said.

"That is her request."

Later that evening, when the family was settled, and the servants had left the main house, Cornelius sat at the desk, trying to decide how to respond to Margaret's letter. What she asked was a hard thing. While his heart went out to his beloved Grace, it would take some major maneuvering. It was not appropriate for a man to travel with a colored woman without the company of another female companion. He paced the floor for a long time, weighing the pros and cons of the situation. Finally, he decided that once again; he needed to talk with Hannah.

After breakfast, Beatrice was going to town to the mercantile with her mother and sister. Adam and Rebekah would play with their cousins at the maternal grandparents' home. "Play?" he thought. James was probably reading and writing, and in a garden learning about fruits and vegetables. He tried to do away with the thought.

After being certain Beatrice and the children were off the grounds, Cornelius went to find Hannah. He explained his dilemma after she read the letter. Hannah was quiet for a few seconds and finally covered her face with both hands. Taking her hands away, she simply said, "I can do it. I will take Mary to New York to see Grace. I can do what I wanted to do anyway, have Grace make my wedding dress."

"How do you think you can tell mother you're going to choose a wedding dress without her?"

"That will be up to you and father to keep her from coming with us," Hannah said sternly.

"Perhaps we can get Father to take mother away for a day or two. When you get back, you can tell her you wanted the dress to be a surprise." Cornelius was very serious.

"The only caveat, my dear brother, is if Mary decides to stay. You know she won't want to leave once they see each other and now with the addition of…"

"James," he said, nodding slowly.

They discussed the pros and cons of the situation, and concluded telling the truth would be the way to handle it. Susannah would just have to understand. The other servants would talk among themselves but not question Mary being gone. They always thought Grace had been sold and with Tapper now deceased, nobody would blame Mary for leaving, or blame the Fines for sending her away. Cornelius told Hannah he would talk with their father and ask him to tell Susannah. He would also write Margaret Muncy that they would deliver the package between Thanksgiving and Christmas. He asked Hannah to tell Mary. She agreed.

"Dear Mrs. Muncy, we sincerely appreciate your order. The Fine China Company is grateful for your business. We will deliver the order between Thanksgiving and Christmas. I'm sure your holiday table will indeed be lovely. Best regards, Cornelius Fine."

CHAPTER 20

Charlotte, North Carolina

A few days after Nina and Wilson met with Dr. Rasmus, a very tall, handsome, blond, blue-eyed gentleman walked into the Midtown Family Clinic.

"Morning! I'm Dr. Erik Rasmus here to see Natalie Joyner, please."

When Natalie came into the waiting area, she was stunned. First because she wasn't expecting Dr. Rasmus, but mostly because he was gorgeous. Natalie was tongue tied for a few seconds but finally recovered, extended her hand, and spoke. "Dr. Rasmus, I'm Natalie Joyner. It's a pleasure to meet you."

"The pleasure is mine, Ms. Joyner." His accent was noticeable, but not so heavy he was hard to understand. Erik explained how he ended up there today unannounced, and obviously unexpected. Natalie invited him to her office.

As Erik followed Natalie to her small office, she was glad to have dressed up today and applied a lightly scented lotion after washing her hands. Instead of sitting behind her desk, Natalie sat in the guest chair beside Erik, told him about the clinic, and asked him questions. The clinic needed his help, but he needed to be an asset to the culture.

They talked for about fifteen minutes. She gave him a tour, and then Natalie showed Erik the schedule. He told her what his availability would be for the next two weeks.

"My sister will come by tomorrow, and my dad at some point. Aldona's schedule is busy. Dad is retired. He has time. He should be able to give you significant hours. Take advantage of him."

"What does that mean?" Natalie asked seriously. Erik laughed.

"He has time and my mother, my sister and I would appreciate you giving him something to do, so he will stop creating things for us to do!" Natalie relaxed and laughed too.

"And Dr. Kasper, as we so affectionately call him," he said, laughing again, "has many friends who are retired too, and can give you hours. Some of them need to contribute, anyway! Helping some people who can't pay will be good for them." Erik smiled, but Natalie knew he was serious.

They talked a few minutes more, and he left, restating he would see her the next day. He thought as he left, "this is going to work out nicely for a couple of reasons."

Natalie sent Nina and Wilson a text message to say thank you and tell them she met Erik.

"You should respond first," Nina said to Wilson. "I hardly ever respond right away."

Wilson laughed and reached for his phone. He replied to Natalie's message and then pulled Nina back into his arms. He had convinced her to have lunch with him at her house.

CHAPTER 21

"Mary! Mary!" Hannah started calling Mary's name in a singsong voice coming down the stairs. That was what she did growing up. Usually, alternating between saying Mary and Grace.

"Woo hoo," Mary called in response.

When Hannah walked in, she realized how long it had been since visiting Mary in her space; only one other time since Tapper passed. They hugged.

"What can I get you?" Mary asked.

"Nothing, I need to tell you something." Mary motioned toward a chair. They both sat. Hannah didn't beat around the bush.

"Cornelius told me…" Hannah's voice was just above a whisper, and she was choosing her words carefully… "that he saw Grace." Mary half smiled, but didn't take her eyes off Hannah, who kept talking. "The lady who Grace was with wrote him a letter to say Grace wants you to come for the holidays."

"Oh Lord," Mary said. "Come to New York?" Now Mary was whispering. Grace knows that ain't possible.

"We're going to make it work, Mary."

"Whatcha talkin' 'bout Hannah?"

"I'm going to take you to New York. We talked to Mother and Father about it, and they agreed. And you can stay there with Grace if you want to."

"Whatcha mean stay?"

"If you don't want to come back home…" Hannah cleared her throat. "… back here you won't have to."

"You know I was born on this land, and I spent my life here. I never been off the Fine's prop'ty. I don' know if I can live anywhere else. But God knows I miss my Grace."

"Mary, she is fine, has a job and … lives with a nice lady, according to Cornelius. Hannah couldn't tell Mary about Grace's son. It wasn't her place.

"I don't know a lot about it, but I know I can't just leave here," Mary said, looking at Hannah.

"No, but you can travel with me. That's why I'm going. I want to see Grace too. I want her to make my wedding dress."

For the first time in the conversation, Mary smiled. "Yes, I know you would want that."

They talked for a few more minutes, and it was decided. Hannah and Mary would travel to New York by train. Hannah advised her not to tell anybody, and pack anything of value in case she decided to stay. "Get ready. I don't know when we'll leave."

After Hannah was gone, Mary made a cup of tea and sat to think. Never expecting to see Grace again, and when Tapper died, thinking that was the end, Mary was alone and always expected to be. The warmth of holding that teacup in both hands was the warmth she wanted to feel in her heart again. Being with Grace would give her that. That's what had been missing since Tapper passed away. Mary finished her tea. The sun was setting. She got a lantern, lit it, reached behind the curtain, and brought out a bag. "Pack anything of value," Mary recalled Hannah saying. There were only a few things.

The night before Mary and Hannah were to leave, Mary didn't sleep at all thinking about Tapper and how he would be so excited. But the reality was if Tapper was still living, she wouldn't be leaving. Looking over at her packed bag, and on the chair beside it was the skirt and blouse to travel in, and the cape and hat Grace made for her. She could hardly wait to wear it.

Mary watched the sun rise and when the rooster crowed, got to her feet, dressed, and went upstairs to prepare breakfast. It was her last official duty for the family. The moment was bittersweet. When breakfast was finished and the kitchen cleaned, Mary went back downstairs, changed clothes, and waited for Hannah. It was Cornelius who came for her. He carried her bag and walked to the carriage, where Hannah and Mrs. Fine were waiting. Cornelius and Mrs. Fine would accompany them to the train.

As they traveled the thirty minutes to the depot, Mary marveled at all she saw. In fifty-plus years of life, she hadn't ever been a mile off the plantation. There wasn't a reason for her to, and now, on her first trip, the experience was more than was imagined. It was overwhelming. When they arrived at the train depot, Mary was so nervous her hands trembled, and her heart pounded. Not only was this her first time off the plantation and first time on the train, but it was also her first time being exposed to blatant racism. A man younger than her daughter called her "girl," another called her "Auntie."

Before they left the plantation, Susannah Fine had hugged Mary, thanked her for taking care of her family for so many years and told her she loved her. Now Mary understood why. At the station, Mary was their servant, accompanying Hannah on her journey to New York to buy a wedding dress.

"Your maid has to go to the back," a very arrogant man said to Hannah.

"This is her first time on the train. I will make sure she's comfortable!" Hannah responded to him.

"No, ma'am, you won't," the clerk said. Hannah ignored him and walked toward the back car. Mary was right behind her, but didn't look back. Cornelius would handle it.

"My sister requires time with her attendant, and we appreciate you obliging her," Cornelius told the man, in a tone that didn't require a response.

There were only a few people in the "colored car," and Hannah found Mary a seat by a window. There wouldn't be much to see, but it was better than nothing. Mary had food and water in her bag. She would be fine for a while.

As Hannah was heading back to the front where her seat was, there was another lady appearing to be around her age with a colored woman, older than Mary. The older woman had obviously ridden the train before. Hannah heard the younger woman remark that she would talk to her when they reached Maryland. The younger woman hugged an older man and boarded. Sitting across the aisle from Hannah, they spoke and chatted briefly.

"Excuse me," Hannah said. "But I overheard you say to your… companion you would talk to her in Maryland. This is my attendant's first time traveling. I'm not sure she will know what to do."

"Yes, that is right. The colored riders can only use the bathroom on stops until we reach Maryland. Then they can join us as long as we allow them to." The lady laughed a little.

"Don't worry, somebody will tell her what to expect. They look out for each other. Probably be my Glory who tells her what to do. She's a busybody!"

Mary gasped when the train started to move.

"Ya first ride?" Glory asked Mary.

"Yes, ma'am." Mary replied.

"Well, jus axe me if ya need anything. I been on this trip nearly dozen times."

"Glory's my name. Pleased to meet ya."

"Mary's my name. Thank you. Please to meet ya."

"Where y'all headed?"

"To New York…" Mary had to think before saying anymore.

"Yep, been there 2 or 3 times. Gone to Phildefty this trip. Mosly whey we go. Yo Missus got kin in New York?"

"No. She lookin' for a weddin' dress."

"Lawd, hope you brung yo patience. If she anything like my Missus, take her days to make her mind." Glory laughed again.

Glory stopped talking when a white man came through the door. "Who you traveling with, girl?" He asked Glory, who simply said a name, putting Miss in front of it. He asked the same question to the other passengers, asking Mary next to last. "Miss Hannah Fine,"

Mary said politely. The man didn't respond, just went on to the last person.

When he left, Glory reached into her bag and took out a smaller bag with yarn and long needles. She was knitting. There was a big portion already done. It was yellow with a few small blocks of blue and pink.

"Missus having a baby," Glory said. "First one."

Mary thought of James. "That's excitin.'"

As Glory concentrated on her knitting, Mary kept her eyes on the window, wanting to see as much as possible; to take it all in. She thought of some things Grace wrote in her letter about her journey on the ship all those years ago.

After a few hours, the train made its first stop. Glory showed Mary to the restroom, and then they walked a few feet outside to stretch their legs. Glory was obviously older than Mary, but "very spry," Mary thought. They were back in their seats before the whistle blew for the first time. Glory resumed her knitting and Mary continued to look at everything they passed. She was a little hungry, but wasn't sure about taking her sandwich from the bag. Looking across the aisle and seeing a woman eating an apple, decided it was okay.

"Would ya have some?" Mary asked Glory, taking the food from her bag.

"Much obliged, but have something right here." They ate mostly in silence, and then Glory leaned her head back and closed her eyes. It was getting dark, and Mary knew she wouldn't see much more and finally dozed off.

The second stop on the journey was in the state of Maryland.

"Use the bathroom befo you meet up with yo Missus. You can sit with her but can't use they toilet," Glory said to Mary. Her tone was firm.

Mary waited outside the "colored" car for Hannah to come get her. Hannah didn't have her wait long. She wanted Mary to get a seat by a window. This trip was a new experience for her.

Once seated, Mary by the window, Hannah asked how things went in the back.

"Fine, no problems."

"Good," Hannah replied.

Alone with their own thoughts, neither Mary nor Hannah knew what to expect. Mary just wanted to see Grace and hold James in her arms. Her baby's baby. Hannah and Susannah said she could stay in New York. Not even there yet, but Mary knew she wouldn't leave.

CHAPTER 22

The first day Erik spent in the clinic was hectic, to put it mildly. One thing he determined immediately; Natalie's heart was in the right place and the clinic had major potential, but she needed more than a few free doctors. He also knew that if his father and especially his sister were going to help, the ship needed to be righted. The only option Erik had was to be perfectly honest with Natalie.

The door was opened, but he knocked anyway. Natalie looked up, and smiled, "Yes, Dr. Rasmus." Closing her laptop and looked directly into his eyes.

"May I?" he asked, gesturing toward the chairs in front of her desk.

"Yes, of course."

Looking at him closely, she saw an uneasiness in his face. "How was your first day?"

He didn't beat around the bush. "Natalie, the clinic has the potential to be a major force in this community, but the operation needs to be tightened." Natalie looked embarrassed. She couldn't think of anything to say. There was an uncomfortable silence between them. Natalie swallowed hard. Erik broke the silence.

"The Rasmus family is not trying to take over your business, but my sister wouldn't have made it through the day, and you need her." Natalie nodded. "I would like to ask my mother to come over and help you get more organized." He told Natalie what, in his estimation or opinions could be corrected. Erik chose his words carefully. At the end of the conversation, she agreed to meet with his mother. There wasn't a choice. She needed to keep the three Rasmus doctors. Wilson Peters sent them, and he needed to be on her side.

"Now, how about we get out of here? I'll buy you a drink." He stood and stretched slightly. She couldn't believe he just switched gears so casually. "Thanks, but I have plans," Natalie lied.

Over the next few weeks, Natalie and Natasha had a gigantic dose of the Ramus family. Natasha was grateful for the help, finally feeling like she was in a real medical facility. Natalie resigned herself to the fact that they were not going anywhere. Dr. Erik and Dr. Aldona in and out, but Dr. Kasper and Mrs. Rasmus were there Monday through Thursday, for at least four hours. Natalie didn't appreciate how much Mrs. Rasmus helped her until five weeks in they went on vacation for a week.

"I guess lunch will be peanut butter crackers and coffee," Natasha said to Natalie from the vending machine.

Natalie just grunted. It was raining hard and neither of them wanted to go out. There were a couple of patients in the clinic, and then a lot of paperwork to catch up on. Natasha walked away to see one of the patients. Headed back to her office, Natalie met Erik coming in the opposite direction with a big bag of what was obviously food. He followed her to her office.

"I know you don't want to get your hair wet. So, I brought you lunch."

"Thank you!"

He started unpacking the bag. "Where's Natasha?" Before Natalie could answer, she appeared at the door.

"I was not imagining I smelled food." She looked at Erik. "You are my hero!"

He laughed, "I know you two would be hungry before you go out in the rain."

"That's probably true, but what do you know about it?"

"I know water is the black woman's kryptonite!" He said it with great pride in the information. Natasha and Natalie laughed.

After they ate, Erik talked with Natasha about a patient. As he was preparing to leave, Natalie stopped him. "Since you brought me lunch, I'll buy you dinner."

"We can use my umbrella," he responded with a sly smile.

CHAPTER 23

New Amsterdam, New York

Mary finally dozed off. Hannah looked over and smiled. She was awake for almost twenty-four hours. When the conductor walked through to let them know they were 30 minutes from the depot in New Amsterdam, Hannah took a deep breath and lightly tapped Mary's arm.

When they were off the train, Mary's heart was beating so hard she could hear it. Cornelius gave Hannah specific instructions about how to get to Margaret Muncy's house. There was a car stand right outside the station. He told her to wait, not to walk.

Being very quiet, Mary drew the cape tighter around her shoulders. She wasn't sure if the chill was the weather or her nervousness. Hannah was a little nervous too; for a few reasons, including arriving at Mrs. Muncy's house unannounced with Mary and seeing Grace after all those years. They waited only a few minutes when a colored man pulled up and addressed Hannah.

"Ma'am, could I take you somewhere?"

"Yes, thank you." She gave him Margaret's name and address.

The man opened the door for Hannah and put her bag in an open compartment in the back. Then he opened the door for Mary and took her bag. He finally made eye contact with her.

In about ten minutes, they arrived in front of a modest home. The residence of Margaret Muncy and Grace and James Fine.

Tears welled up in Mary's eyes. She sat still, not so much because Hannah would get out first, but because her feet wouldn't move. It was almost eight years since Grace left. A long time. But not as long as they imagined. Mary never expected to see Grace again. As much as she missed Tapper, she knew if he was alive, this time would not have come.

The driver took their bags to the porch and knocked on the door. As he walked back to the buggy, Hannah paid him. He thanked her and tipped his hat to her and then to Mary. A second later, the door opened. Hannah knew this was Margaret. Cornelius described her perfectly. "Mrs. Muncy, I am Hannah Fine."

Margaret laughed loudly and opened the door wider. "Come in, Miss Fine." Hannah looked back at Mary, who was standing at the edge of the property by the road. Margaret stepped onto the porch and realized Mary was there.

"Should she go to the back door?" Hannah asked.

Margaret was surprised by the question, and walked out the door, pass Hannah toward Mary. Smiling at her, she said, "Mary, welcome. I'm Margaret." The tears that were in Mary's eyes spilled over her lower lids. Margaret squeezed both Mary's hands and walked her to the side door of the house. Hannah followed a few feet behind.

Margaret could feel Mary trembling and put an arm around her tightly. James walked into the room. Mary gasped. "Hello," he said, looking from one of them to the other. "I see you have more friends," he said to Margaret. That was what they called the people who came and went over the years through the Quakers network. "My name is James Tapper Fine! I will get my mama." Mary exhaled when he walked away. "Oh, sweet Jesus," Mary whispered. She would have known that child anywhere.

"Mama! Miss Margaret has friends here." Grace came from the sewing machine, walked to the kitchen, and stopped in her tracks. Her hand flew to her mouth. She closed her eyes, shook her head, and opened her eyes again. This time, seeing Hannah standing behind her mother. Grace started crying. Mary opened her arms and Grace practically fell into them. They held each other for a long time. Then Grace reached for Hannah, and they hugged for a long while. Margaret was standing aside and holding James' hand. After a few moments, Margaret said softly, "Grace." She looked at Margaret and then realized James was standing there with a puzzled expression on his face.

Grace kneeled in front of him. "James, I want you to meet someone very special." He nodded. "This is my Mama, your Grandmama, and this is my... my friend Miss Hannah." James looked at Mary and then he looked at Hannah, then he looked at his mother.

"She's your mama like you my mama?" Mary remembered Cornelius remarked how smart he is for his age.

"Yes, son. That's right." He hugged Mary around her waist. "Hello Grandmama."

"Hello James. I am so happy to meet you." He looked up and smiled. Then James took a few steps and said hello to Hannah.

Margaret walked away from the group to put the kettle on the wood stove, then asked everyone to the parlor. Mary and Grace held on to each other. They sat and Hannah sat on the other side of Grace. Margaret sat in her chair and James sat on the floor at Grace's feet.

When the teakettle whistled, Margaret asked James to help her. She knew Grace needed a minute. When James left the room, Grace laid her head on Mary's shoulder and took Hannah's hand. A little while later, Grace told James it was time for bed.

"Good night, Miss Hannah, and Good night Grandmama." A few steps out of the room, James looked back.

"Grandmama, will you be here when I wake up?"

"Yes, baby. I will."

Hannah, Grace, and Mary stayed up late talking, and when Hannah went to bed, Mary and Grace stayed up even later.

The next morning, as Grace walked James to school, Mary, Hannah, and Margaret discussed their day. "First thing, we need to send a telegram to Mr. Fine and let him know you are here safely. Then we will go to the mercantile." Mary looked puzzled.

Hannah spoke up, "You are here as my companion Mary. It's okay." Mary's shoulders relaxed. Margaret continued, "Tomorrow we'll go to Bergman to a mercantile with the best fabric. The folks there are accustomed to seeing Grace, and they let her move around the store freely. They know she works for me. Mary, you just stay close to me or Grace.

"Yes ma'am," Mary said, quite overwhelmed.

"Theodore will take us, and he will keep an eye on James after school. The store doesn't welcome children, and especially not colored children."

"Who's Theodore?" Hannah asked.

"The car driver who brought you here. He works for a friend of mine, a member of the society. I think he's sweet on Grace." Margaret laughed a hearty laugh. Hannah laughed too and covered her mouth with both hands. Mary just looked from one to the other.

A little later that evening, Mary and Grace went to the shop. Margaret and Hannah went to the post office. They sent a telegram to Cornelius. "Mr. Fine, the package arrived safely. It will be a beautiful holiday celebration here. Pray the same for your family and you."

The following day at the Bergman Mercantile, Mary was overwhelmed at first. She hadn't ever been in a store and hadn't been anywhere this large with this much stuff. Even in a household with seven people. The white people looked at her, but nobody said anything. They acted like she was invisible. Mary and Grace looked at white satin, silk, lace, ribbon and tulle. Mary quietly gave Grace her opinion, but couldn't verbalize her feelings.

As they looked at fabric, Margaret and Hannah looked at adornments. The store's proprietor greeted them enthusiastically. He knew Margaret would spend money today. "Miss Margaret, I see you have a new gal working for you. Business must be good."

"Yes," Margaret said and kept walking. The wooden floor creaked under her weight. Hannah was excited, and that made Grace happy. They looked and planned and drew a sketch. When they were all satisfied, Grace figured the amount of fabric, and Margaret placed the order. She told Mr. Bergman to have it cut and delivered to her shop the next morning.

"Miss Margaret, the pearls and other ornamentations are in the city. I can have them here day after tomorrow."

"That's acceptable," Margaret said, looking at Hannah, who simply nodded. The four ladies left the mercantile, went back to the house for lunch and then to the shop. A few customers came in. Margaret attended to their needs. She wanted Grace to enjoy her time with Hannah. Over the first few days they were there, James became Mary's door to the world. He read to her, showed her the vegetables and flowers in the garden. Grace thanked Hannah over and over for bringing her mother to New York and back to her. They took long walks, held hands, and talked. They cried and talked about Tapper.

For three days, they worked on Hannah's dress. Margaret thought Grace was a beautiful seamstress, but Mary was amazing. Her seams were flawless. Sewing seemed to make her very happy. The embellishments arrived as promised. It took Grace, Mary, and Margaret a full day to get the stitching done; all by hand. Hannah waited on a few customers to allow Margaret and Grace not to be interrupted.

On the fifth day, Hannah tried on the gown. Two slight adjustments and it was perfect. Standing before the full-length mirror, Hannah cried.

"It is so beautiful."

"It was made with love," Grace replied.

CHAPTER 24

Paris and Wilson had dinner with her parents. They did that from time to time. Wilson didn't care for the dinner dates, he did it for Paris. He also didn't care for the way Paris acted when she was with her mother. They were both so superficial. They talked about everybody. Mrs. Motley, who wore a variety of wigs, had the nerve to talk about another woman's weave. Wilson checked his phone twice before Paris said anything.

"Is something wrong, sweetheart?"

"No. I'm expecting a text from Tokyo," he lied.

The truth, Wilson texted Nina early in the day, but no response. He wanted to know where she was. He hadn't talked to her in days.

Nina checked out of the hotel in Manhattan after four days. She was ready to go home, but the long weekend had been exhilarating. It was a shame the other dancer, Reba, wasn't able to perform at the last minute, but Nina was grateful for the opportunity. Rumor had it Reba was a victim of domestic abuse. Nina hoped it was just a rumor. Reba checked out of the hospital at the same time.

On the ride to the airport, Nina re-read and responded to Wilson's message. She saw it when he originally sent it, early that day. "Why did he send it? Why does he 'need' to know where I am?" Trying to decide what to do, Nina exhaled loudly, and texted back; "Headed home from New York," and pressed send.

Wilson went to the man cave to watch basketball, and Paris was in the den watching the daily recording of "The View." He could finally look at his phone alone. He read Nina's text message. "New York?" he thought. "Why was she in New York?" He went to favorites in his contacts and tapped her name. The call rang five or six times and went to voicemail. He left a message. "Let me know when you land and let me know why you were in New York." The tone of his voice was a little demanding.

A few minutes after Wilson left the message for Nina, his text message indicator sounded. He reached for the phone, smiling slightly. To his surprise, it wasn't Nina; it was Paris sexting him a picture and inviting him to join her upstairs for half time.

Nina was home when she heard Wilson's message. "How dare his 'may as well be married ass' ask me why I was in New York!" In the middle of the night, when Wilson checked his phone, there was no response from Nina. He called several times a day for the next few days. There was no answer.

Natalie and Erik's first dinner date led to more dates. They didn't tell his parents or her sisters. She wasn't sure if Erik wanted to pursue a relationship with her, so from her perspective, there was no need to involve anyone else. What Natalie couldn't discern was if Erik was seeing someone else or if he wasn't sure about an interracial relationship. As much as they enjoyed each other's company, something was missing.

"It seems like my turn comes around too quickly," Nina said to Natalie on the phone. Natalie called to see where they were meeting for Sunday brunch. "Keep in mind you missed two Sundays."

"True." Nina had gone back to New York to fill in again. Reba still wasn't available to perform because she missed rehearsal.

Natalie and Nina confirmed their plans. Natalie promised to call Natasha, and they hung up. Nina really forgot about brunch. She had been busy. The trips to New York were great, but being gone caused her to get behind on things at her studio and at the clinic.

Brunch was good. They laughed and talked, caught up on everything, and ate and drank more than they should have. It was fun.

As they were getting into their cars, Nina ran into an acquaintance. Her sisters waved goodbye, and Nina stood talking for another minute or two. Unlocking her car, someone called her name. Looking around, she saw Robin Peters, Wilson's sister, and her son, Will. Robin remarked they were meeting "everybody" for lunch. "Everybody" was Nina's cue to leave, but she didn't quite make it. Without warning, he was standing there.

"How are you, Nina?"

"Fine, thanks. How are you?" The three of them chatted for a couple of minutes, and Robin excused herself.

"Nina, I've been trying to catch up with you. Why won't you take my calls?"

She closed her eyes for a couple of seconds, took a deep breath and said, "I don't want to do this, Wilson. We've been here too many times before. Make a decision and stick to it. And so you don't have to ask. Yes, I'm giving you an ultimatum."

"My family is waiting for me, but you and I need to talk. I will call you when I finish here."

She shrugged and reached for her door handle.

He opened the door, stood there until her seat belt was fastened, and watched her pull away. "Dammit!" he said out loud, walking towards the restaurant door. Driving away, Nina wondered if Paris was included in "everybody."

CHAPTER 25

Hannah Fine paid extra to transport her wedding gown with her on the train, refusing to be away from it. She sent a telegram to her father to let him know of her return plans.

On the ride back to North Carolina, Hannah had time to think about her conversations with Grace. They talked about James. Grace told Hannah that Cornelius was James' father. Hannah admitted to knowing. Grace came clean about all the years she and Cornelius had a relationship and told Hannah about being glad to be free of Cornelius. "I loved him, he loved me, but not the lie we were living," Grace had said. It was like old times. They talked like they did as girls. They were honest with each other and kept each other's secrets.

Hannah made Grace promise to send her a telegram if anything happened or if she, James, or Mary needed anything. Grace promised and meant it. Hannah gave Grace money and told her to keep it for James. "I will make sure you get more. I will send it to Margaret," Hannah told her. The last thing they talked about, Hannah put in perspective for Grace.

"What are you going to do if Margaret says you can't live here anymore? Where will you live?"

"Miss Margaret says we don't have to leave. We always have a home here."

"You have a good life here now, but what if Margaret passes on?" Grace admitted, thinking about that, but didn't know how to bring it up to Margaret. Hannah advised her against it.

"Margaret loves you, but will resent you for asking. Personal feelings aside, you work for her, and you live in her home. You owe everything to her. I will have Cornelius take it up with her. I will discuss it with him when I am back at home."

"Thank you, Hannah, but please don't bother Cornelius with this. He may not see the need to meddle in Miss Margaret's business. And I'm not sure he will talk to you about any of this."

"He will. I'm the only person he can talk to."

The change in climate was immediately noticeable the further south the train traveled. Hannah removed her cape and stood to stretch her legs. Looking out the window as the train came to a complete stop, she noticed the white people waiting on the covered gravel area and the colored people waiting on the uncovered area standing on the dirt. There was a little boy holding a woman's hand. Hannah immediately thought of James. Her nephew James.

At the train depot in Charlotte, Beatrice, Adam, and Rebekah were there to meet Hannah. Definitely not expecting them, she hugged the children and took both Beatrice's hands in hers. Beatrice was quick to explain there was a death in the community, and the rest of the family was attending the service. The family's servant, Paul, waited by the carriage. He had loaded Hannah's things carefully, laying the long unidentifiable package on top of everything else. Paul took over many things of Tapper's duties after he passed, including being Augustus' confidant. Before they left for the funeral, Augustus instructed Paul to pick up Hannah and that she was bringing back her wedding dress. He also made sure Paul knew not to mention it to Beatrice. They made small talk on the ride back to the plantation. Once they were home, Paul took Hannah's things in the house and one of the female servants unpacked everything except the wedding dress. Hannah freshened up, had a cup of tea, and waited for her family.

As the weeks and months went by, Mary settled in, and Margaret gave her more to do in the shop. Mary didn't ask for anything, so the day she approached Margaret "to ask a favor" there was no way to say no.

"I would like to make a wedding quilt for Miss Hannah and her new husband," Mary said.

"I'll do all the work. Get Grace to help me, not on your time. On our own time. But will need you to send it. Be much obliged, if you will."

"Mary, that is a splendid idea. You and Grace work on it here in the shop, I don't mind. And use any fabric you want."

A huge smile crossed Grace's face when Mary told her about the idea for the quilt and after dinner that evening, Grace drew a sketch based on her thoughts and Mary's.

Margaret walked into the parlor, where they sat with a concerned expression on her face. Sitting in her favorite chair, she asked what they decided about the quilt. Mary answered her, but Grace noticed her body language.

"What is it, Miss Margaret?" Grace asked quietly.

"I received a post from Mr. Cornelius Fine." Mary and Grace looked at each other.

Hannah only let her mother see her wedding dress. Susannah Fine agreed it was the most beautiful gown she'd ever seen. Her mother was satisfied with what was paid to Margaret Muncy for the dress. "That is a very fair price." Hannah didn't share that she gave Grace money as well. They talked about Grace and Mary, and how happy they were to be together again. "We will miss her, but being with Grace is best," Susannah said with a slight smile.

A few days after Hannah was home, she finally talked with Cornelius alone and updated him on Grace and James. He protested and pretended he didn't want to hear it.

"I don't want to know about what you're saying, sister."

"Brother, because you don't want it to be so, doesn't change that it is so." Cornelius held his head in his hands. Hannah continued to talk, mostly about James.

"I told Grace I would send her more money. And I told her you will make sure she and James and now Mary too have a place to live if something should happen to Miss Margaret."

"Sister! Why would you tell her that? I cannot get involved. I should have nothing to say on the subject." He hit his left fist into the palm of his right hand. Hannah did not back down.

"Yes, you can, and you should. Grace will not have a home, which means James won't have a home! You love her. How can you ignore her future? You think if you disregard James, he will go away? He won't."

Cornelius walked a few steps away from his sister. They were in the barn. One of the places they would play as children. He kicked a bale of hay. He picked up a rock and threw it. The rock hit the side of a stall. The horse whinnied. Hannah leaned against the barn door and waited. Cornelius turned back to face her.

"What do you see as fair, sister?" He sounded defeated.

"I don't have knowledge of such. You will make a good decision."

"I don't know if I ever told you my late husband built this house. He tilled those gardens that James loves so much. He worked on the loading docks." Margaret was staring into space as she talked. Grace was wondering what any of this had to do with Cornelius.

"We opened our home to many. Well, you know that for yourself, Grace."

"Yes, Miss Margaret. What does this have to do with Cornelius?"

Looking at Grace, Margaret told her the content of the letter from Cornelius.

"Mr. Fine wants to know what will happen to you and James and Mary at my demise."

"What?" Mary said and then covered her mouth. Grace looked at Margaret and frowned, knowing Hannah caused Cornelius to write the letter. She recalled their conversation and knew not to say anything.

Margaret continued. "There is no legal means for me to give you this house, as is pointed out to me in this letter. But it's yours. You and James are the daughter and grandson I never had." Looking at Mary, she said, "and you have become a dear, dear friend." Mary smiled. "Mr. Fine wants me to sell him this house so you can continue to live here, and so that James will always have a home." Mary's head was spinning. Grace wasn't saying anything, but understood more than her mother or Margaret suspected she did. Cornelius talked to her about many business things. Grace knew a little about wills and inheritance. He had explained to her how the Fine Plantation and the Fine China Company passed from his grandfather to Augustus to him and would pass on to Adam. Knowing that Cornelius owning the house meant it would stay in the Fine family, and also meant the white local officials could not make her leave if a white man owned the house and said they could stay.

"Miss Margaret, you are upset. I'm sorry the letter made that so. I am much obliged you have allowed me and mine to live in your home, and even more that you would consider us worthy to keep it. Do what's in your heart."

"Grace, I'm upset because Mr. Fine is trying to fix a situation he created and had no thought to change until his sister was here. I'm certain she influenced his decision to write me. His idea is acceptable, but he will have to agree that this home will always belong to James, and any children of his; not to the other Fine children."

The tone of Miss Margaret's voice was almost angry. She was right, and Grace knew it and also knew it would only happen because Miss Margaret would see to it. Grace admired Margaret Muncy. She was in the presence of Susannah and Hannah Fine and their friends all her life, listening to them talk, but didn't see them say the things to the men they said privately. Margaret said whatever she wanted! Grace knew Margaret was right. Cornelius was under pressure from Hannah. Otherwise, he would just live his life.

Grace left her seat, kneeled in front of Margaret, and took both her hands. Smiling, Grace looked directly into Margaret's eyes. "Thank you, Miss Margaret. Thank you for loving me, for loving James, and for providing for us." Mary nodded in agreement and pulled a handkerchief from her pocket to wipe tears. "We will honor your home and take good care of it. I promise." Margaret squeezed her hands. A few days later, Margaret wrote to Cornelius Fine and outlined the stipulations of her agreement to sell her home to him.

CHAPTER 26

Charlotte, North Carolina

Nina knew, looking at her friend's name on the screen, there was a "situation." She laughed and answered. "Good morning, Magnolia! How are you?"

"Hello Nina, my dear. I am physically well, not so much emotionally; actually, very stressed." Nina smiled and rolled her eyes. "You know my show is in ten days and my mother isn't well. She is in hospice. The doctors are keeping her comfortable but only giving her days to live. I must go and attend to her."

Nina sat up and was immediately sorry for rolling her eyes. "What can I do to help, Maggie?"

"I hope you will consent to finish the show for me!"

"Don't you join the troupe for one of the numbers?" Nina shook her head and frowned as she asked.

"Yes, but you can ad-lib the piece." As Magnolia described the dynamics, Nina was lost in her thoughts. She didn't have time, didn't have the energy, didn't have the mental capacity to take on another project.

As Nina tuned back into what Maggie was saying, she was giving her the rehearsal schedule. "Maggie, I really can't. I just cannot take this on."

"But you're the only one I trust. My people are good. Very good, but none of them have produced a show to this magnitude. I cannot be focused on Mother if I'm worried about the performances." Nina sighed loudly, knowing she would regret her decision no matter what.

"I need to leave today, but if you will come to rehearsal tonight; I will adjust my plan and leave tomorrow."

Another sigh.

"I will come tonight and make my decision."

As promised, she went to rehearsal and was absolutely impressed with the show Magnolia was producing. It was very organized, and truthfully, the routine could be improvised. Maggie needed her, too. Nina agreed to help, "this time because of the circumstances."

When Nina told her parents and her sisters at brunch what she intended to do, they couldn't believe it. But they all promised to be there to support her. Even her dad.

Fifth row center, they had great seats. Natasha flipped through the play bill as Natalie and Erik looked around, spotting the local celebrities and dignitaries. Natalie had recently introduced Erik to her parents. His parents were there too, but they were sitting somewhere else.

"Isn't that your board chairman? Peters, right?" Erik pointed to two rows in front of them.

"Sure is," Natalie answered.

Wilson, Paris, her parents, her brother, and his wife were in the third row. The Motley Firm was a benefactor to the Community Arts Association, and they helped sponsor the performance.

After intermission, there was an announcement that Magnolia was away, and Nina Joyner would join the troupe for the finale. Wilson hoped Paris didn't notice his reaction. He was stunned, cleared his throat, and stopped short of squirming in his seat. He didn't want to be here anyway and Nina performing compounded the issue.

He was holding his breath. It seemed like forever before she came on stage wearing a white costume, and the pale pink lighting made it shimmer. Nina sauntered onto mid stage on her toes, stretching her arms high above her head. Wilson could see that the bodice of the leotard was covered in tulle, and her nipples showed through the fabric. Was that his imagination? As she danced, he was mesmerized. He watched the shape of her hips and legs. Raising one leg straight up against her body, he became aroused, remembering her long legs across his shoulders.

The performance seemed to last for an eternity. When it ended, Wilson exhaled. He didn't even realize he was holding his breath. In that instance, he wanted Nina in his arms.

"I need to make some decisions," he thought.

When they got to his house, he told Paris he needed to make an international call. He went to his office and closed the door. He turned on his laptop and put his headphones on his head. Leaning back in his chair, he closed his eyes and envisioned Nina's dance. He remembered her dark skin against the white fabric and how her make up glistened. She was amazing; beautiful and talented, passionate about her craft, and worked hard to perfect it. He also knew how much she silently resented her father for not allowing her to pursue dance as a career. Many times, he told her he wouldn't ever do that to his daughter. Wilson checked his email, trying to decide what to do. After sitting for a minute or two, most of the time with both hands covering his face, he called Nina.

Nina didn't see Wilson until she was back on stage to take her bow at the end of the show and was grateful not to. The audience was on their feet with a rousing ovation. He would have distracted her for sure. Nina didn't actually see Paris, but knew that was how and why he was there.

Following the performance, Nina accepted all the congratulations and accolades graciously, glad to have accepted the invitation. Back in the dressing room, she called Magnolia, who was thankful for the good news and reported her mother had passed. Nina was even more grateful then. Her parents and sisters were waiting to go with her to the cast party. She didn't feel like going, but needed to, and wanted to tell them about Magnolia's mother. Just as Nina walked into the party, her phone rang. She didn't have to look; knowing it was him, but didn't answer. Late that night when Nina was home, she listened to Wilson's message. He complimented her performance and remarked how "pleasantly surprised" he was to see her on stage. He ended the message by saying, "I know it'll be late when you get in. But please call me tomorrow. Please Nina. We need to talk."

CHAPTER 27

Some weeks later, Miss Margaret received a post from Cornelius Fine. The documents confirming the sale of her home and the dress shop to him with the stipulation that James Tapper Fine and Grace Fine and their family could always live there, and Grace could keep the dress shop as long as she wanted. There was a place for her signature and a bank note included for part of the agreed upon sum. The agreement specifically stated the other Fine children had no rights to the property.

Margaret discussed the condition with Grace. The one thing left out of the thought process of Margaret and Cornelius was Grace could do the work in the shop, but the community would not support her being the face of the business. Grace brought these facts to her attention matter-of-factly. Margaret promised to address that to Cornelius in her return letter to him. Grace was satisfied they would handle it.

The response post from Margaret Muncy to Cornelius further disturbed him. He had the feeling Margaret was putting pressure on him because of her knowledge of James. But what could he do? She had the upper hand. In discussing it with Hannah, he expressed his agitation with Margaret. Hannah laughed. "My dear brother, you are overreacting. Miss Margaret is acting out of her love and commitment to Grace and James. She's only doing what we all, as abolitionist say we believe in."

"Be that as it may, I don't want to be this involved."

"You have no choice," Hannah said to Cornelius. He knew she was right.

Cornelius had to make this work without telling Augustus. His father would be furious about his indiscretion.

"Indiscretion?" He thought. This was not a tryst. It was a long-time, long-term love affair. No, not an affair, a relationship, a love relationship.

There was only one way to get this handled. Cornelius would have to go back to New York. He needed to talk to Margaret and find out who she trusted there, who was in the network they could turn to as the face of the business, so Grace could be a colored woman owning a business. Hannah admonished him to tell the truth to their father; at least what he shared needed to be true. Again, he knew his sister was right. If anything happened and Augustus found out any of the information, it would be best for all concerned if he wasn't completely surprised.

After dinner the next evening, as they shared a bourbon and a cigar, Cornelius told Augustus about his business dealings with Margaret Muncy. He left out the part about James. He made the transaction sound simple. Margaret wanted to leave the house and the business to Grace.

"Under the circumstances, that's not possible, so she offered to sell the property to us so that Grace could have it. She knew our family would want to take care of them." Augustus nodded as he listened.

"I need to travel to New York to complete the business, including finding someone in the network to be in charge. It is understandable that the patrons will not support a colored woman." Cornelius waited for his father to respond.

"Understandable indeed," Augustus replied.

"Your mother says Grace and Mary do fine work based on your sister's wedding gown. Women know about such things." Augustus chuckled and then continued talking. "Have you spoken to Beatrice about this?"

"No sir," Cornelius replied truthfully. "I see no need to."

"I agree," Augustus said, taking the last swallow of his drink.

"Your mother and sister are pre-occupied with the wedding; they won't question your absence for a few days. Finalize the business and return as swiftly as possible."

"Yes, sir," Cornelius answered, relieved not to have any further discussion.

After speaking to his father, Cornelius went in to Beatrice, and told her he would be away in New York on business for a few days.

"New York. I would love to accompany you on this trip." Cornelius was caught off guard. Beatrice hadn't ever asked to travel with him. He had to think fast.

"Not this time, my dear. There won't be time for shopping and sightseeing and the big city is not a place for an unaccompanied woman."

Beatrice asked Cornelius to reconsider. "One of the servants will care for the children. You can extend the trip a few days," she said.

"The servants will have their hands full with the wedding preparation..."

Beatrice interrupted Cornelius. "Is that all anybody in this house can think about?" She was being dramatic, and he didn't care for it. Looking at his wife with a scowl on his face, Cornelius said, "No different from when you were planning our wedding." She responded, but he stopped her. "There will be no further discussion on the matter. I will plan a trip to New York for the two of us at another time."

CHAPTER 28

New Amsterdam, New York

Their usual practice was to talk when Margaret was away from the shop, or on the rare occasion she was out of the house when they were home. Mary and Grace learned to do that when they lived on the Fine plantation. This morning, Margaret walked James to school. It was actually a colored church that housed the school in the basement. About once-a-week Margaret would take a basket to the school. Sometimes vegetables from her garden, apples, pears, or plums from her trees, and sometimes bread she baked. Today it was pears.

As Mary and Grace walked to the shop, they talked about what Margaret was having Cornelius do. Mary was nervous about the whole process. Grace assured her Margaret would see to it everything was done well.

"Cornelius won't fight Miss Margaret," Grace laughed. "He knows Miss Margaret will fight back."

"You know he's coming here," Mary said to Grace, looking at her seriously.

"I know, Mama!" Grace responded, but didn't look at her mother.

"Do you know how to stay away from 'em so you two won't make this situation worse?"

"Mama!"

"Grace Fine, I love James. Loved 'em before I ever laid eyes on 'em but be glad this work out wells it did. Don't go actin' on somethin' you can't do nothing with."

Throughout the day, as they worked, Mary hummed. Margaret talked or sang, but Grace thought of Cornelius and what her mother said. She didn't think of him much, but Mary bringing it up gave her pause. Grace knew they loved each other, but Grace also knew Mary was right. She trusted Cornelius, but her mother nor Miss Margaret did. Grace never fancied herself to be equal to Cornelius, but knew she was special to him, and expected him to do right by her. The reality was, though, he had done nothing for James until Hannah prompted him, and he wouldn't be coming except Miss Margaret practically demanded him. She told Hannah she was glad to be rid of Cornelius, and in that moment, meant it. Now, in anticipation of seeing him, Grace wasn't so sure.

CHAPTER 29

Charlotte, North Carolina

Nina waited three days before reaching out to Wilson, and communicated through text message. "My office 9:00?"

He responded, "I'll bring breakfast."

Wilson showed up with grits, salmon patties, biscuits, cinnamon apples, and coffee. He knew it was her favorite. The only thing missing were the fried green tomatoes she would add when cooking this meal at her house.

Sitting in the studio's small kitchen, Wilson complimented her again on the show and her performance. He also admitted to being surprised when she came on stage. Nina told him pointedly how her performing came about.

"Why are we doing this again, Wilson?"

"Having breakfast?"

When Nina didn't respond, he took a big swallow of his coffee. "We're doing this because I want to spend some time with you."

Still nothing from Nina, who held her coffee cup in both hands and stared at Wilson over the steam. He said what he usually did, but when he got to the part about his relationship with Paris being "complicated," she stood and started to clear the table. After a couple of minutes of her slamming the containers in the trash can, Wilson stood and reached for her. She stepped out of his reach.

"Nina!"

"Thank you for breakfast, Wilson. Thank you for the compliments. Consider this our curtain call. I'm done. I'm tired of waiting on you to uncomplicate your life. I'm tired of being single. I want a husband and children. Full disclosure, I want that with you," she said more softly, "but I won't wait any longer."

Wilson couldn't respond because he didn't know what to say. Nina had dismissed him before, but it was years since she said anything about marrying him and having his children.

"Leave please," Nina said.

"Please listen…"

"No. Please leave, Wilson."

She held the tears just long enough for him to close the door between the reception area and the hall.

For some reason, Wilson believed Nina this time. There was something in her eyes that said she was serious. The ringing phone interrupted Wilson's thoughts. It was Paris. He was sure this call was to tell him what they were doing for the evening. He didn't answer. He didn't want to talk to her. She cost him Nina. The "complicated" defense was true. Paris was not only Wilson's longtime lover; but his business partner, owning a portion of the trucking company, limousine company, and the courier service.

A few years prior, Wilson needed an investor to combat a temporary cash flow issue. He discussed it with Paris in general conversation. She offered, and the next day he accepted. Interestingly, they never really talked about it anymore. Paris hadn't asked for her money back or the profit, and it was off Wilson's radar, until now. If he gave it back to her and ended their relationship, she would fight him and probably ask for interest, on top of principal and profit, and would most certainly tie him up in court and cost him a ton of money. She was that person. Paris would not lose; no matter what. Wilson didn't like that about her, but just dealt with it. He couldn't explain why. Wilson called his sister Robin. He needed to talk and help to figure this out.

CHAPTER 30

Cornelius arrived in New Amsterdam, vowing to himself he would handle the business with Margaret Muncy and go back to North Carolina in a few days.

Upon arriving at Mrs. Muncy's shop, and seeing Grace, Mary, and James, he was sure he couldn't walk away so quickly. He would never admit it, not even to himself, but James and Grace tugged at his heartstrings.

He was genuinely glad to know Mary was settled and at home there. He told her his parents sent their regards, and Hannah sent her love and gifts. Along with the larger packages, Cornelius gave Grace a small drawstring pouch. There was money in it. She wasn't surprised that he gave it to her, but surprised at the amount. Late that night, Grace sewed it into the hem of the old skirt with the other money. Money that had been saved for years. Grace intended to give it to James. It was his inheritance. Cornelius often spoke to her about the importance of a legacy. She fully understood the impact, and without knowing it, Cornelius Fine was leaving an inheritance for his son, James Fine.

The night before the appointment with the lawyer, Margaret invited Cornelius for dinner. For the first time in his life, he sat at a table with only women, with colored people, and colored women at that. James sat at a small table a few feet away.

Mary served Cornelius as she had for most of his life. Grace served Margaret, then James, and then took her seat to Cornelius' left. His being uncomfortable wasn't lost on Mary or Margaret. Mary wouldn't ever draw attention to it, but she didn't know what Margaret might say!

After dinner, Margaret and Cornelius had coffee in the parlor. Mary sat in the kitchen in case they needed anything. Grace was in the back of the house with James. She didn't know when Cornelius left.

The business with the attorney didn't take long. He was a member of the Society and didn't ask questions not related to the transaction. He also didn't seem surprised to see the caveat of the home going to Grace and James. Cornelius told Margaret the addendum wasn't necessary, but she didn't trust him, and didn't care that he knew it. He left New Amsterdam later that day.

CHAPTER 31

Robin was furious with Wilson, and let him know. She absolutely understood his needing the money, but told him, "combining sex and money outside of marriage is a recipe for disaster."

"Why didn't you ask me for the money? Why didn't you ask anybody but her?" Robin seldom raised her voice, but right now was yelling at her big brother.

"Rob please!"

To add fuel to the fire, she called their sisters and told them about the "insane" decision Wilson made. The three of them were equally appalled. While he tried to defend his decision, they discussed a way to undo the situation.

Wilson finally got his sister's attention. "I have the money; I can repay her myself."

"Why haven't you?" His sister Rita asked.

"There was no need until now."

"Why now?" Rita asked again softly.

Wilson exhaled deeply. His sisters waited. Judith, Jeannette, and Rita were on the phone, and Robin sat beside him on the office sofa.

"I'm getting out of the relationship with Paris."

"Good, but why? And why now?" Judith asked.

"Nina, Robin said. Nina Joyner. The only somebody who can make you crazier than Paris makes you…"

"…. But for all the right reasons," Rita finished the sentence.

Wilson dropped his head. He loved his sisters more than life itself, but he hated when they were exactly right about him. Paris often commented on how they were too involved in his personal life.

"So what's the plan? 'Cause you know she won't go away quietly?" Jeanette said this time.

"I don't know yet," Wilson responded, which wasn't true. He had a plan, but chose not to share it. If they knew he had a plan, they would want to know the timeline. That was the part he hadn't figured out.

CHAPTER 32

James Tapper Fine finished school. He was almost sixteen years old. Over the years, he became a good gardener, and Margaret taught him how to buy and then sell at a profit. He gave the money to his mother, who put it away.

Mary and Margaret didn't go to the shop everyday anymore. Grace was very busy and needed help. James helped with keeping things clean and making deliveries, but she needed more help with the actual sewing. Margaret complained often of her knees hurting. Grace knew it was her age and weight, and Mary stayed around to attend to her.

A friend of Margaret's came to call one day unexpectedly, with a request that gave her a second thought. Since Grace came to live with her all those years ago, she had denied requests from the Society of Friends to take in colored families who were escaping slavery. Though the practice was now outlawed, there were still owners who broke the law and did not allow their slaves to leave. And there wasn't much the slaves could do. There weren't many people in power who would take their side publicly, and most of them had no means to go out on their own.

The friend told Margaret of a girl who was about seventeen years old. She could read, write, and was a beautiful seamstress. This was all too familiar to Margaret. Fifteen years ago Grace came to live with her, with the same "credentials," except she had a young son.

Mary sat in the kitchen and could hear the conversation between Margaret and her friend, thinking the same thing as Margaret. Just as the thought cleared her mind, Margaret asked her friend, "is this young girl expecting or have a child?"

Her friend frowned, "No, Margaret, nothing like that. I realize this is a lot to ask; your home is full," the friend looked around before finishing her statement, "but she will fit nicely here I think."

Margaret used both hands to lift herself out of the chair. Balancing on her walking cane, addressed her visitor. "I am obliged to consider your request, and will respond to you in a day or two." Margaret walked toward the door, indicating to her guest it was time to leave.

Late that night, Mary told Grace about the visit and the request. "I hope Miss Margaret says yes," Grace whispered to her mother. "She could have a good life here too, and I can use the help in the shop." "But don't ya think that mix up thangs when Miss Margaret pass on?"

"No, ma'am." Grace's whisper was forceful, and she grabbed her mother's hands. "This house and the shop belong to James. That's legal now. Cornelius and Miss Margaret sign the papers. Ain't no need to worry."

Margaret decided to talk over her decision with James. Mary and Grace noticed she had done that before. "I think it's a fine idea, Miss Margaret," he said. Mary had remarked to Grace that James was smart and would be a leader and in charge of other people, like his grandfather had been. Grace reminded her, "James is free, though. He can work wherever he wants to." Mary just nodded. Grace continued talking. "Mama, I know you don't want me to talk about Cornelius, but let me tell you this." Mary's face was expressionless. Grace was right. Mary didn't want to hear about Cornelius. "We talked a lot. He told me about money and business. Knew he won't spose to, but he did." She laughed. "Used to say I couldn't do nothin' with what I know anyhow. I never comment, just listen, and remember everything he told me. The money he give me, Hannah give me, I put it up. Savin' it for James. Even before Miss Margaret said for me to. Gone give it to 'em, so he can buy land and be a farmer. Sell food to stores and such." Mary looked at her daughter. Her daddy used to call her headstrong. That was one reason he wanted her off the plantation and out of the Fine's house. He knew she was bound to say something and get herself in trouble. Mary knew Grace meant what she said, and would convince James that was the right thing to do.

James accompanied their family friend Theodore in picking up two people brought to New Amsterdam, New York through the Society of Friends network. One of them was Ruth Austin.

CHAPTER 33

Charlotte, North Carolina

Paris frowned when Wilson gave her the cashier's check. Finally, saying "What do I need to do with this?" Her tone was casual.

"That's the money you invested. Plus, the profit percentage we agreed on. And I need your signature here. I'm buying back your interest in Fine Transportation." She looked at the check, briefly looked at the document, and signed, genuinely puzzled. "Just think it's time to get that handled," he said casually. Paris shrugged but didn't comment. She opened her portfolio and slipped the check into a pocket, zipped it shut and left the room.

Wilson knew her well enough to know the subject wasn't closed. Paris was surprised. A place she didn't care to be and needed to contemplate her response. He changed, grabbed a basketball and went outside through the garage.

After hitting 20 free throws in a row, Wilson stopped and thought about his next step. He needed to move his things from her house to his, and vice versa. He needed to tell her, not just disappear, but there were some things he needed to gather without having to debate her.

The garage door opened, and his phone rang simultaneously. He answered as Paris backed the car out. The call was business. She waited patiently and when he disconnected the call, simply asked, "Do you want salmon or steak with the shrimp?"

"Steak, and get me beer instead of wine."

"Got it," she said and backed out past him.

Driving to the store, and while shopping, Paris thought about Wilson's gesture, having actually forgotten about the money. "Robin," she thought. "His nosey ass sister, who's always minding his business." At that point, Paris dismissed the whole incident.

Paris cooked, they ate, and then played chess until time for Wilson's overseas call. "I'm going home to take my call. I'll talk to you tomorrow." He kissed her forehead, not giving her time to react or say she would go with him.

Wilson finished his call and then went upstairs to his bedroom. Looking around, he realized how much "Paris" was infused into his room. Truth be told, his entire house. He started picking up things and making a pile on the sofa. Walking into the closet, there were clothes and shoes. Over the next couple of hours, he went into every room and gathered her things and some things that were theirs. He didn't want to fight with her about things, and he found himself laughing about items he wasn't sure belonged to who. It didn't matter. He had to totally undo his situation with Paris if he wanted a chance with Nina. The thought of her brought a smile to his face.

Paris was baffled by Wilson's mood, but figured it would blow over by morning. They had plans for the weekend, which should help. He had been really busy, and a getaway was probably what he needed. Getting settled for the night, she remembered that her work bag was in his truck.

"I will leave in time to go by his house on my way downtown in the morning."

There was a car in the driveway that Paris didn't recognize. She eased past it and pushed the button on the garage door opener.

Walking through the mudroom into the kitchen, she could smell waffles. Wilson looked up from his plate. Probably a thousand times this scene had played out, but this time he didn't want it to.

"Hey babe," Paris said, smiling at him.

"Good morning."

"I left my bag in the truck."

"Where you headed?" He asked, getting up from the breakfast table. She leaned in, but he didn't touch her. Paris turned on one heel.

"What is wrong with you?" Paris raised her voice at Wilson.

They heard laughter before he could respond. Two female voices. Zora, the housekeeper, entered first, and a beautiful young woman behind her. "I'll take that. Oh, Miss Paris, how are you? Can I get you some breakfast?" Zora laid Wilson's dishes in the sink.

"No, thank you," Paris said. Zora introduced her daughter to Paris, who had been holding her breath, and was nervous about who the lady was in Wilson's home, and she could see him smiling at her. That had to be her car in the driveway. The four of them chatted briefly, and Zora and her daughter walked outside. Paris noticed the time. "I have to go; can I have your keys?"

"I'll walk out with you." Giving her the bag, he asked, "Can you meet me back here for lunch?"

"Why can't I just see you this evening?"

"I have some things I need to tell you, and the sooner the better."

Paris was absolutely puzzled, but didn't have time to deal with it right then. "I can't get all the way back out here for lunch and make my afternoon appointments."

"I'll meet you at your place at 6:00."

"Fine." At this point, she was angry, but wanted to gather her thoughts.

Wilson worked at home, just calling Robin for some information he needed. He only told her he had a repairman coming and needed to be at home. He found a bin in the storage room and filled it with Paris' things. He put another one in the truck to bring back what belonged to him. Meeting at her house was strategic. He wanted to leave on his terms.

The first thing he did when he got to her house was lay the garage door opener and keys to her house on the kitchen table. He was on the phone when Paris walked in. She walked past him without stopping and came back, wearing sweats, a t-shirt and no shoes. She saw the bin and walked right by it, but stopped in her tracks, noticing the keys and garage door opener.
"Wilson, what the hell is going on?"

He took a deep breath. "Paris, you and I have run our course. I'm not happy, and I don't want to do this anymore." His voice was steady. It was obvious she was shocked, but recovered quickly. "Years in and you decide you're not happy. What's really the problem, Wilson?"

"When we were good, we were good, but I've hit a plateau, and don't see a future with you."

Paris knew Wilson well and knew he didn't act on anything haphazardly. She really didn't know what to say or do. Paris was hurt. She loved Wilson, but if his mind was made up, there was very little chance of changing it. "Let's deal with this after we get back. We have invested a lot of time, a lot of life, into each other. I love you. I'm not willing to just give up or walk away without unpacking this some more." Her voice was steady, too. They were both quiet for a few minutes. Wilson finally broke the silence.

"You can go if you want to. Everything's covered, but I'm not going."

Paris started to reply, but he interrupted her.

Pointing to the bins, he said, "your clothes and stuff are in there, and I packed up my things out of the bedroom. If you're missing anything, let me know and if I left anything, I will get it later."

He rose to his feet and started out the door. Paris was right on his heels. He wasn't going to ask for the keys or garage door remote. He would just replace them. He put the bin in the truck and turned around just in time to see Paris throw the garage door opener and keys at him. Because his reflexes were quick, he caught the remote before it hit the window, but the keys hit the pavement.

Paris couldn't sleep. This had come out of nowhere, and this time, she couldn't blame Robin. This was something else. In all their years together, they hadn't ever had a real fight. There had been a couple of "separations" but never to the extent of giving back keys and bringing back clothes. Wilson was a good man. Her mother even said he wasn't like her father; he wasn't philandering, he didn't even flirt with other women. She laid there looking at the ceiling for a long time, honestly not knowing what to do.

In the office the next morning, Paris told her brother the whole story, and asked if he had heard from Wilson. To keep their relationships compartmentalized, Wilson engaged Paris' brother as his attorney. "No. We aren't working on anything, so I'm not surprised I haven't heard from him. If he was severing our arrangement, he would have to put it in writing, anyway. He wouldn't have to call."

Paris exhaled loudly. She was grasping at straws.

"Give him a few days," her brother told her, "then call him."

Wilson spent the next couple of days changing passwords on accounts, and requesting new cards, and account numbers. He transferred her half the money in a joint account they had and closed it. Robin continuously cautioned Wilson about his "entanglements" with Paris. He never gave it much thought. He knew Paris wasn't Robin's favorite person. But through this process, he realized his sister was right. Being extra diligent, he had everything covered. Now he could go to Nina with a clear head—and heart.

CHAPTER 34

New Amsterdam, New York

Margaret eventually agreed to receive the new lady into her home. It took some doing, but they rearranged things and made it work. James and Theodore made a space for James to sleep in a corner of the back porch. Theodore was around a lot more recently.

Ruth was nervous as expected, but became friends with James immediately, being about the same age. She warmed up to Mary and Grace, but seemed intimidated by Margaret. James assured her there was nothing to worry about. "If she was a bad person, you wouldna been able to come."

The thing they all noticed about Ruth immediately was her very dark complexion. Mary and Grace were brown, the color of a paper bag, and James a caramel color, but Ruth's skin was the color of coffee with no milk. Ruth was polite and unassuming. She was also a little overwhelmed with all the goings on in Miss Margaret's house. James was immediately smitten with her, and took it upon himself to show her the ropes.

As the first few days and then weeks went by, Ruth was given more responsibility in the shop. She really sewed well, and Grace was thankful for the help. There was also a transition going on at the shop. Margaret had brought in a new "manager," a white woman, who she wanted to be in charge so there wouldn't be a problem for Grace and James.

They all knew this would happen eventually, but Margaret sprang it on them. Her name was Eleanor. She was nice enough, and there to do a job. About a month in, James told Margaret that he didn't think Eleanor was a good fit for the shop.

Eleanor Macy was a member of the Society of Friends, who Margaret had known most of her life. Her mother and Margaret were friends. Eleanor was smart and committed to the work of the Society. Margaret trusted her and knew her affairs would be cared for.

"That boy jus like his mama. Talk too much. Lawd a mercy," Mary said. The only person in the room was Ruth.

"Miss Mary, a man 'spose to speak his mind."

"Not a colored man."

"Yes, ma'am colored men too." Mary looked over her shoulder at Ruth, not knowing where that notion came from. She was more like Grace than Mary wanted her to be.

Later that same evening, Ruth was helping James in the garden. Her voice was low, telling him about the conversation with his grandmother. He listened as he showed her the difference between the two types of lettuce.

"James, you gone do good 'cause you a thinker. My daddy say a man with a strong mind not jus' strong back get by in this world."

"Why you leave yo daddy?"

Ruth looked sad. "Cause Massa Austin's son was payin' me too much 'tention. My daddy say he don't want no trouble and he don't want no white blood in his family." James stopped what he was doing and looked at Ruth.

"My daddy a white man," James said soberly.

"I knowed that when I first saw ya. My daddy and granddaddy colored men and proud."

"My mama don't think I know, but Miss Margaret told me."

"My great granddaddy African," Ruth said, squaring her shoulders.

"That why yo skin so dark?" James put his hand next to Ruth's.

"Yes," said Ruth softly.

"My granddaddy colored, but his daddy white."

Ruth nodded knowingly.

"So, you sayin' if I wanna marry you, yo daddy won't like it cause I got white blood?

Ruth smiled. "I'm sayin, if you wanna marry me James Fine, you axe me proper, no mind 'bout blood."

James nodded and turned back to his vegetables.

Theodore Miller came to New Amsterdam from Boston. He was born free. His parents had worked for the Miller family all their lives and all his life. He was sent to New York with the Miller's son, who was attending seminary. After Reverend Miller graduated and settled in New Amsterdam, he gave Theodore charge of his church. Theodore kept the grounds, cleaned, and handled the maintenance. Because he was so efficient, he had time to do other things, so he provided transportation in the community.

Theodore had been keeping company with Grace Fine most of her time living with Miss Margaret. She liked him, but thought adding him to her already complicated life was too much to think about. Of late, being with him wasn't so challenging anymore. Ruth asked her one day if Theodore proposed to her what would she say. Grace laughed.

"I don't know."

"Ya need to think 'bout it."

Ruth was right. Two Sundays later, he asked. Grace said yes. Shortly after, they were married, and she moved into Theodore's house. For the first time, James and Grace lived apart. Though they were within walking distance of each other, the dynamic of Margaret's house and of all their relationships changed. Although not realizing it, Mary worried if Margaret died, and Grace no longer lived there, what would become of the house that was supposed to belong to James?

Six months after getting married, Grace and Theodore told the family they were expecting a baby. Mary and Margaret were thrilled. James and Ruth were surprised; shocked, in fact. He was nineteen years old, and never expected to have a sibling. The emotion was overwhelming. He felt a sense of responsibility that was foreign to him.

Very early on a Sunday morning, seven months later, Theodore came to get Mary.

"The baby coming Miss Mary!"

The birth of Rose Mary Miller brought an energy to all their lives. Mary and Margaret kept the baby. Grace and Ruth went to work, and James and Theodore helped between at the shop and their other jobs. And Eleanor was around.

For Rose's first birthday, the family had a big party. For her second birthday, James proposed to Ruth. She said yes.

Mary made Ruth a beautiful white dress. Margaret gave James her wedding band to give Ruth. The only thing Ruth wanted that she didn't have was her parents. Knowing they couldn't come, but wishing to at least get a message to them. Grace felt the pang in her heart. She knew how Ruth felt, having longed for her parents while away from them, and remembering how much she wanted them to know when James was born. Grace didn't know what to do. Her first thought was Cornelius; to ask Miss Margaret to write him and have him contact the Austins. They would tell Ruth's parents. Her second thought was, ask Theodore to have Reverend Miller send a telegram to the Austins. "Theodore is my husband," she thought. "Cornelius is out of my life."

Reverend Miller agreed immediately to reach out to The Austins with the news of Ruth and James getting married. Two days later, he brought a telegram to the shop and gave it to Ruth.

"Congratulations on your marriage. Our love always, Elias, Sallie, Lemuel and Emerline." Lemuel and Emerline were Ruth's parents. She cried hard.

Two years after James and Ruth were married, Margaret Muncy died. She went to bed one night and did not wake up the next morning. James was the most devastated. This was the first time in his life he experienced death. Margaret had been as consistent in his life as his mother. For days, he threw himself into his gardening. One of the last things Margaret had done was buy an acre of land for James to work. The garden in her backyard and on the adjacent lot were no longer adequate. He told Ruth he was going to plant flowers "all colors" in the backyard garden, to remind him of Margaret. For the first time, they were all glad Eleanor was there. Margaret left detailed instructions for her memorial service and business affairs. Eleanor was the one who could execute everything.

At the memorial service, Reverend Miller talked about Margaret's love for people and her social activism. Grace wiped tears. Mary held her hand and James covered his face with both his hands from their seats in the third row. Eleanor made sure the seating arrangements were exactly as Margaret wanted them. In a quiet moment, Eleanor told James that he and his mom were Margaret's family, but it was not appropriate for them to sit in the front row.

"Becuz we colored..." Eleanor didn't answer... "I know I'm right."

Immediately after Margaret's death, business in the shop slowed down. Only a handful of regular customers came, mostly members from the Society of Friends. Mary stayed home with Rose, and some days, Ruth stayed and helped James in the garden. He was doing well, selling vegetables to a regular group of people, and to one restaurant. Theodore fixed up an old truck he had and on Saturday they would park at the church and sell from the back of the truck.

Ruth had an idea she talked over with Mary.

"I'm gone arrange flowers in these here pots, and sell out the back a da truck too."

"They's pretty, but you needa talk to James' bout it."

"He be fine!" Ruth laughed.

The first Saturday, Ruth joined them, she sold out, and took an order for a birthday party the next weekend. For the party, Ruth decided to go to the shop, get scraps of fabric and cover some of the bigger pots, and make bows to tie around the smaller ones.

With Ruth's new flower business, Grace was alone in the shop a lot. Most days Eleanor would drop in for a couple hours and then leave. Theodore came by every day for lunch. Sometimes James would come too.

Hearing the bell on the door, Grace put down what she was working on and walked out of the back room to the front of the shop. A white man stood there who looked real official.

"Yes sir, may I help ya?"

"Who's in charge here?"

"Miss Eleanor Macy sir."

"Get her."

"She's not here now, be back directly. You wanna leave a note?" Grace asked, reaching for a piece of paper and pencil. The man scribbled a name and address.

"Have her call on me soon."

"Yes, sir."

When he left, Grace looked at the note. His name was Albert Sullivan. Grace took the note to the back with her, wondering what he wanted.

The next morning, before Eleanor could make her way to see Albert Sullivan, he came back to the shop, and got straight to the point.

"I know Margaret Muncy died, so who do I need to talk to about buying this place?"

"The shop is not for sale, Mr. Sullivan," Eleanor said evenly.

"Why not? Mrs. Muncy has no family."

Eleanor was prepared. "Before Miss Margaret passed, she sold the business to Mr. Cornelius Fine, who resides in North Carolina."

"North Carolina? Why would he want a business in New York?"

Eleanor did not answer.

"Give me his address. I will write to him today." Giving the information to Mr. Sullivan, Eleanor wanted him to leave, so she could go to the post office and send Cornelius a telegram.

Grace's heart was pounding, listening to the exchange between Eleanor and Albert Sullivan. She wasn't surprised that he said he wanted to buy the shop, but was surprised it happened so quickly. It had only been three months since Margaret died.

Receiving the telegram from Eleanor made Cornelius uneasy, but he would have to deal with Albert Sullivan. By the time the letter reached him, Cornelius had had time to think of a response and returned a post to Sullivan the following day. He simply stated Margaret Muncy's late husband was a relative, and it was her desire to keep the property in the family, and therefore he would not consider selling. The letter thanked him for his inquiry and considered the matter closed. As he signed and sealed the letter, Cornelius thought of James and Grace.

CHAPTER 35

Charlotte, North Carolina

The note on the card read; "It's NOT complicated anymore." It was attached to a beautiful bouquet; sunflowers, daises, carnations, roses and tulips. Nina patted Oreo on his head and sat on a bar stool. She re-read the card, laid it down, and walked away. The card laid on the bar two days. More of the blooms in the bouquet had opened, making it stunning. The fragrance was subtle, but pleasant. This whole gesture was "so him." He always wanted the best.

"I need to at least say thank you." Taking a deep breath and closing her eyes for two seconds, she called him. Wilson took a deep breath and closed his eyes for two seconds before he answered.

"Hey sweetie."

"Hi Wilson."

"How are you?" He asked, holding the phone tighter than he needed to, as he reached for the remote and hit pause.

"Doing fine. How are you?"

The small talk was not only unusual, but unnecessary. Nina and Wilson had known each other for years, had a brief relationship, and saw each other at other intervals.

"I'm good," Wilson said, reaching for his glass.

"Are you busy?"

"Naw, having a drink and listening to some music."

Nina smiled, picturing him in gym shorts and a T-shirt, biceps bulging, swirling the ice around in the glass. She responded, "bourbon, with one ice cube, and jazz or Jack and coke with R& B!"

They both laughed.

"You know me well. It's a jazz and bourbon kinda night."

"Thank you for the flowers. The bouquet is gorgeous."

"Gorgeous flowers for gorgeous you."

She smiled, but didn't say anything.

"Did you read the card?"

"Yes, but I'm not sure I understand."

"What do you think it means?" He took another sip.

"The last time we talked, you said your relationship with Paris was still complicated. So either you are not together anymore or you're getting married."

"We're not getting married."

"Wow! You broke up?"

"Gorgeous and smart!" He finished his cocktail. Nina heard the ice clink in the glass.

Wilson told Nina about the breakup with Paris, including the part about the money. The last thing he said was, "I did it to be with you."

"Wilson, I really don't know what to say."

"Say you will have dinner with me tomorrow."

"I will have dinner with you tomorrow."

They talked a few more minutes, worked out the details, and hung up. Nina was nervous, not sure she did the right thing.

Wilson was elated. Sure, he did the right thing.

Sitting by a window in the restaurant, he had a clear view of her dance studio. He would see her come across the street. They had done this a dozen times, but he felt like it was a first date. The flash of purple caught his eye. He was distracted briefly and when he looked up, Nina was walking under the canopy at the door. The purple jumpsuit fit her figure snuggly. Her high heel shoes made her long legs look even longer, and Wilson loved the look.

He rose from the table and made a few steps to meet her. Nina was glad to see him, even more than she expected to be. He was wearing a suit but no tie; the jacket hugged his biceps.

Their greeting hug was brief, but their body language was easy. He pulled out her chair and then took his seat across from her.

"You look beautiful, and thanks for coming."

She smiled, looking directly into his eyes. "Thank you. I'm glad you invited me."

A few hours later, they exited the restaurant, holding hands. Wilson admitted to Nina he knew he had to earn her trust, and her love. He promised he was prepared to do just that. From that dinner, Nina and Wilson saw each other almost every day. The only days they didn't were the few days he traveled. He invited her to join him both times, but she declined. As much as Nina wanted Wilson, wanted to be in his life, and wanted him in hers, her heart still needed protecting.

A couple of weeks after Wilson broke off things with Paris, he came home to find a box at the garage door with more of his things from her house. Instinctively, he looked around. He had not heard from Paris at all. It wasn't her personality to beg or be vulnerable. Even hurt, she would suffer in silence. Looking at his watch, he let go of the thought of Paris. He was headed to see Nina's show. She wasn't performing this time, but had choreographed the production.

Wilson took his reserved seat and a minute later, Nina's parents were seated on the same row. He didn't know what she had told them. They were cordial as always and made small talk. Nina's sisters, Natalie and Natasha, came in a few minutes later and sat right behind them. Mrs. Joyner asked Natasha about her husband and children. Her answer had to do with weeknight and homework. Wilson was quiet, and glad the attention wasn't on him. She asked Natalie about Erik. Her answer had to do with his schedule.

Coming out of the restroom at intermission, Wilson saw Paris' mother across the foyer. He hadn't considered she would be there, or for that matter, Paris may be there. For a second, he was going to pretend he didn't see her.

"Why would I?" He thought, "I don't have anything to hide."

As Wilson crossed the lobby to speak to Mrs. Motley, he saw her sister with her, which probably meant Paris was not there. "Auntie" was more of a busybody than Mrs. Motley.

Wilson spoke to "Auntie" first. She was closer to him when he approached, and then to Paris' mother. They were cordial but didn't engage him. He was surprised. He expected one of them to question why he was there and ask about the breakup. Neither of them did. But what he knew for sure, Mrs. Motley would tell Paris about seeing Wilson. At the curtain call, Nina came on stage. She wore a stunning royal blue skin tight dress. The V-shaped opening in front went from her neck to her navel. He hoped her parents didn't notice him squirm in his seat. Following the show, Wilson waited for Nina with flowers. Her smile was huge, and he complimented her. "You are brilliant. The show was flawless." He knew why Nina wanted to dance. She was good at it. Really good. Just as they headed to their cars to leave, her phone rang. She laughed and answered. It was Magnolia. Nina thought Maggie was calling about the show, but wondered how she knew.

"No dahling! I wasn't aware you had a show tonight. Please send me the video. I'm sure it was amazing." Nina knew from the tone of Magnolia's voice there was a problem.

"Maggie, what's wrong?"

"I need you to come to New York. Reba is out again; in the hospital. We need a replacement dancer. You are the only one I trust."

"When is the show?" She asked, looking at Wilson. He looked puzzled. They talked a few minutes more, and Maggie promised to send Nina the rehearsal schedule and Nina promised to let her know in "a couple of days."

Over a drink on her deck, snuggled under a lightweight blanket, Nina explained to Wilson what Magnolia asked her to do.

"I can't move to New York for a month! Natalie will freak out if I'm away from the clinic that long, and what am I supposed to do about my students?" He took her hand, entwined his fingers in hers, and kissed it.

"You can move to New York for a month. I'll pay for it."

Nina looked at him and frowned. "It's not the money. I can stay at Maggie's apartment. I have a life here; and responsibilities…"

"And a man," Wilson said, looking directly into her eyes.

"And a man," Nina repeated, barely above a whisper. "And I will miss you."

Pulling her closer, Wilson said in her ear, "I will go to the city with you."

"And stay for a month. How will you work?"

"Babe, as long as I have a phone and my laptop, I can work."

They talked a few minutes about how to make a month in New York work. Wilson convinced her it could be done.

CHAPTER 36

New Amsterdam, New York

At dinner on Sunday, James announced to the family that Ruth was going to have a baby. Amid the celebration, Mary started to cry. Rose noticed first, climbed into her lap, and wiped her tears.

"Why you cryin' Grandmama?" asked James.

Mary closed her eyes and held Rose tight for a few minutes.

"When yo mama left, neva thought I see her again. Then I come here, find you, and then Rose, now my great grands, Lawd I'm jus' happy James. Jus' happy."

Prior to James' good news, Grace had shared with everybody the news about the visit from Albert Sullivan. "I knowed it boun' ta happen, jus' not so soon," Theodore said.

"Same I said," Grace remarked, "but Cornelius gone handle it." Mary didn't know how much Grace told Theodore about her relationship with Cornelius, but hearing her mention his name made Mary uneasy.

"I told Reverend Miller about it when Grace told me, so he on the lookout too," Theodore wanted to reassure them all.

Albert Sullivan was not at all pleased with Cornelius' response to his letter. His sentiment was how dare a Southerner tell him no. Cornelius Fine did not live in New Amsterdam and he didn't know how it looked for those colored people to be the face of a business in this community. He decided to research Margaret Muncy's will.

The county register of deeds didn't tell Albert anything he didn't already know. Yet he wasn't satisfied or done with his investigation. The Will stated all property would transfer ownership to Cornelius Fine, including a new one acre of land purchased a few months before she died. Sullivan was curious why in all the years he knew Margaret Muncy and her husband, he had never made the acquaintance of Mr. Fine. He decided to look into this new land purchase and see what he could find.

Margaret and Cornelius had covered their bases, except Cornelius didn't know about the last land purchase until she passed. He had reviewed the packet of papers Eleanor sent him upon Margaret's death and found things in order. Receiving the post from Albert Sullivan, he looked over things again. He dreaded being involved with any of this, but he had no choice.

In talking to the man who sold Margaret the acre of land, Sullivan found out it was located beside the church, and across from the church's handyman's house. He paid Reverend Miller a visit. Thinking as he walked the few blocks, he knew Reverend Miller was a white man who was sympathetic to the coloreds and especially to Theodore. He had to approach him carefully.

After the small talk, Sullivan asked Reverend Miller, who was working that "prime acreage."

"My handyman, Theodore, and his son, James." Reverend Miller knew not to say anything.

"Profit to the church, I 'spose?"

"Some; and son get wages, and some food to the colored school."

"Hope the church is not giving away too much," Sullivan said with a chuckle.

"Just following the desire of Mrs. Muncy to do, according to the scripture, 'to feed the hungry.'" Sullivan decided not to debate scripture with Reverend Miller.

"Who can I speak to about buying that land? I'll keep those boys on to work it."

"Far as I know, it's not for sale."

"With all due respect, Reverend, everything has a price."

A few minutes more passed, but Albert Sullivan wasn't getting anywhere with Reverend Miller. He finally gave up, and bid Miller "good day." In his gut, he knew there was more to this story than he was being told.

CHAPTER 37

New York, New York

Wilson made arrangements with a business associate to stay in a corporate apartment. The unit was about 1000 square feet, with an office and access to a gym and pool. He described it to Nina as "cozy." She didn't care, just grateful he was willing to do all this to be with her.

The two toughest decisions were what to do with her dog, and if they should take a car. Finally, she "hired" her niece and nephew to keep the dog, after bribing her sister. Wilson decided they would try to go without a car for a while to see if they could make it work. "But I'll get a car if I have to."

The first week of rehearsal was tough, and Nina came in every night exhausted. At one point, telling Wilson she was going to get out of her agreement with Maggie. He talked her down.

The second week was better until Nina heard two of the dancers talking about Reba.

"... of course he did. I don't know why she won't leave that bastard."

"Right. There is no way I would stay with a man who hit me once, and he has put her in the hospital for the second time!"

Nina was stunned, wondering if Maggie knew why Reba was in the hospital.

"Yes, dahling, I heard the rumors, but Reba didn't tell me that so I couldn't bring it up."

"So, what do you intend to do?"

"I don't know Nina. What do you suggest?"

"I suggest calling the police."

"That is impossible without a complainant," Maggie said, throwing up her hands.

"Can we go to the hospital and talk to her?"

Maggie put her hands on Nina's shoulder, shaking them slightly. "I just don't think we should get involved."

Nina didn't debate the subject with Magnolia any longer. She was content to take matters into her own hands. Discussing the situation with Wilson, he encouraged her to check on Reba. Finding out which hospital Reba was in wouldn't be easy. This was New York City with five boroughs and at least ten hospitals in each. Nina had to narrow down the search. One dead end, after another, and Nina finally gave up on finding Reba at the hospital, and found her at home. The last few days of rehearsal were intense. Magnolia demanded perfection. Most nights Nina came in and went straight to bed, feeling so guilty. Wilson was there to be with her, and she was neglecting him.

On Monday, before the Thursday of opening night, Wilson told Nina he had to go home for a couple of days. "I promise I will be back for opening night." What he didn't tell her, he was meeting with his attorney, Paris' brother Townsend Motley. The meeting would be awkward enough without having to explain it to Nina.

Taking a deep breath, Wilson stepped off the elevator and walked into the offices of Motley and Motley, P.A. The receptionist greeted him by name and asked him to have a seat. In about five minutes, Townsend came down the hall and greeted Wilson with a handshake. In his office, he was all about business. When they finished, Wilson felt he needed to at least ask about Paris.

"How are your parents?" Wilson asked.

"Good! Of course, Daddy hates retirement, mostly because Mama plans his days!" They both laughed.

"How is Paris?"

"Man, she's ok. Working a hell of a case. This woman killed her abusive husband."

"Damn." Wilson shook his head.

"It's so crazy. A production company is following the case and doing a documentary about it."

"Wow. Too bad it's under those circumstances, but I'm sure Paris appreciates the impact of publicity."

"And you know my sister well. She likes a good drama!"

Wilson appreciated Townsend's perspective on the situation. He couldn't have said it better himself. Wilson also appreciated knowing Paris was in court, and there wasn't much chance of running into her.

Townsend walked with Wilson to the elevator. They had a brief chat about Hornets basketball, and Wilson left. Walking to his car, he saw Paris across the parking lot. She didn't see him, and he could have ignored her. He didn't. As volatile as their relationship was, they were together for almost five years. Why would he act like he didn't see her? His decision to end things with Paris was what was best for him. Nothing personal against her.

"Hey Paris," he said as he approached her. "How are you?"

CHAPTER 38

New Amsterdam, New York

Albert Sullivan asked enough people enough questions to finally discover that the last names of James and Mary were Fine, and Grace's maiden name was also Fine. He put two and two together and determined Cornelius Fine was connected to them. Sullivan wanted to know how and why Margaret Muncy was involved. He expected the "coloreds to lie," so he went back to Reverend Miller.

This time Sullivan was not coy; spent no time beating around the bush. "Reverend, I know your boy and his boy are related to this Cornelius Fine from North Carolina. I want to know what that connection is." Reverend Miller didn't appreciate the repeated inquiry or the tone of Albert Sullivan's voice. He decided the only way to deal with this was to play hardball.

"Mr. Sullivan, stop insisting on information you are not entitled to. Understand I am not threatened by you, and I will protect Theodore and his family. As I previously stated to you, the property is not for sale. Reverend Miller did not address the connection between Margaret Muncy and the Fine family. I suggest you move on."

Miller wasn't surprised that Sullivan eventually came upon the information he wanted. New Amsterdam was a small town and a fairly tight community.

Over the next few months, Ruth's flower business picked up. The residual effects for James' vegetable sales were noticeable, and vice versa. Over dinner one evening, they discussed the need for more space, and Theodore suggested building a shed with storage in back and a place to pick up orders in front.

"We could sell some of Grandmama's preserves too."

"Good idea Ruthie," James said.

As they talked, Grace watched and listened. She was so proud of James.

Their family had grown so much, and they were all so busy. James and Grace seldom had time alone, but Grace needed to talk to him. He was a grown man now, with a wife and baby on the way. There were things he needed to know.

Earlier in the week, business at the shop was slow, and Grace asked Ruth to stay so she could run an errand. Walking the two blocks to the farm, Grace brought lunch for James.

"Hey Mama, what ya doin' here? Is Ruth alright?"

"Hey sweetheart. Yeah, she's fine. I need to talk to ya."

As they ate, Grace started to talk. "There was never no good time to talk 'bout this…"

"What's wrong Ma?"

Grace explained to James how she came to leave the Fine plantation and move in with Miss Margaret. She told him about the Fine China delivery. "James, son, Cornelius Fine, your real daddy. I'm sorry to keep it from ya all these years, but one a them thangs ya don't talk about."

"I knowed it already. Miss Margaret told me."

Grace chuckled. "I shoulda knowed."

"Ma, I ain't got no shame 'bout none of that. I got a good life wit my wife, baby comin', you, my baby sister and Theodore and Grandma. Why ya brang this up now?" James looked at his mother, who right then realized how grown up he really was.

"Over the years Cornelius give me money, then Hannah made sho he starts sendin' some reglar, and I been savin' it. Got it put up, should be enough for ya to build the shed, you talkin' to Theodore 'bout, and jus use the rest for whatever ya need to or put it away"

James was quiet. "I kin make thangs work wit what I got. Ya need to save that money for Rose. She needa go to school."

"No son. That yo money. Ain't proper for me to use it on Rose. Theodore won't like it nohow."

After a few minutes more of talking, James agreed to take the money from his mother. Later that night when he was home and told Ruth about it, they talked about expanding his business, and hers, possibly buying more land. Ruth made James feel better about the whole situation. He was glad he married her.

As the weeks passed, and Ruth's delivery time was nearing, she was more and more uncomfortable. One Saturday afternoon, sitting in the shade beside James' truck, a woman approached and wanted to purchase a few of the potted arrangements Ruth had on display.

"Sorry ma'am, they ain't for sale, ordered by a customer. Ones ova here for sale."

"Gal, are you refusing to sell me what I asked for?"

Ruth took a deep breath. "No, ma'am, not refusing." Ruth shifted her weight from one foot to the other. "Jus sayin' the ones on this side for sale." She pointed to the last few.

"That's not what I want, and I know you need the money. I will take four of these."

Ruthie rubbed her big belly. "Ma'am, I kin have four made by next Saturday for ya, or maybe even delivered to ya by Thursday."

"No today," the woman said.

"No, not today," Ruth said, as a pain shot around her back to her stomach. She groaned.

Just then, the customer who ordered the dozen plants showed up. Ruth walked away to greet her customer just as another pain came. She held on to the side of the truck to let it subside. James came out of the garden to load the flowers into the wagon. The customer paid Ruth, remarked how beautiful the flowers were arranged, and left. The first woman was standing there, astonished that Ruth was telling the truth, but couldn't under any circumstances admit Ruth was right, and certainly couldn't purchase what was left. Turning her attention back to the first customer, Ruth asked what she decided.

"Since you are so rude to walk away from me when I wanted to make a purchase, I am leaving and not buying anything."

"Suit yourself," Ruth mumbled under her breath.

"What did you say gal?" The lady raised her voice.

Before Ruth could answer, Mrs. Miller, the Reverend's wife, approached. The tension was obvious; she spoke pleasantly.

"Hello Mrs. Sullivan, lovely afternoon, isn't it?"

"Sullivan," Ruth thought. "She must be Albert Sullivan's wife."

"Yes, lovely, Mrs. Miller. I was admiring these floral arrangements, but girlie wouldn't sell me what I wanted…" Ruth spun around on one foot. Mrs. Miller shook her head slightly to signal Ruth not to respond.

"Yes, Ruth prepared those as decorations for a special dinner. I'm certain it will be quite nice." Mrs. Sullivan simply nodded as she walked away.

"I think you may want to call it a day, Ruth."

"Yes, ma'am."

Rose laid in bed sucking her thumb, twirling her hair around her finger and looking out the window at the sky. She did that often, drifting off to sleep, but tonight there was a very bright light. Her screams awakened her parents. The garden was on fire.

CHAPTER 39

Charlotte, North Carolina

Paris grabbed her bag and was hurrying out of the car when she got a whiff of a familiar scent. Then heard his voice. She stopped and stood there two to three seconds before turning around, knowing it was Wilson.

As small as this town was, and their circle of friends, they had not seen each other since he left her house that night. She put a smile on her face and turned around.

"I'm well, thank you. How are you?"

"Good." Wilson responded. There was an awkward silence between them.

"Townsend told me about your new case."

Paris took a deep breath and let it out. "Yep, it's pretty tragic… on a lot of levels."

"I have full confidence you'll get her off."

"Thanks. I need to go, have a lot to do."

"Understand… it's good to see you, Paris."

She walked away without responding. Once in the elevator, Paris took another deep breath and blew it out, not clear of her emotions right then, and she didn't have the luxury to deal with that right now. A woman's life was in her hands.

As Wilson left the parking lot, it occurred to him he was really over Paris. He hadn't been sure how he would feel when he saw her. He didn't feel anything. He called Nina to see what she needed from his house or hers and told her he would be back the next day.

"Love you beautiful."

"Love you more."

Paris walked into the suite through a private entrance. She didn't want to see anybody, and barely made it into her office before the tears came. Paris wasn't sure if they were angry tears or sad tears. Seeing Wilson startled her. She thought her hurt was gone, her heart was healed. It wasn't.

CHAPTER 40

New Amsterdam, New York

It took hours and the entire community to put out the fire. The crop damage was severe. Mary was grateful nobody was hurt. Grace was angry and scared. Ruthie felt guilty and kept apologizing. "If I hada jus' let that crazy lady buy them flowers, she wouldna told her husban' and he wouldna burned the garden." James and the rest of the family tried to console her and convince her the fire was not her fault. Eleanor was very emotional about the whole situation and determined to rectify it. After confirming that everyone was okay, she went home and crafted a telegram to send Cornelius Fine, asking him to come to New Amsterdam and deal with Albert Sullivan.

At the insistence of Reverend Miller, law enforcement talked to James, but nothing concrete came of it. James was hurt to his bones. He had worked hard, done everything Miss Margaret taught him. He was thoughtful, respectful, and fair. He sold quality produce at a reasonable price. He thought the people in their community respected him. Now he knew that wasn't true. He never positioned himself or fathomed himself as equal, but he was an honest, hardworking farmer. What he got for that was his crops burned and his land and livelihood destroyed. Most of the money his mother had saved, and some she brought all the way from North Carolina and held on to all those years he used to buy seeds and plants. Now it was up in smoke. James' emotions were teetering all over the place.

Almost immediately, James went to work. He started at one end raking the burned ground, and was determined not to stop until the whole acre was done. The tears streamed down his face, and he was glad Ruth couldn't see him. He didn't want his wife to see him cry.

Adam Fine stopped in the post office to pick up the mail about the time the telegram came in. He read it. Who was Eleanor? Who was James? Why did his dad need to go to New York? Adam tucked the telegram into his pocket.

Arriving home from running errands and making deliveries, Adam found his aunt Hannah there visiting his grandmother. He was glad to see her. They were close and had been his whole life. Hannah was his confidant and supporter. His mother was too busy with her daughter. She left raising a son to his father.

"Aunt Hannah, I'm going to the shop if you want a ride back to town. No hurry, I will wait until you're ready to go."

On the ride to town, Adam and Hannah caught up on things, and then he showed her the telegram.

"Buddy, you know I always tell you the truth, but this is a conversation you need to have with your father."

"You sound like my mother."

"I don't mean to." Hannah patted his shoulder. "But let's give him a chance to explain."

Seeing Hannah walk in with Adam, Cornelius knew something was wrong. She rarely came to the shop. "Is something wrong?" Cornelius asked without even greeting his sister. Adam handed him the telegram. He read it and looked up at Hannah. A few seconds of silence passed before Adam asked his dad about the telegram. "Who is Eleanor, and why is she asking you to come to New York? And who is James?" Hannah shifted in her seat. Cornelius was still quiet.

"Father?"

Cornelius leaned back in his chair and looked at the ceiling. He sat that way for a full minute. Hannah and Adam waited. When he sat up, his initial thought was to lie, but he knew that was pointless. Hannah knew the truth.

"Adam, do you remember Miss Mary, who worked for us when you were little?"

"Not really why?"

"Miss Mary and her husband, Tapper, worked for our family for a long time."

"What does that have to do with New York, James, and Eleanor?"

"They had a daughter named Grace." Cornelius took a deep breath and continued. "Grace and I spent some time together." He was stalling. Hannah folded her arms. She was getting impatient. Cornelius knew it. "Son, what I'm about to tell you can't leave this room."

"Yes, sir."

"James is Grace's son…and my son." Hannah blew out a soft breath. Adam looked directly at his father.

"James is my brother."

"Half-brother!"

"How old is he?"

"Two years younger than you."

"How could you have an association with a woman other than your wife?"

"It was an indiscretion."

It was obvious by Adam's body language he was not satisfied with his father's answer.

For about thirty minutes, they talked. Adam asked questions, Cornelius answered. Then, using Grace as the example, Cornelius told Adam the year's old story of their family's work to free slaves through deliveries for the company. Adam listened intently, making eye contact with his aunt Hannah from time to time. Cornelius was actually glad to get some of it off his chest. Cornelius told Adam about the land and the shop, which explained the telegram from Eleanor.

"I'm going to New York with you."

"What do you mean, it burned? How much damage?"

"We burned it up like she told us to."

"Who told you to?"

"Anna. She told us that darkie gal needed to be taught a lesson, so we did it… showed her and her husband not to fool with our sister."

"You jack asses ruined my plan." Albert Sullivan walked away from his brothers-in-law and into the house.

"Anna! Anna!"

"What are you yelling about, Albert?"

"You told your brothers to burn that land? I intended to take that land from them. That was a prime piece of property. I was even willing to pay something for it if I had to. Now it's no good.

"Well, I didn't…"

"No, you didn't and those numb skull brothers of yours…"

"Don't say that, and I didn't tell them to burn it."

"No, but you knew they would go to the extreme."

"Albert, I am sorry."

"And you did all that over some flowers."

"She disrespected me!"

"And you disrespected me. You took money out of my pocket and food off this family's table. Stay in your place, Anna. I told you to let me take care of it. Now what are you going to do if the law come snooping around here?"

"The law? The sheriff won't look at an upstanding family like us because of something said from a colored boy and his pregnant wife."

"Anna, you don't know the entire story. There are white people in this town who will stand up for that family. Starting with that Reverend Miller."

Anna's face flushed. "What do you want me to do, Albert?"

He looked at her for a long moment. "Nothing. Stay out of this. Keep your mouth shut, stay away from those people, and tell your dough for brains brothers to leave town."

CHAPTER 41

The performances were superb. Magnolia was ecstatic. So much so, she asked Nina to stay in New York indefinitely and continue to dance with the troupe. Nina declined without giving it a second thought. They landed in Charlotte on Sunday afternoon, both tired and glad to be back. Nina went to her house rather than staying with Wilson. He pouted, she laughed.

"I'll see you tomorrow."

"Promise?"

"Yes, I promise."

The past month was a whirlwind. Nina couldn't have ever imagined where her life was right now. The only man she had ever really loved, loved her too. After all the ups and downs, they were together. But he had history. He had dated and lived with Paris for about five years, and he cut out on her. At one point with Nina. "If he will cut out with me, he will cut out on me." Her heart sank. One thing they had going for them, they communicated well, and always honestly. The only way to manage her fear, to let him know what was bothering her, was to tell him.

Wilson flipped through the mail Zora left on his desk. She had also left food in the refrigerator for him to heat if he was hungry. He was glad to be home, but missed Nina. Wilson never second guessed his decision to leave Paris to be with Nina, and after their month together, he was more sure than ever he made the right decision. He sent a group message to his sisters, letting them know he was back in town and would see all of them for dinner this week. Dinner was a pre-emptive move. He knew Rita, Judith, or Jeanette would ask. Robin wouldn't, because he would see her in the office the next morning.

Just as he started upstairs, the doorbell rang. He smiled, thinking Nina decided to stay at his house after all. He walked to the door, wondering why she came to the front rather than through the garage and, much to his surprise, it was Paris at the door. He took two steps back into the foyer as she stepped inside.

"Hi Wilson."

"Hey Paris. What's wrong? Why are you here? Uninvited is not your style."

"Nothing is wrong. We need to talk." There was an awkward silence.

"You should have called. Now is not a good time. I can probably meet you for lunch tomorrow."

"No, uninvited is not my style, but I needed to see you and didn't think you would be receptive. Can we go in and have a seat?"

"No. What's going on, Paris?"

"I am still not clear about why you ended our relationship when nothing was wrong."

"I won't go over that with you again tonight. I told you I wasn't happy, and…"

"Are you happy now, away from me?"

"Yes."

"Is this about me not wanting to have kids?"

"No."

"Dammit Wilson. What's with the one-word answers?"

"We don't need to talk about this anymore, and please don't come here without calling."

"Wilson, will you marry me?"

CHAPTER 42

Pansy Margaret Fine was born two days after the fire. Mary helped the midwife deliver her.

"I done delivered my grandchild and my great gran. That's enough!" She laughed.

"That Ruth, a strong gal, didn't mind the pain seems like." Mary was talking to Grace.

"And James beside hisself," Grace laughed. I never seen him grin so much!

Pansy didn't cry a lot and Ruth needed little downtime. In a couple of weeks, she was back to work, the baby at the shop with her to nurse. James visited daily. A month after Pansy's birth, Ruth took orders again for flower arrangements.

Pansy's birth gave James energy. He worked harder and longer every day to get the lot ready and then to start planting again. A month in, he had replanted part of it. Now he had to pray for rain and find some temporary work in between.

For a few weeks, he did some odd jobs around the post office. One evening, as he was cleaning up to leave, the postmaster handed him a telegram and told him to deliver it to Eleanor.

"Do that have to do wit Miss Margaret's house or anything?"

"I sent for Mr. Cornelius Fine to come see about this fire situation."

"He comin'?"

"Yes, be here end of the week."

James didn't say anything; but he was glad Cornelius was coming. He was headed home to tell Ruth and talk to her about letting Cornelius know he knew the truth.

The train ride to New Amsterdam was tense. Cornelius was worried. Adam was anxious. He wanted to check out the community, get to the bottom of the fire foolishness, and meet James. More than anything, Adam was curious about James. He knew he would have to take things into his own hands. His dad probably wanted to keep them apart.

Upon arriving at the station, Cornelius immediately spotted Theodore's carriage. He was hoping there would be someone else.

"Mr. Fine, afternoon sir." Theodore tipped his hat. "Be glad to getcha to the hotel." The situation didn't seem to affect Theodore, but it was awkward for Cornelius. Theodore was, after all, Grace's husband. Feeling guilty made things even more uncomfortable. Before Theodore could respond, Adam walked around the buggy, tipped his hat to Theodore, and introduced himself.

"Adam Fine, glad to make your acquaintance."

"Theodore Miller, thank you, sir. Glad to meet ya." Theodore loaded the two bags in the back while Adam and Cornelius climbed in. Theodore didn't know if Adam was Cornelius' brother or son, but he would bet on son. No sooner than the thought was through his mind, Adam spoke again. "My father and I will be meeting Miss

Eleanor Macy at the seamstress shop formerly of Miss Margaret Muncy. Can you get us there tomorrow morning?"

"Yes sir. What time?

"Ten o'clock."

"That be fine. I'll be at the hotel, fifteen to. Trip take us about ten minutes."

Cornelius was undone that Adam was talking so much and wanted him to stop.

After dropping Adam and Cornelius at the hotel, Theodore went straight home to tell Grace that Cornelius and his son Adam were in town.

"Lawd a mercy. I knowed Miss Eleanor was up to something, but didn't reckon she sent for Cornelius."

"They meetin' her at the shop in the morning. Axe me to pick 'em up and get 'em there befo 10:00."

"I guess I needa tell James. I know they gone axe bout the fire."

Theodore, Rose and Grace walked the couple of blocks to James' house, and found him and Ruth in the flower garden, and deep in conversation. Grace took Rose inside to Mary, who was rocking Pansy.

"Grandma won't let Pansy go to sleep on her own. Insist on rocking her," Ruth laughed.

"It's ok, she did the same with Rose! Just let her be!"

Theodore was updating James on what he knew, and James told them about the telegram.

"James wanna tell Cornelius Fine he his son," Ruth said.

"He need ta know," James responded.

"Eleanor gone make sure he get to bottom of who set that fire. The rest is personal and I need to be the one who has the talk with him, Grace said."

"No Mama. I need to talk to him, man to man."

"James you…"

"I know he a white man. I talk to white men every day. But he still my daddy and he need to hold Albert Sullivan to account for his actions. Truth be told, some a that money got burned up was his money."

Grace felt bad because James was saying all this in front of Theodore. None of it was anything Theodore didn't know, but they just didn't talk about it.

"Ruth's daddy tell her a man ought speak his mind, and that 'xactly what I'm lookin' to do."

Ruth nodded in agreement.

While Cornelius and Adam had dinner in the hotel restaurant, Cornelius expressed to Adam his displeasure in how he was so friendly with Theodore and admonished him not to repeat the behavior the next day.

"Father, I will make no such vow to you. I thought we came here to help James and his family; my brother and his family."

"You don't need to refer to James as your brother. I doubt he knows, and if anybody finds out, it will create problems for me."

Adam didn't debate his father or comment further, but he fully intended to get James alone and discuss everything with him.

Cornelius didn't sleep much that night. The thought of seeing Grace disturbed him. After all these years, he still had feelings for her. He wished Margaret Muncy had not involved him in all this. He would rather have forgotten about James and Grace and gone on with his life. At 9:55 A.M., Adam and Cornelius arrived at the shop. Before they could get out of the buggy, they saw a young woman standing in the door. They went through the front and Theodore drove around back, parked and went in where Grace, James, and Ruth were waiting.

Eleanor introduced herself to Cornelius and Adam and showed them to a seat in the waiting area. A minute later, Grace came in with tea on a tray, and looking up, gasped audibly. Not at seeing Cornelius, but at seeing Adam. She hadn't seen him since he was a baby. Knowing he was with Cornelius had not lessened her surprise. His resemblance to James was astounding. Grace prayed for a brown baby so he wouldn't look so much like Cornelius, and she didn't think he did until she saw Adam.

Grace recovered quickly, hoping nobody heard her, and sat the tray on the coffee table. Turning to leave, Adam spoke up, "You must be Grace."

She stopped and turned to face him. "Yes."

"I don't know if you remember me. I'm Adam Fine." Grace could see Cornelius out of the corner of her eye, looking uncomfortable.

"Yes, sir. I remember you as a baby."

Cornelius couldn't take his eyes off Grace. She was still beautiful. He had to divert his eyes from looking at her breasts. Adam laughed. Grace was uneasy, not knowing whether to stand there or leave.

"Is the rest of your family here?"

"Yes, sir."

"Please ask them to join us."

Cornelius and Adam locked eyes. Cornelius was the one who looked away. Grace walked away for a minute, coming back with Theodore, James and Ruth following, holding hands. They all sat.

Eleanor explained the events leading to the fire. She told Adam and Cornelius what happened after Albert Sullivan received notice from Cornelius that the shop was not for sale. Adam didn't know about the correspondence between Sullivan and his father. "The sheriff didn't do anything and I'm concerned Mr. Sullivan will try something else," Eleanor said.

Finally, Cornelius joined the conversation. "I don't trust him either, but I don't know what I can do. He doesn't respect Southerners, and I don't think he believed me about being related to Mrs. Muncy." To this point, Ruth, James, Grace, or Theodore hadn't said anything.

"I don't much care about his respect or what he believes. He can be made to understand he will not be the one who disrespects us," Adam said firmly.

"James, when will the land be ready for planting again?" Adam asked.

"Part ready now, I 'spect other part in a few months."

"Will you show me the property when we finish here?"

"Be glad to." James had an agenda and Adam had one, too.

Adam tuned to Cornelius. "Father, what is the plan to deal with Sullivan?"

"I will meet with him today…"

"I will accompany you to that meeting." Cornelius cleared his throat. Adam didn't flinch.

"Miss Eleanor, can you tell me where to find Sullivan?" Cornelius asked.

"Yes."

"Theodore, are you available to drive us there?"

"Yes, sir."

Adam finished his tea and turned to James. "May I have a word?"

"Yes. Outside."

Grace's heart was pounding.

Cornelius' heart was pounding.

"We have a lot to discuss," Adam said.

"Yes, we do." James agreed.

"I will accompany my father," Adam paused, "Our father…" James didn't change his expression… "to meet with Sullivan. I am going to make this right for you." Still no response from James. "After that meeting, I will meet you back at the garden. Is that acceptable?"

"Yes, it is." Adam extended his hand. James shook it.

Repeating back to his wife and mother, James told them Adam referred to Cornelius as "our father."

"Lawd a mercy James, I ain't never seen no white man show as much respect." Ruth said.

"He from a good family," Grace said, "been raised right. The Fines was good to me, my mama and daddy, but the world was not good. Cornelius a decent man, but don't like to fight."

"Seem like Adam don't mind a fight," Ruth laughed.

"But is he fighting for me or against Cornelius?" James asked.

CHAPTER 43

Charlotte, North Carolina

Wilson laughed, a loud, deep belly laugh. "Are you kidding Paris?" Before she could answer, he grew very serious. "I asked you to marry me four times, and four times you turned me down. We didn't need to be married. Our relationship is fine as it is," he said sarcastically, mocking her. "Then, months after we break up, you show up with no warning and ask me to marry you! You are out of your mind or drunk!"

Paris was nervous, but determined not to show it. "I am neither drunk nor out of my mind. Upon reflection, I guess I took you and our relationship for granted. I realize now that these months have passed, how much I miss you. Since I saw you the last time, I have longed for you. For us."

"Are you horny Paris?"

"Wilson!"

As soon as it was out of his mouth, he regretted saying it. "I apologize. That was uncalled for."

"You didn't answer my question."

"No Paris. I will not marry you."

"Why? Are you in love with someone else?"

"You've been here long enough, and you've asked enough questions. Please leave." He opened the door. "Please don't come back without an invitation."

She stepped onto the porch. He closed the door and walked away.

Looking out the window upstairs, Wilson watched Paris drive away. He sat, clearly puzzled why she came and why out of nowhere would ask him to marry her. Perhaps his explanation to her around his ending the relationship wasn't adequate, but he didn't want or need any scrutiny from her. Creating a solid foundation with Nina was paramount, as was being honest with her. He reached for the phone to call her.

Wilson asked Nina to come over via pleading his undying love, and her laughing, saying she would see him the next day. As he talked about his unexpected guest, Nina listened attentively and didn't ask questions until he finished.

"Thank you for telling me. Are we a secret?"

"Absolutely not. Paris just doesn't need to be all in my life like that. I love you. Nothing else, nobody else matters."

"I love you too."

"You want to meet for lunch tomorrow?"

"No. I have to go to the clinic. Natalie has been blowing up my phone. I'll see you for dinner, though. Why don't you come over here and plan to stay the night?"

"That sounds like a plan I can get behind." Wilson laughed. "But how am I going to sleep tonight without you in my arms for the first time in months?"

"Just think about us being together tomorrow."

"Ok, I'm going to bed right now so morning will hurry and get here!"

Wilson couldn't sleep. His mind raced from one thing to another, but it was all related to Paris. Her stunt was odd. What was she up to? Paris was cunning but not manipulative. Maybe she did still love him.

Paris couldn't sleep. Her mind replaying the exchange with Wilson one minute and going over the court case the next. She needed to push aside the situation with Wilson and concentrate on her preliminary arguments for the trial, which started in a few hours.

The next morning while he was working out, Wilson watched the news. During the local news break, the lead story was the trial of Erica Dawn Brooks, a woman accused of pre-meditated murder for killing her abusive husband. The reporter talked about Paris representing her and about the documentary being filmed. There was a quick shot of Paris. Wilson realized it was from the day he saw her in the office parking lot. He remembered what she was wearing. On one hand, he was proud of Paris, on the other, concerned for her. This could make or break her career. "We should have talked about this." Then Wilson realized he was out of her life by the time all this came up. For a short time, he felt the need to protect Paris, to be there to listen as she talked through the elements of the case. In the next moment, he felt bad; guilty for reflecting on their old life together.

Over dinner that evening. Nina mentioned Erica Brooks and Paris. "Natalie told me Erica Brooks came to the clinic a couple of times. Once for an STD. Another time for a broken finger."

"All courtesy of the man she killed, I assume."

"Yep."

"Does Natalie have to testify?"

"I don't know yet. One attorney on Paris' team had reached out to her, indicating they would probably subpoena the medical records."

"The whole situation stinks." Wilson made the comment genuinely concerned about Paris.

CHAPTER 44

New Amsterdam, New York

Again, Cornelius reminded Adam to let him deal with Albert Sullivan.

"If you tell him, even let on to him James is related to us…"

"Your son."

"Sullivan will take that out on him."

Adam knew his father was right. "Yes Father, I understand." That was the first concession Adam had made all day. Arriving at Sullivan's place of business, Cornelius walked in, suddenly feeling empowered. He didn't waste any time on pleasant greetings. "Mr. Sullivan, I am Cornelius Fine. This is Adam, my son. I am here to inquire about the fire set to my land, and the continued exploration of the sale of the Muncy shop." Sullivan was caught a little off guard. He wasn't expecting Cornelius and wasn't expecting him to be so assertive. Adam noticed it immediately. Sullivan stood and offered his hand. Cornelius did not respond. Sullivan cleared his throat and gestured toward a chair. Neither Cornelius nor Adam moved or said anything.

"Mr. Fine, it's a pleasure to make your acquaintance in person." When they again didn't reply, he moved on.

"I don't know anything about the fire except what I've heard in the community." Sullivan noticed Adam looking around, sizing up the place. Sullivan hated their demeanor, but he had to be careful.

He didn't know what they knew, but they didn't know what he knew either.

"I doubt that's true. We're aware of your wife's encounter with Ruth about some flowers," Adam spoke.

"Ah yes, Ruth Fine." He put emphasis on "Fine." Cornelius didn't react. Adam kept talking.

"Yes. Do you deny it happened and then the next day, the very land they stood on was torched? Crops included?"

"I deny any involvement, but I am curious why you care. Who are the coloreds to you?" Adam let Cornelius answer. He wanted to let his father determine how much information to disseminate.

"I own that land. They work for me. I have to protect my investment in the land and in the workers. And I have the promise to Margaret to uphold. She sold me the land partly because I promised to keep her employees." He had sidestepped the question of the last names.

"Please be on notice, Mr. Sullivan. We will be in town for a few more days, investigating our loss. If it is determined you are involved, there will be ramifications," Adam said.

"You didn't answer my question, Mr. Fine." Sullivan was looking at Cornelius.

"I don't owe you an explanation, Mr. Sullivan. And if you know who destroyed my land, you should deliver my son's message." Cornelius and Adam walked out.

Albert Sullivan slammed his fist on the desk. He was utterly pissed at Cornelius and Adam Fine.

"The gall of two damn Southerners to confront me in defense of some colored hired hands," he hissed aloud. But somewhere in the recesses of his brain he believed the Fine's. Particularly the young one. He had to contemplate his next move extremely carefully.

On the ride back, Adam asked Theodore to stop at the post office. He needed to send a telegram.

"Greetings. Hope all is well. How is Grandfather? Work here is going well but not complete. Will be extending at least two more days. Tell the children we will bring presents. Love to all."

Adam had promised his aunt Hannah he would check in to let her know how things were going in New Amsterdam. Asking about his grandfather was code for he and Cornelius were not at odds. Presents for the children was code for Cornelius was in control as far as dealing with Grace. Adam knew well that for all his business acumen, Cornelius did not make good decisions in his personal life, he did not like confrontation and he was still in love with Grace. Hannah was worried that being in Grace's presence would rattle Cornelius to the point he would make a bad decision or do something he shouldn't.

Cornelius didn't want to go back to see James, and he didn't want Adam to go, but he knew he couldn't stop him. Theodore dropped him at the hotel and took Adam to meet James. Adam took the few minutes of opportunity he had alone with Theodore to reassure him of his commitment to James and to getting to the bottom of the situation.

"I know you and your family have every right to mistrust us, but we mean no harm. I also know my father isn't as aggressive as I am, but he understands business, and he will not allow that land to be unharvested."

"'Preciate yo words, but know James don't trust easy. Love him like he my blood. Some days he hard to figa out."

"He is my blood, and he deserves his share of what the Fine name can give him. Even if my father won't do more after this, I won't let James and his family down." Theodore just nodded.

They found James in the field, checking his crops. Theodore went across the road to the church. Adam walked out toward the end of the lot, where James stood with a hoe in his hand. Adam took out a handkerchief, wiped his forehead, and replaced his hat.

"Looking like you want it to?"

"Not too bad. Could use some more rain."

"When will you start on the other half?"

"Don't know yet. This bean crop will tell me if the under soil is too damaged to use."

"If it is?" Adam furrowed his brow.

"Then I have no crop this season and maybe not next season. The equipment I need cost hundreds. I will have to cultivate the garden by hand. Can't afford no help, and will have to do some kinda work to make money."

Adam wiped his head and face again. James wanted to laugh, but he didn't. It was obvious Adam hadn't ever worked outside. James nodded toward a shed behind the church. They walked over in silence. Adam contemplating his response. Being indoors, Adam immediately appreciated the cool air. James wiped off a bench for Adam to sit and then positioned himself atop a work table opposite his brother.

"James, I will give you the money to purchase the equipment you need. Not just to repair the damage but to work the land the way you need to, and money to take care of your family in the meantime."

James didn't immediately answer. "Why would you do that?" he asked, following a contemplative pause.

"It's the right thing to do. You are family. You, your wife and daughter deserve your portion of the Fine family fortune."

"Cornelius may not agree."

"He won't disagree. He can't afford to."

Before James could respond, Adam spoke again. He told James how he discovered him, how he insisted on accompanying Cornelius to New York, and that his grandparents nor his mother knew the real story about their trip, and didn't know about James.

"What do they think happened to my mama?"

Adam laughed. "Grandfather knows officially. Grandmother knows, and she knows Hannah left Miss Mary here unofficially. My mother knows nothing and we intend to keep it that way. My aunt Hannah knows everything."

"Yeah, Miss Margaret said Miss Hannah is the reason Cornelius would take care of everything."

"Miss Margaret was right, and now I will also make sure things are fair for you."

James was still apprehensive about Adam. He couldn't understand why Adam was so adamant about helping him and about them being "family." Borrowing Theodore's buggy, James drove Adam back to the hotel. They finished their conversations in the few minutes' ride.

Adam explained he would purchase the equipment James needed. James had written a detailed description for him. As Adam talked about sending money to Eleanor for James' family, and how it would be called a salary. James pressed Adam. "With that kinda equipment, I can work more land."

Before he could finish, Adam jumped in. "If you know of another plot we can buy, I will inquire about it while I'm here."

"I will find out tomorrow." James was eager to get home and tell Ruth about all this.

CHAPTER 45

Charlotte, North Carolina

"The bad thing is, we have three or four patients who I'm sure are victims of domestic violence and abuse, but we can't do anything." Natalie and Nina were talking about the Erica Brooks case.

"Do you have a referral process?"

"Not really. I sent a family to a shelter, but the guy found them and they moved away."

"It would be good if there was something in place," Nina said.

She paused and then told her sister about Reba.

"Yep, I wish we could afford a social worker."

"Well, we can't. But what we can do is offer office space to someone from the crisis center or Safety Alliance and make a satellite here."

"Nina, that's a great idea. I am going to work on that today."

At home that evening, Nina updated Wilson on some things at the clinic, and her conversation with Natalie.

"I am just floored. This is such a big problem. What I really don't understand is women who stay." Nina shrugged her shoulders.

"Baby, you can't judge the decisions people make."

"I don't mean to judge. I really don't. But how can somebody go to work every day and not tell anybody or call the police or just never go back? Like Reba for example."

"Speaking of… have you heard anything else about her?"

"No, Maggie hasn't mentioned her, so I haven't asked."

"You realize everybody is not as headstrong as you are," Wilson said as he played with one of her locks.

"When we were growing up, my mom said I was headstrong, and it wasn't a compliment!" She laughed.

"Whatever you need from me, let me know."

"I will. Thanks, babe."

In the middle of the night, Wilson awakened. He realized he had been dreaming about Paris. He looked over at Nina. She slept soundly, her hair framing her face. Wilson felt bad, and he was puzzled by why Paris was on his mind. He snuggled close to Nina and closed his eyes, hoping he could go back to sleep.

The ringing phone startled Paris. She half opened her eyes and didn't look at the screen. "Yes," she answered, just above a whisper.

"You better lose this case…" Paris had the presence of mind to push the button. "… that bitch needs to go to jail for what happened to my man!"

After the first threatening call, Townsend loaded an app on Paris' phone that wouldn't disconnect the phone for an additional ten seconds. The originating phone number would be traced, and the call recorded. Paris went back to sleep. The next day, Townsend checked the app and reported the information to the police. Erica was getting death threats, too.

Wilson was on an international video call when his mobile phone vibrated and he saw Paris' face on the screen. He chuckled. "She won't quit," he thought. Then the ping of the text message. "Call me. Important." He decided he wouldn't.

An hour later, Paris called again. Wilson blew out a long, slow breath and picked up the phone. "Wilson Peters." The formal greeting was to let her know he couldn't talk. She didn't bother with greetings. "I need to get my gun from your house." Wilson took a beat to process what he heard. "What's going on?" She gave him the cliff notes version of the past few days, including broken glass behind all four of her car tires.

"Have you notified the authorities?"

"Yes."

"Where are you?"

"My office."

"Give me a few minutes to call you back." He had to figure out how best to handle this.

A few years before, Wilson and Paris took a concealed carry class, and he brought her an automatic Beretta 380. They went to the firing range a few times, but other than that, she hadn't even held the gun. It was in a strongbox at the top of his downstairs closet. He carried a Beretta 9mm most of the time, but he didn't encourage her to.

He went home to get it and take it to her at the office. He called her back, but was glad when he didn't get an answer. "I'll bring it to you" was the message he left. Nina would be at the studio late. Wilson knew he could run the errand and get back home before she got there. He would tell her, though. No secrets. He wouldn't hold anything from Nina the way he did from Paris.

Wilson called Paris and asked her to let him in through the private entrance.

"Thanks Wilson. I hate to even do this, but they know my phone number and my car."

"The court won't hire security for you?"

"No."

"Does your dad know about this? You know he will hire somebody."

"I know…" Paris sighed. "I'm trying not to worry him."

"You don't want him to find out on his own."

"You're right." She took the pistol from the holster.

"Do you remember how to use it?"

"Yes." She checked the ammunition. The magazine was full. Click, click. Paris cocked it to put one round in the chamber. Wilson walked behind her and put his arm around her so that his hands were holding the gun too; on top of her hands.

Raising the gun, he said, "head," lowering it some, "heart, close range will yield greater input."

"I remember."

"Center mass."

He lowered it again. "Don't pull the weapon unless you intend to use it."

"I know. You've told me that a hundred times!"

He stepped back. "Put the safety on," and handed her the holster. "The whole thing should fit in your purse."

"Yes, it will. Thank you for bringing it."

"You're welcome, but I wish you didn't need it."

"Me too, but I do."

Nina's class went a little long. When she called, Wilson let her know dinner would be waiting.

Over dinner, they shared the events of their respective day. She told him about having to change a portion of her show because the dancers, "just couldn't get it. I am so frustrated."

"You shouldn't change it. When I was playing ball and coach designed a play, we practiced it until we got it!" Wilson was serious.

"All of them are younger than me…."

"But they're not as fine as you, or as good a ballerina as you." He put his arms around Nina and kissed her forehead. She laid her head on his shoulder.

"Paris called me today."

"Again," Nina thought, but didn't say anything. He kept talking. When he mentioned the gun, Nina gasped and sat up. "Babe, that's scary."

"Yep."

"She's fighting for right and people hate her for it. That sucks."

"I just want her to get some protection." Wilson's heart sank at the thought of Paris being in danger.

CHAPTER 46

On the way to his room, Adam passed the hotel bar and saw Cornelius inside. He joined him. Now was as good of a time as any to tell his father what he committed to James.

"Scotch neat," Adam told the waitress, taking the seat across from his dad. The scantily clad cigarette girl walked over, opened the case around her neck and waved her hand across the array of cigarettes and cigars. Adam chose a cigar, laid a bill in the box, and turned his back to her.

Adam surveyed the room, took a sip of his drink and then asked his father to repeat what he just said. Cornelius grunted. "Are you just leaving James?"

"Yes sir. We had a good conversation. He knows he's a 'Fine,' and he will receive a portion of the Fine fortune. For starters, I am going to order him some farm equipment and purchase another plot of land for him."

"Adam, you had no right to promise that boy—"

"Boy!" James is a grown man, just like me. He has a family. "Unlike me, he is not living under the continued scrutiny of his parents. I want to be more like him."

Cornelius took a pause before he responded to Adam. He wanted to choose his words carefully. Motioning for the waitress to bring another drink, Cornelius looked at Adam seriously. "Son, I know you have a desire to help people, and that's good. Our family has always been especially good to the coloreds. The tenants of our faith admonish us to treat people fairly."

Adam was looking at his father in disbelief. "Is he actually lecturing me?" Adam thought. He downed the last of the scotch and forcefully slammed the glass on the table. Cornelius was startled, and stopped talking mid-sentence.

"There is no need to lecture me on the protocols of dealing with colored people. I know and have known all my life. James is not just a colored man we know. He is my brother, your son --- your indiscretion. You cannot ignore that fact. Face the truth!"

"Facing the truth will cause more harm than good, and in the end could cost us our business and cost you your inheritance. Is that your desire? Is your fight for James more important than the well-being of the whole family? Whatever you want to do for James and his family is at stake, too. Keep that in mind."

Adam took a few seconds to consider his father's words. "No, that is not my desire, but I intend to keep my word to him. Discreetly, of course. You can help me figure out the best way to accomplish that."

"The best way to accomplish it would have been to discuss it with me before you made him any promises."

"A promise I fully intend to keep."

"I won't try to change any of that. Just be very careful how you execute the arrangement."

As Cornelius and Adam continued to talk, they were interrupted by loud, obnoxious laughter. For a few seconds, all eyes were on the two men who had disturbed everybody in the bar. About the same time, the waitress came back to the table.

"Sorry about that, gentlemen," she said. "A couple of locals. They talking about that fire the other night, but didn't know why they think that's funny."

Cornelius spoke up. "We just got into town yesterday. What about a fire?" Adam looked at the waitress.

"Those fools say they set fire to some crops over by that church, cross town. I don't know much about it, just heard some people talking, that's all. Can I get you another drink, hon?" She was addressing Adam.

"Yes ma'am, please."

She touched her finger to his cheek. "Be right back." Adam smiled. The second the waitress turned her back, he leaned across the table. "What are we going to do?" He was speaking in a forceful whisper.

"We need more information. Let's see what else we can buy from the waitress," Cornelius said. Adam sat back just as she returned. Adam pulled out one of the empty chairs at the table.

"Sit with me for a minute." She didn't hesitate.

"Tell us what you heard about that fire," Cornelius said. She made a face. He slid a coin across the table. Her demeanor changed.

In the few minutes the waitress sat with Adam and Cornelius, she told them what Sullivan's brothers-in-law said about their involvement in the fire. A few minutes later, the cigarette girl appeared, wanting to sell more information, which filled in most of the blanks.

Now they had to determine what to do with what they knew. The only people they could trust were Eleanor, James, and his family.

No advantages there. James was colored and Eleanor was a woman, and a member of the Society of Friends. They left the bar and went to Cornelius' room to devise a plan.

"The problem we will encounter is getting the local law to do anything about all this," Adam said.

Cornelius sighed. "The additional problem; exposing our family ties."

"Father, that may not be a problem. That may be our advantage."

CHAPTER 47

The Erica Brooks trial started under top security. The local and national media swarmed. Paris arranged for a decoy car to stop in front of the courthouse and had a deputy sheriff friend take Erica into the courthouse through the jail entrance.

Erica looked over at the jury. Paris had assured her that was an acceptable jury based on the pool they had to choose from. There were seven women and five men. Four of the women were Erica's age, and four of them were black, the same race as Erica. There were two black men. The same race as the man she killed.

Days one and two were fairly uneventful. There were no surprises, as the Prosecution presented police evidence and testimony. Paris stipulated to most of it. Their entire case was to undo the defense case that Erica killed him in self-defense.

Day three. It was the defense's turn to present their side of the story. Paris had everything meticulously laid out; exhibits, experts, and witnesses. She was probably over prepared, but leaving nothing to chance. The jury was engaged, and the prosecution knew it. They objected several times and only once did the judge sustain the objection. Paris knew he would, but it was fine. Like her dad taught her, you can't unring the bell. The jury heard her, despite the judge admonishing them to "disregard the comment."

For two days police officers, emergency department doctors and nurses, psychiatrists, and battered women's counselors testified that Erica's circumstances and series of events and her behavior were consistent with Battered Woman Syndrome. The prosecution objected fourteen times. The judge overruled thirteen.

That evening Nina, Natashia, Natalie, and Wilson sat in the conference room at the clinic watching the local news and heard the recap of the day's events in court. Ironically, they were eating pizza and waiting to start their monthly board meeting. On the agenda was allocating space in the clinic for a domestic violence crisis center.

The court room was packed for closing arguments. The prosecution painted a picture of Erica as a villain who devised a plan to kill her husband. They made no mention of the broken bones and other various abuses. They implied Erica had the opportunity to leave, but chose to stay and commit murder.

Then it was Paris' turn.

"Erica Brooks married the man she intended to spend her life with. The man who busted her lip in a drunken rage on their first anniversary because he didn't want steak for dinner. The same man who broke her rib because she rode with a tow truck driver when her car broke down. The very same man who caused Erica to break an ankle when he pushed her down a flight of stairs. Ladies and gentlemen of the jury, as you have heard, my client left Mr. Brooks and came back on numerous occasions, a symptom of Battered Woman's Syndrome. The last straw for her after almost three years of physical, psychological, AND financial abuse was the night of June first last year. Erica was discharged from the hospital earlier that day after a one-day stay. She had a concussion, AND had suffered a miscarriage. The prosecution would have you believe it was an accident. It was not. When the deceased, Mr. Brooks came in and remarked he was glad she wasn't "havin' no kid," Erica snapped, went to the closet, got the gun he had threatened her with a dozen times and fired all six shots, hitting him twice." Paris made eye contact with all the jurors, one by one, then continued. "He was an awful man. Who, on top of being an abusive husband, was an adulterer." She had to get her final statement in quickly. "What proof do I have? Two women from two different phone numbers have been calling Erica AND me with death threats if I don't lose this case because Erica killed their man."

"Your honor, I object. Nothing was entered into trial about death threats and should not be included in closing arguments," the prosecutor said, slamming his fist on the table.

"Ms. Motley!"

"I'm done Your Honor."

"The jury will disregard Ms. Motley's final statement."

Paris walked back to her table. "You can't unring the bell, she thought," looking at her father who was in the gallery.

CHAPTER 48

New Amsterdam, New York

Adam reminded Cornelius what the cigarette girl told them about Albert Sullivan's brother-in-law being known around town for having a colored son and daughter. She thought that should make him "nicer to colored people."

"Father, we don't need to expose our family until we can expose theirs if they won't cooperate."

At the time the cigarette girl mentioned it, Cornelius felt guilty. He put it out of his mind.

Cornelius and Adam went back to see Albert Sullivan the next day. Cornelius didn't waste any time. "Sullivan, we know your brothers-in-laws were the culprits behind the fire on my land. Now we can do this the hard way; your way or you can pay for the damage."

Sullivan laughed. "Fine, I don't know where you're getting your information…" Adam didn't let him finish. "From the same place, we were informed about your niece and nephew. The children of the teacher at the colored school." Sullivan's face reddened. Adam knew he had his attention. There was a long, thick silence.

"I know nothing about them setting that fire, and I'm certainly not going to waste my time on your accusations." He side stepped the comment about the children.

"As we understand it, your wife fancies herself as a very prominent person in New Amsterdam. How would she feel about her brother's crime and indiscretion being known among her friends, church members, and bridge partners? That would put a blemish on her reputation. Don't you think?" Adam said seriously.

"Mr. Sullivan, an offer to cover the cost of damages, and equipment to refurbish the land, including crops, will be sufficient to keep what we know away from your neighbors," Cornelius spoke.

Albert Sullivan snorted. "I will do no such thing. Make no such offer. You gentlemen should kindly leave my place of business."

"We will give you time to reconsider. Expect us tomorrow," Adam said, making direct eye contact with Cornelius.

Cornelius went back to the hotel, but Adam went to see if he could find James. He found Theodore first, who informed him James was doing work at the white hospital. The thought that James was having to work all over town infuriated Adam. "Would you be so kind to let him know I need to see him tonight?"

"Yes sir, I will."

Adam accepted Ruth's invitation to dinner. He didn't know what to expect, but on the way over, decided to be okay with it. Cornelius declined the invitation. Upon arrival, Adam immediately noticed the immaculate gardens. Flowers in the front and on the side of the house, and vegetables in the back.

The house was modest, cozy, and well kept. When thinking it was a little larger and more nicely furnished than he expected, he remembered it was Mrs. Muncy's home originally.

They all sat at the table in the dining room. Ruth served James, and Mary served Adam before serving their own plates. The meat and vegetables were spectacular. Ruth bragged on James, telling

Adam the vegetables and the seasonings came from his garden. Adam ate a hearty portion of everything.

When the meal was done and Adam thanked Ruth profusely, he and James went outside to the garden on the side of the house. There were two benches there. James loved being in that space. He and Margaret sat there many days as she taught him to read, write and how to count money. Adam lit a cigar, told James what he and Cornelius found out about the fire, and about their meeting with Albert Sullivan. Listening and contemplating how he should respond, James sighed deeply and kept his eyes on the ground. Adam kept talking. We are going back to see him tomorrow morning.

"What if he don't budge?"

"He will. But on the outside chance he does not, it won't matter. The equipment you need is on the way here."

James' face lit up. Reaching into his jacket pocket, Adam retrieved an envelope and gave it to James, who hesitated before he looked inside.

"That is three months' salary. You don't need to work all those odd jobs. You are a farmer. A businessman, not a handyman. You and Ruth can make a good living with your flowers and vegetables." James looked at Adam. Even in the dim light of dusk, he could see himself in Adam's face.

"I'm much obliged at what you doin.' Much obliged. I jus' ain't sure why and why you doin' and not Cornelius."

Adam paused before he answered. "Brother, I am a man of faith. The good book teaches we should treat others the way we want to be treated. That is what I am extending to you. We live in a society that does not value all as equals, but my faith says we are. All I want to do is help you, your wife and daughter, live the way God intended for you to." He was silent for a moment. "I cannot answer for Father. He knows what's right. He will have to make amends in his own time."

James stuffed the envelope in his pocket. "When will you return to North Carolina?"

"Father will return the day after tomorrow. I will decide if I go then or remain more days based on Albert Sullivan's response."

On the ride back to the hotel, James and Adam talked about the arrival of the farming equipment, and Adam reiterated his commitment to buy an additional plot of land.

"Your numb skull brothers are blabbing about setting that fire," Albert Sullivan said to his wife in a forceful whisper, even though they were home alone. He went home to find her as soon as the Fine's left.

"And you believe those people over my family?"

"They know about the children."

"Hmph!" She waved her hand at him flippantly. "That's a rumor."

"Is it a rumor you want spread around town?"

"They wouldn't dare."

"Oh yeah, they would. Fine lost good money on that land."

"Well, I…"

"Listen to me!" Sullivan didn't let her finish her statement. "You find them and tell them to get out-of-town once and for all." She looked at her husband, but decided not to argue. Sullivan sat to ponder his response to Cornelius Fine.

CHAPTER 49

"Not guilty." The verdict was delivered after eight hours of deliberation. Townsend got Erica out of the courtroom with the help of the same deputy friend, and Paris went out to meet the press. There was a barrage of questions, and one reporter asked about the death threats. "The police know who they are," was her response.

After a few weeks, Erica moved and was ready to get on with her life, and reached out to Paris about helping her find a job. "I want to do something different," she told Paris, who agreed. Previously, her job was in retail, and that was more raw exposure to the public than she needed. In the days following the conversation with Erica, Paris reached out to some people about employing Erica, and a couple of things were in the works. One afternoon, in the office supply store, Paris ran into Nina and Natalie.

"Congratulations on the verdict in the Brooks case," Natalie was saying when Nina walked up.

"Thank you."

"That had to be tough," Nina said.

"Yeah, it was, and it changed her life forever. Some people will only remember her as a murderer."

"What's she doing now?" Natalie asked.

"Looking for a job."

Nina and Natalie looked at each other. Nina spoke up. Standing there talking to Wilson's ex was awkward for her, but it didn't seem to be for Paris. "That's interesting because we're buying all this stuff to set up our new office. The clinic is going to house a branch of the Safety Alliance. They're sending a part-time counselor, but they will need a full-time person to answer the phone, do intake, make referrals, make appointments, stuff like that."

"That would be great for her," Paris replied with a huge smile. "May I have her call you?"

Natalie gave Paris her business card. "Yes. Ask her to call me."

"Whew! That was strange."

"What?" Natalie responded, frowning.

"Having a conversation with Paris."

"Oh! Dang sis. I forgot. I didn't mean to put you in a situation."

"It wasn't a 'situation,'" Nina said with air quotes, and closed the car door. "She didn't seem to be bothered at all." Just then, they saw Paris come out of the store and put her bag in the trunk of a very sleek, very expensive automobile.

"Wonder if Wilson bought her that car?" Natalie remarked somewhat absentmindedly.

"Nat! You are so messy!"

"I don't mean to be…"

"She is a very prominent, and I'm sure very well paid attorney who can buy her own car."

"You his woman and you certainly don't drive a car like that!" Natalie rolled her eyes at Nina and backed out of the parking space.

Back at the clinic, Natalie talked with Natasha about Erica Brooks coming to work there. "That's a decision Safety Alliance needs to make. Not us. They need to decide how all the publicity around her case affects them and what they do. Don't make a hasty decision. Let's take a beat and consider all the pros and cons."

"I saw Paris today." Nina told Wilson.

"Oh, yeah?"

Nina told him about the conversation with Paris, and what she and Natalie wanted to do with Erica.

"I like the idea, but Natasha is right. Safety Alliance needs to make that decision." They talked a few more minutes and then Nina circled back to Paris.

"It was a little weird seeing Paris."

"Why?"

"Wondering if she wanted to ask about us."

"That's not her style. It could be eating her up inside, but she won't show it. But with that being said, how would Paris know about us? We don't travel in the same circles. My question is, why do you care and why wouldn't you want to answer?"

"I never said I wouldn't answer!" Nina rolled her eyes.

"What would you say, baby?" Wilson was laughing.

"I'm sure Ms. Motley has bigger fish to fry than us!"

"I'm sure you're right." Wilson changed the subject, but in his gut he wondered what Paris thought. At some point, their paths were going to cross.

That point came sooner than Wilson thought it would. Unbeknownst to him, Natalie invited the Safety Alliance representative to the next board meeting for discussion on their partnership. Safety Alliance had asked Paris to join their board. She agreed, and Natalie was unaware they asked her to attend the meeting.

It was a little awkward. Nina and Wilson were sitting side by side at the conference room table, having a private moment. They were forehead to forehead when the others walked in, Paris being the second to enter. "Get a room," Natasha said, and laughed. A couple of seconds passed before Wilson realized Paris was in the room.

Natalie didn't waste any time getting started, making the appropriate introductions. As the meeting progressed, Nina sized up Paris. They couldn't be more different. Paris was glamorous, with nails, lashes, and jewelry, and her perfume was pleasant from across the table.

Wilson was watching Paris too. She was professionally impressive. There were things about her he would always admire, but he didn't miss all that was Paris Motley; the pretentiousness, the glamor she paid for, and her air. From this new perspective, he wondered what originally attracted him to her. Paris felt all eyes on her. What they didn't understand, she wanted the meeting to be over and to leave. Looking at her phone the second time for emphasis, Paris finally announced to the group; looking at Natalie, "I have to leave." Leaning over, Paris whispered something to the Safety Alliance representative, then reached for her bag and left the room. Once inside her car, she sat for a moment and took a deep, deliberate breath, then drove home with the music too loud to hear her thoughts. Nina waited for Wilson to address Paris being at the meeting. He didn't, so she did.

"Another awkward encounter with Paris."

Wilson shrugged. "Awkward?" He shrugged again. Nina looked impatient, so he needed to respond.

"Babe, it wasn't 'awkward' to me. My time with Paris is over. I don't have any connection to her anymore. She is a member of the Safety Alliance board now. I'm sure we will be in her presence again." He paused. "I love you. I don't care who's around or what the situation is."

Ultimately, the board and Safety Alliance agreed to make an offer of employment to Erica Brooks, and she accepted. Her impact was immediate. The clinic was glad to have this partnership, and the community was glad to have a place to go.

In the shower, Paris allowed herself to think now, knowing Wilson left her for Nina. Of all the scenarios she had contemplated, that wasn't one. "Nina Joyner, young, attractive, smart, big family.

That's it. He wants children. I shouldn't have told him I didn't want kids. I should have told him I couldn't have kids." Then the dam broke. She didn't sleep much that night.

"Hello." Wilson wasn't surprised to see Paris' face on the caller id screen.

"Hi Wilson."

"Paris."

"Can we talk for a couple minutes?" She was beating around the bush to gauge his mood.

"Okay."

"I guess I… I know now that you left me for Nina." He didn't respond. "I just don't understand why."

Wilson took a beat. "Paris, our relationship ended for the reason I told you. I wasn't happy. The relationship wasn't for me. I had outgrown it. None of that had anything to do with Nina; she came later."

"Later! It's only been a few months!" She caught herself. Raising her voice was not going to get her anywhere with him. "I'm sorry for raising my voice."

Wilson didn't respond directly to that comment. "Look, my relationship with Nina, the timing, whatever has zero to do with you, or what used to be us." He paused, but she didn't comment. "Obviously we will see each other from time to time, so I ask that you respect Nina, and respect our relationship." When a long pause had passed and Paris didn't say anything. Wilson ended the call.

CHAPTER 50

Charlotte, North Carolina

"Hello Miss Brooks, my name is Luisa Fernanda and I need your help." Erica had heard this refrain dozens of times since she started working for Safety Alliance, but this one hit her in the gut because the caller was whispering, and then the call disconnected. Erica was able to capture the phone number and call the police. The call was traced to a fast-food restaurant only about a mile from the clinic. Erica got Natalie to go with her and pretend they were customers. None of the name tags of the people they could see said "Luisa."

They both ordered fries and vanilla shakes, and took a seat. After a few minutes, a young lady brought them napkins. Written on the second napkin in the stack was a phone number and the letters "LF." Erica turned her back to the counter and called the number. The same voice answered.

"Can you come to my office?" Erica asked.

"I'm afraid."

"I will wait here for you if I need to."

"Okay, I get off in one hour," Luisa whispered.

An hour and ten minutes later, Luisa sat on the loveseat in Erica's office. "I don't want to go back home, but I don't got nowhere to go." Luisa was crying.

"Are you willing to press charges against him?"

Luisa was quiet for a moment. "Miss Brooks, we are illegal. If I press charges, I will be deported." Her speech slurred because of her busted lip.

"Do you have children, Luisa?"

"Si. One daughter."

"How old?"

"Ocho."

"We need to get her from school."

Erica stood to go. Luisa didn't. She just didn't know what to do. "I know you're afraid, Luisa, but you can't stay with a man who hurts you." By this time, Erica could see the police officer in the lobby.

"You need to decide. I'm here to support your decision."

A few minutes later, Luisa, Erica, and the officer arrived at the school to get Valeria, who wasn't there. "Mr. Fernanda signed her out right after lunch. He told us she had a doctor's appointment." Luisa cried. "There is no doctor's appointment, Erica said. He wanted to get her away from Mrs. Fernanda."

"Do you have a picture of Señor Fernanda?" The officer asked.

Luisa pulled out her phone, hands shaking. Erica took it from her. They found a couple of pictures, one of the three of them. "Don't worry, ma'am, we'll find them."

Through the course of the questions the officer found out that Mr. Fernanda did not own a car and didn't have much money, which meant he couldn't get away fast, but the flip side was he could be on a bus or in a taxi, headed in any direction.

Erica took Luisa back to her office to wait for the police. Erica took pictures of her half-healed lip, and the bruises on her arm, and Luisa shared pictures from her phone of a knot on her forehead from months before.

Erica was taken aback when Luisa asked her about killing her husband. "Don't go down that road Luisa." Erica told her sincerely. "Don't let my story, or my outcome, persuade you to do that. I took a man's life."

"But he was trying to kill you!"

"You're right. That doesn't make it easier, though. I think about it every day. I dream about it. People still harass me about it."

Before they knew it, the clinic was closing, and it was getting dark outside. They hadn't heard anything from the police.

"I think you should go home in case Valeria comes back."

"I'm afraid to be there with him by myself."

"One of our volunteers will stay with you. We wouldn't leave you alone, and tomorrow I want you to talk with our lawyer, Ms. Motley."

"She the one who help you not go to jail," Luisa smiled. Erica was nervous; Luisa wanted her husband dead and wanted Paris to get her exonerated, too. Erica needed to talk to Paris before she met with Luisa.

It had been eight hours and no sign of Mr. Fernanda and Valeria. Luisa had cried, and now was laying across the bed wide awake. The volunteer from Safety Alliance was on the sofa in the other room, where Valeria usually slept.

A little before 10:00 P.M. an alarm from Luisa's phone startled her. It was a reminder for her to wake her husband. Tonight was one of the nights he helped clean the floors in the mall. He would always do the job because he was paid in cash when they finished. Luisa bounded from the bed and told the Safety Alliance volunteer she knew he would show up for the job because of how much they paid. They alerted the police and Erica.

Shortly after midnight, the police found Mr. Fernanda at the mall, and Valeria was asleep in the employees' locker room. Fernanda couldn't actually be arrested; Valeria was his daughter. Luisa wanted to press charges, but their illegal status complicated things. For the night, she went to the apartment with Valeria and Mr. Fernanda agreed to stay away.

Erica knew the arrangement wouldn't last. Luisa needed another plan; Paris knew that, too. Paris made sure the school principal knew that only Mrs. Fernanda was to pick up Valeria from school. The truth, there was no judge's order or legal document, but Paris made the statement sound official.

Paris awakened in the middle of the night. "I know what would work for Luisa." Sitting up in bed, she made notes on the pad from her nightstand. "And Wilson will be impressed."

CHAPTER 51

The day following Cornelius and Adam's visit to Sullivan; he found them and said he would pay to cover the damage and equipment. "Not because anybody I know is guilty, but because I don't need your kind spreading rumors around this town. I have to live here and you will be gone. I can afford it, and looks like that's a problem for you."

Cornelius smirked. "However you need to satisfy your own conscience. Our only interest is our land." They agreed on a price and walked the few blocks to the bank. Albert Sullivan averted a community scandal. Cornelius, Adam, and James Fine recovered what they were owed.

The following day, Adam and Cornelius left New Amsterdam. Prior to, Adam had a long talk with James and Ruth, and with Eleanor. They assured Adam they would keep him abreast of the sequence of events leading to getting things resolved. Adam assured them he would come back at a minute's notice. Cornelius' departure was less intimate, fairly formal actually. Upon their return to North Carolina, Adam and Cornelius got caught up on things there. It was business as usual until Adam talked with his aunt Hannah. Her news startled him. His mother had committed him to escort Miss Dove Kelley to her ball.

"Without asking me?" Adam raised his voice.

"Yes, and be quiet," Hannah whispered.

"That's why I'm telling you. So you can prepare your response.

Later that same evening, Beatrice approached Adam and announced that he would escort Dove. He was glad he already knew, so she couldn't see his actual reaction, which was more directed at her audacity than the event itself.

"Do I understand, Mother, that you have committed me to this task?"

"Time was of the essence, and you were away so long. Mrs. Kelley called on me personally and was so gracious and kind. She wants her daughter to be in the company of the most eligible bachelor in the area." Those kinds of compliments were flattering and important to Beatrice, and Adam knew it.

"Please share the details, Mother."

The cotillion was an outstanding event. There was dancing, good food, and wine. Adam had a delightful time despite his reservations, and Dove was good company. He thought she would be unattractive or shy or socially awkward since her mother chose an escort for her. At the end of the night, Adam asked Dove if he could call on her at home. She said yes.

Two weeks after getting back from North Carolina, Adam received a post from Eleanor. The letter confirmed the arrival of equipment for James' garden and let him know the process was going well. She updated him on everything going on in the community, including Sullivan's brothers-in-law, not being seen for weeks. The end of the letter was the most exciting part. She wrote that James and Ruth were expecting another baby.

In his return post addressed to Eleanor, but written to James, Adam exclaimed his utter joy in being an uncle again and told James he would continue to pray for them. He also renewed his commitment to do anything he could to help them. The end of his letter told James about Dove.

As Adam spent more time with Dove, he became more interested in her worldview. She was an accomplished musician, playing the piano and harp, and liked to read, but he was specifically interested in her opinion on slavery and racial issues. He wanted to know if the relationship was to head to marriage, could he tell her about James, or would he have to treat her like they did his mother and keep that information from her? He prayed for the former. He had to figure out a way to ask her. Interestingly, he wanted to talk to James. A month later, he sent a telegram to Eleanor informing her of his plans to travel to New Amsterdam.

Adam was very impressed with the progress James had made. He was also amused with how much Pansy had grown, and he was a little envious of Ruth and James having another baby. The evening before he was to leave, Adam had dinner with the family and then had a talk with James in the garden.

James assured him he was fine financially, but Adam gave him money, anyway. Then James asked him why he was really there. "I know you ain't come all dis way to check on my garden. What on ya mind?"

Adam chuckled. James waited. Adam finally started talking."Her name is Dove."

"Like a bird?" James asked, laughing.

"Yes." Adam laughed too.

"I want to tell her about you and your family, but first I need to know how she thinks."

James understood.

"Don't make no problems for yosef on my account. You and me, we okay. Any trouble she may cause could come back on Cornelius, and even Aunt Hannah."

Adam sighed. "Or our grandfather."

"And even you."

"I don't like living in untruth like Father."

"I thank ya jus' axe 'er. If she give ya a straight answer, then ya know. If not, ya still know." Adam shook his head in agreement. James continued. "But ya know she gonna 'spect a answer to the same question."

"I'm prepared to tell her I believe all men are equal in the sight of God, and while I understand society and business, I oppose slavery and any kind of forced servitude."

"Even if it cost ya her hand?"

"Yes. At whatever cost."

Four months later, Eleanor received an announcement from Mr. and Mrs. Paul Kelley informing her of the marriage of their daughter Dove Pauline to Mr. Adam Cornelius Fine. She immediately sent back a note of congratulations.

A month before the wedding, Adam came to New Amsterdam to visit again. He knew he wouldn't be able to visit as much once he and Dove were married. He reviewed James' records, which were in great shape. Adam was pleasantly surprised, but he shouldn't have been. James and Ruth's life was very organized. Despite everything, the farm was showing a monthly profit, as was the flower stand. Adam was relieved to tell James that he and Dove had talked, and she shared his views on the abhorrent nature of forced servitude, and told him that her parents allowed those in their "employ" to learn to read and write, have days off, medical care, and religious services. Adam had confided in Dove that his father had a son with a former slave and his mother didn't know. She confided in him that her father had more than one child with a former slave, and her mother was well aware. Adam stopped short of telling Dove he had a relationship with his father's other son.

When Adam and Dove returned from their honeymoon, they found among the congratulatory telegrams, one from Eleanor announcing the birth of Ruth and James' son, Lemuel James Fine. Interestingly, he was born the day of Adam and Dove's wedding.

CHAPTER 52

Over the years, Adam made two or three annual visits to New Amsterdam. He and Dove had two children, like James and Ruth, but both boys.

Adam noted in every visit how advanced Pansy was. She read very young and was good with numbers. Ruth told Adam how quickly she was advancing through the colored church school. The problem was, there was no public school for colored children in their community. Fortunately for Pansy, Adam was able to find a Quaker teacher who agreed to tutor her privately.

"What all dis mean, Adam?" Ruth asked.

"It means Pansy can get the education she deserves, and not be bound by the limits here in New Amsterdam."

Ruth looked at James. "Lawd a mercy. What ya thank, James?"

"I agree wit Adam, this be good for 'er."

After a couple years of marriage, Adam confided in Dove that he and James had a relationship. She was surprised, but not shocked. Dove came to see Adam in the shop one afternoon and brought lunch. As they ate and discussed matters with their sons, she asked to accompany him on the next trip to New York. "I would like to meet Ruth and James." Her request caught Adam off guard, but he expected it to come at some point. "Yes. On my next trip."

Three months later and a week before his trip to New York, Adam sent a telegram to Eleanor alerting her to his arrival. There wasn't anything unusual about that, as that was standard practice. The unusual part was the last sentence of the message; "Dove will accompany me on this trip. Eleanor was amazed when she read it. James and Ruth were stunned when they heard it.

Ruth liked Dove immediately. The feeling was mutual and Dove recognized right away that James was right about Pansy. Dove taught her a scale, on the old out of tune piano in the living room, which she played correctly on the first try.

At seventeen, Pansy Fine was admitted to Bennett College in Greensboro, North Carolina, a long way from her family in New Amsterdam, New York. The only comfort James and Ruth had, she would be close to Adam and Dove. It was Adam's suggestion that Pansy enroll at Bennett, and he paid her tuition. He told them he knew someone who worked there. James was having a hard time with her leaving. The nucleus around him seemed to be constantly changing. Mary had passed away. His baby sister Rose had married a serviceman and moved away. Lemuel was good at farming, but was even better at machines, and was going to enlist in the military.

After leaving her parents in North Carolina at 20, traveling by boat to Ontario, Canada and then moving to New Amsterdam, New York, Grace Fine Miller had a full life. Now standing over her mother's grave crying, all she wanted now was to settle into a quiet life with Theodore.

James and Ruth's businesses flourished over the years and Eleanor found she didn't have to "protect" them and their interests as much. Eventually, she met a gentleman in church. They married and had 2 children. But in all of their minds and hearts, they knew Eleanor would come on a moment's notice. She had promised Miss Margaret.

Supposedly, Albert Sullivan's brothers-in-law never returned to New Amsterdam, but the whispers persisted about the two black children, one of them fathered. Sullivan died a few years after he had the run in with James, Cornelius and Adam about the fire. Shortly before he died, he had a dispute with another black family in the town, precipitated by his wife.

CHAPTER 53

Pansy did well in college. Like her mother, she was very organized, and adapted quickly to the academic rigor. But she was terribly homesick. Almost every day, writing a letter to someone in her family; her grandmother Grace, her brother Lemuel, or her parents. Sometimes writing them separately.

Lemuel encouraged her to join a club on campus. She wasn't shy and had made friends, but she was afraid to do anything to impede her progress in her classes. "Jus' try it. If it don't work, you feel better 'cause you try." He had been her biggest supporter and helped convince their parents that going to college was good for her. From time to time, he would send her money from the odd jobs he did around the community, fixing things.

Taking her brother's advice, Pansy joined the choir as one of the accompanists, and eventually was initiated into Alpha Kappa Alpha Sorority. One of the highlights of Pansy's years at Bennett was the monthly visits to see Adam, Dove and their sons in Charlotte. She would board the train on Friday and go back to Greensboro on Sunday evening. The transit time allowed her to read or study.

James and Ruth told Pansy and Lemuel the whole story about Adam when they were teens. They never met Cornelius, but on her first visit, Pansy met their great Aunt Hannah.

While in Charlotte, Pansy stayed in a basement area in the Fine's home. When she described it to Grace, her grandmother told her that was where her family lived. Based on Pansy's account of the plantation, they had downsized the number of servants and now had a dozen or so sharecropper families.

Cornelius was managing the plantation business, and Adam was managing the retail businesses. As was their practice, Adam and Pansy would review any challenges she was having in her bookkeeping or accounting classes. They also talked about Fine China. Pansy probably knew more about the company than anyone except Adam.

James, Ruth, and Lemuel rode the train from New Amsterdam to Greensboro to see Pansy graduate. Adam and Dove came too. It was a grand occasion. Topping it off was the opportunity for Pansy to introduce her family to Thomas Wilson, with whom she had been "keeping company."

James described him to Adam as "sturdy with working man's hands." They learned Thomas worked for the Post Office and was from Rock Hill, South Carolina. He had come to Greensboro to attend North Carolina Agriculture and Technical State University, and graduated the year before.

A job in the office of Bennett College was offered to Pansy as a bookkeeper. She accepted it and moved into a boarding house close to campus. She continued to make her monthly visits to see Adam. Now, during her visits, Adam had work for her to do. He valued her input, and her help in better organizing his accounts. They worked well together. Just like her grandmother, Pansy absorbed everything her Uncle Adam taught her. She made notes and studied the notes in her spare time. Fine China's profits soared until 1930, when the country fell into the Great Depression.

CHAPTER 54

The Fine Plantation's farming business survived during the depression. James' farms did well too. People had to eat, but they didn't order flower arrangements from Ruth or buy China from Adam. It was a tough season, but they managed. As the country dealt with the end of the depression, Thomas Wilson proposed to Pansy. They went to New Amsterdam to be married, then moved back to Greensboro. Adam made sure they had no issues being able to buy a house. Pansy was now the supervisor of the accounts department at the college and Thomas was still working at the Post Office.

By the time World War II started, Lemuel was old enough to go. Ruth was sick about it. Pansy was worried too, but she tried not to let her parents know. Her cousins, Adam's sons, were both enlisted, too. Lemuel had a hard time in the war. The black soldiers were treated unfairly, and paid less than the white soldiers. But, after four years, he came back home. Tragedy hit the other Fines. Both of Adam's sons were killed in the war. The news of the second death came when Thomas and Pansy were visiting Charlotte. They died three months apart.

Pansy wrote her parents, *"Aunt Dove is inconsolable. I don't know that she will ever be the same again. She cries a lot, barely eats or talks. Uncle Adam drinks a lot and is often not at home. He hasn't been sober for weeks. The business would suffer if I were not helping. My time is limited to be there with him."*

Pansy was distressed watching Fine China suffer because of Adam's absences, and lack of interest. She went to Charlotte and talked to Hannah. Together, they confronted Adam. The result; Pansy quit her job at the college, moved to Charlotte and took over operating Fine China.

In the midst of the move and getting settled, Pansy realized she was expecting. There was just too much going on. Thomas was still in Greensboro, so he could keep his job. She was having a baby, and the company was on the brink of ruin. Her mother couldn't come help her with the baby. They didn't know, even after all these years, what might happen since Ruth had left the plantation through the Quaker network.

On one of Adam's better days, Hannah told him some of what was going on with Pansy and the store. He didn't immediately react or respond, but later that day he went to the shop to see Pansy. She was there alone, as he had hoped. "Pansy."

"Hello Uncle Adam."

"I hope you can forgive me for leaving you with my disarray. I appreciate you and your loyalty to the family business."

"I couldn't let you lose everything. You are in a terrible situation."

"Pansy, my dear niece, the pain of burying your child is beyond anything you can imagine, but having to do it two times made me not want to live." He had tears in his eyes, and Pansy's tears streamed down her face. She could hear the pain in his voice.

"Take the time you need. I have brought order to things here. Aunt Hannah has been here to help with the customers who don't want to see me," Pansy said. "And she brought her daughter, my cousin Sarah. She has been very helpful." Adam loved the kindness in her voice.

He sighed deeply. "I'm sorry for abandoning you and the business, and I'm sorry you have to deal with hateful people." He placed his hands on her shoulder. "Have you heard from my brother?" They changed the subject to talk about James, Ruth, and Lemuel.

Adam was sober and clear-eyed, so Pansy showed him the books, the payables and receivables. He realized right then how negligent he had been, but the company had survived and made a profit. He asked to see the payroll. When Pansy showed him the ledger, he gasped. "You did not pay yourself fairly. I insist that your wage be the same at least as you were paid at the college."

"Thank you. I wanted to allow the profit to recover."

"No need. Without you, there is no company, money, or profit." They were quiet for a few minutes while Adam continued to study the ledgers.

Pansy broke the silence. "Uncle, I have a request."

"Anything."

"Thomas and I are having a baby."

Adam looked at her. He had not even noticed. He took her hands. "That's wonderful. I know your parents are delighted."

She smiled. "Yes sir, they are. But we are afraid for my mother to come here, and I will need some help."

Adam thought briefly. "Don't fret. I will get you some help, and I will figure out a way for James and Ruth to visit."

CHAPTER 55

Charlotte, North Carolina

Over the next couple of days, Paris made meticulous notes. Once her plan was developed, she called Natalie and asked her to arrange a call meeting with Wilson, Nina, Natasha, Erik, and herself. We can meet in my office's conference room. Paris wanted to be on offense. She had to convince Wilson and he would convince the others.

Over the months that followed Erica's acquittal, Paris had an onslaught of requests to defend someone in a domestic violence situation. Attorneys in other states called and offered to give her temporary license to practice if she did not have credentials. There were even a few requests from men who were being battered by their female partners.

One case very similar to Erica's, the woman killed her abusive live-in boyfriend, but her case ended in a hung jury. She was hiding from him, had to quit her job and stay away from her family and friends. There had to be a better way to help these victims.

Two days later, they all assembled in the conference room at Motley and Motley, P.A.. Wilson had come under protest. Natalie had to convince him. He just didn't know what to expect from Paris. "You know her, Wilson. If she's up to something, you can diffuse it," Nina said to him.

Wilson knew Nina was right, but he had a gut feeling this wasn't going to go well. Paris' style was not impromptu. She was a planner, an organizer and liked bells and whistles presentations. He had to decide to give her the benefit of the doubt.

Paris was ready. She had her written proposal and Power Point presentation set up. The intent was convincing Wilson to embrace her vision, and in doing so, have time with him. The ultimate goal was to have him back in her life–full time. She would accept his proposal and if he couldn't be steered otherwise, she would agree to have one child.

The instant Wilson saw Paris; he knew there was a full-fledged plan. She was dressed in navy, her signature kick ass color. He and Nina walked in together. Natalie and Erik came a minute later. Erica Brooks was already there. Wilson studied Erica's body language. He was trying to determine if she knew what was going on. As everyone was getting settled, Natalie announced Natasha would be late and they should start without her.

CHAPTER 56

Pansy and Thomas' daughter was born four months after she told her uncle Adam about the baby. They named her Belle. True to his word, Adam got Ruth into town for a month. Lemuel and James came separately for a short time each. While Pansy was out, Hannah's daughter Sarah took charge of the retail side of the business and Adam kept the operations side moving.

Most days Pansy didn't think about the fact that she owned Fine China. Adam rewarded Pansy's loyalty by giving her the store. No matter how she protested, he insisted. Being completely honest, Pansy told Adam about her fear of owning the business.

"I know the business, but I know white people take businesses from colored people."

"You are not wrong, my niece, but I have taken precautions to avoid that circumstance."

Pansy had only told Thomas and Lemuel, who agreed her parents would worry if they knew she actually owned the business.

As per his will, Augustus Fine, Adam's grandfather, left the Fine China Company to him. Cornelius was aware, and relieved not to have that responsibility. He wanted his father to sell the store and concentrate on farming. That part of the business was more lucrative in his opinion, especially since he had planted acres of trees, including pine trees, which were becoming popular as Christmas trees. And he was selling manure to other farms who didn't have cattle. The retail portion in Cornelius' opinion was too top heavy, having to keep inventory, and it required more human resources to work in the store and fill orders. Cornelius was never a fan of hard work. He was perfectly fine watching other people do the work and reaping the benefits. Adam having the store also kept him out of Cornelius' personal business.

Adam knew the store was his to do with as he pleased. After the deaths of his and Dove's sons, he really didn't care what happened to it or anything else. All the china in the country and all the money in the world wouldn't give him back his children or the life he had known with Dove. Many times he wished Pansy had let the business "go to hell" he told Dove. "Pansy is just like her parents. Loyal, hardworking, true." Not until after the transaction was done did he even tell Dove. He never officially told Cornelius. He wrote a letter and attached it to his will.

Belle Wilson followed her mother to Bennett College and two years after graduating with a degree in education, married John Peters. John worked for Fine China. Her mother hired him as the delivery driver and stock clerk. He quickly learned the business and took on more responsibility.

Belle and John had one son, who they named Wilson. He took over the business in his twenties and expanded it. He rebranded it as The Fine Companies and added tobacco and wine. Wilson and his wife, Joyce, had five children. Two daughters older and two daughters younger than their only son, Wilson Peters, Jr. who inherited The Fine Companies.

Though not formally educated, John Peters was smart, and he understood the retail business. Early in their years of working together and when it was clear to Pansy and Thomas that John intended to marry Belle, they told the young couple the truth about the ownership of Fine China. They explained that Pansy's uncle Adam had given the business to her. They showed them the official documents signed by Adam Fine and a lawyer. Their desire was to will the company to Belle and John. Working with a friend John had at the local bank, a document was created stating Pansy Fine Wilson's desire to give the Fine China Company to her daughter and son-in-law upon her death. The final caveat in the document stated the store was to remain in Pansy's bloodline. The wording copied verbatim from the document Adam had given her all those years before.

CHAPTER 57

"Around 1830, a Quaker family in Charlotte took a 19-year-old girl on a ship and sent her to Canada. She was the last of the slaves released into freedom by Augustus Fine, under the auspice of a delivery from the Fine China Company." Paris was talking. Wilson was stunned, and couldn't find his words to ask her why she was telling his family's history.

"Each generation of the Fine family used their resources for social justice initiatives…"

Nina was totally blindsided. In all the years she had known Wilson, they hadn't ever discussed any of this. She was totally unaware of his family's activism. The more Paris talked, the more astonished Nina became.

"The Fines used their company to smuggle civil rights activists out of the country in the sixties, used their financial leverage to help other budding entrepreneurs get business loans and buy homes in the seventies. Mr. Wilson Peters, Sr. helped organize the Million Man March in the 1990s."

By now, everyone in the room could feel the tension. Natasha had come in and sat beside Nina, but no one even noticed. As Paris talked, Natasha could see how offended Nina looked. She wondered if Nina didn't know or couldn't believe Paris was using this scheme to get Wilson's attention.

Everyone also knew where Paris was going with this. She wanted The Fine Companies–Wilson's company to use the concept of making deliveries as a front to help victims of domestic violence. Paris also wanted Nina to know she knew Wilson's family. Under other circumstances, it would have been a good idea, but why present it like this?

Wilson shifted in his seat and put his arm around the back of Nina's chair. He knew she wasn't aware of any of this. Not that he didn't want her to know or had purposefully not told her. It never came up. The only reason Paris knew was because his cousin had brought it up in a speech she gave at a family reunion one year.

The only persons in the audience who looked supportive were Erica and Lisa from Safety Alliance. As Paris went on, Nina shifted in her seat. Wilson could see her in his periphery. He reached for her hand. He rubbed her thumb with his.

The presentation included creating a network of businesses and individuals across the country. She finally admitted it, "to move victims of domestic violence." At this point, shifting to talking about what the partners would look like.

Wilson squeezed Nina's hand slightly and then let it go. He leaned forward with both forearms on the table and made eye contact with Paris. She braced herself. He interrupted her. His voice was raised. "Paris, you have *NO* right to use my family's history or *MY* business to capitalize on this effort. No matter how noble it may be." Nina patted his back. He lowered his voice minimally. "And you, of all people, know this is illegal. It was illegal when my ancestors engaged initially and by the grace of God, they didn't get caught or worse. I have absolutely no intention of participating in your plan." He was loud again. The tension in the room was thick. Nobody was saying anything. All eyes were on Wilson.

Paris jumped in. "I'm not trying to capitalize and there are legal ways to make it happen."

When Wilson talked, everyone listened intently. Erik, not knowing the history of Wilson and Paris, was simply listening. Natalie was fidgeting. Erica was afraid for Paris. She did not know of Wilson and Paris' past either, but it didn't sound like her plan was a good idea.

Wilson was so angry. He was embarrassed that Paris had done all this in front of Nina and they hadn't ever talked about it. He would have to apologize and answer all her questions as soon as possible.

"Paris, the courteous thing to do was to talk to me about this first, before you unveiled my family's secrets. I don't fully understand your intent, but I know you thrive on the element of surprise. What is it you and your dad always say? 'You can't unring the bell.'"

"Wilson, my intent is only to help victims of domestic violence," Paris responded, looking at Lisa and then Erica.

"That may be your secondary intent, but your primary intent is to make sure you have an inroad to me, and to insure Nina knows about it."

The room was completely silent for a long moment. "Ladies and gentleman this presentation is over." He looked directly at Paris. "To everybody in this room…" he looked around, making eye contact with Lisa and then Erica. "…if this moves forward, I will withdraw my support from the clinic."

An audible gasp. It was Natalie. "Wilson!" Nina said, leaning toward him and frowning.

Natasha patted her back. Lisa didn't look at Paris. She just closed her portfolio, got her purse, and left. Erica dropped her head but didn't move. Erik said something to Natalie in her ear. She looked back at her sisters. Natasha nodded, and Natalie and Erik left the room. A minute later, Natasha hugged Nina and left, too. Erica took a deep breath and sat for another couple of minutes before grabbing her bag and leaving.

"Nina, will you excuse us, please?"

"Say what you want to say in front of her," Wilson told Paris.

Paris sat. She had been standing since the presentation started. Deep sigh. Offense. "I had absolutely no ill intent in thinking this was a good way to help domestic violence victims escape their abusers. And how would I know Nina wasn't aware of your family history?"

"That's fucking irrelevant! You just wanted to put on a show at Nina's expense.

Nina was surprised at Wilson's language, but Paris wasn't. She was also puzzled by why he was so angry.

"Nina! Wrong. I'm not remotely interested in doing anything at Nina's expense," Paris said with air quotes. "I think you're trying to save face because you never told her.

"Don't talk about me like I'm not here!" Nina said firmly, looking at Paris. "Trying to find an avenue for domestic violence victims is certainly a lofty goal, and if you thought using the process of the Fine family was the way to go, you should have discussed it with Wilson first not blindsided him in front of the group. You know him well enough to know he doesn't like surprises!" Nina stood. "What you don't get is, if your intention was pure, you blew it. He will never agree now under any circumstances, and the victims don't have an advocate."

Paris didn't respond.

Nina looked at Wilson. "Let's go. We'll talk about this at home."

The words "at home" tugged at the pit of Paris' stomach.

CHAPTER 58

"Man! What's up? I haven't seen you in what, ten years?" They laughed. "This is Nina Joyner...."

Nina and Wilson stopped to eat after they left Paris' office. He ran into an old teammate, and just like that, he was in a good mood. He told Nina about their days playing college basketball together and playing against each other in Europe. As she listened and laughed, Nina waited until they were home to broach the subject of Paris Motely and her plan.

Paris sat alone in her office's conference room for a long while, eyes closed, both hands covering her face. No tears. She just didn't understand what went wrong. "The plan is good. It would work. Wilson didn't give it a chance. Why is this about him and not the people we could help?" Her mind raced from one thought to another. A few more minutes passed. She shrugged, gathered her things, and said out loud, "Wilson just won't think outside the box."

"Let's sit on the deck," Nina said to Wilson. She got lime sparkling water and a beer from the refrigerator. They settled in their usual spot on the lounge chair. It was extra-long because Wilson was so tall. He sat with her between his legs.

“We need to deal with the elephant in the room.”

“Okay.”

“I know Paris didn’t handle the proposal well, but it’s really not a bad idea.” She waited for his response. He adjusted his body in the chair but didn’t say anything. “I agree with you that Paris absolutely should not be involved, but I think Safety Alliance could use the strategy in the most extreme cases.” She paused again. Still nothing from him. “I know your family made major sacrifices to see this through, but baby, they were activists, and you should be proud.” Nina had been leaning back, laying on Wilson’s chest. She sat up and looked over her shoulder at him. Wilson let out a big sigh and pulled her back to him. With his arms around Nina, he finally responded.

“First, I’m sorry for never telling you about this part of my family’s history. When I first learned about it, I was proud, but as I got older and understood the legal ramifications, I was uneasy. My dad and I talked over the years about whether the business was really ours. The two of us never saw any legal or official documents. How did we know some of the white Fines wouldn’t try to take everything away from us? My great-great-grandfather’s half-brother gave my great grandmother the store in the 1930s after the depression. God only knows if there was any documentation.”

“Babe, I understand your concern, and it’s legitimate. And let me say this: you don’t owe me an apology. I’m glad I know now, and that’s a significant part of who you are. How many people do you know who inherited a business that passed through so many generations and have been able to expand it at the level you have? The Fine Companies belong to you.”

For over an hour, they discussed the pros and cons of putting an operation in place that could be used as a vehicle to get victims of domestic violence away from their abusers. They called Natalie and Erik, who had been living together for a few months now. Natalie had a myriad of ideas. The one thing they could not decide on was whether to involve Safety Alliance because Paris was on their board now. Wilson didn't think they should or could trust her. He knew she wouldn't take kindly to them executing the plan she initially created without her.

At the conclusion of the conversation, Erik had committed his parents and their resources to the project; and convinced the other three that his mother would be the perfect person to oversee the process. They didn't decide what to do with Paris.

Months later, the plan was in full effect. Luisa and Valeria Fernanda were the first to pass through the network, and their process went smoothly.

CHAPTER 59

Charlotte, North Carolina

"Nina, dahling, how in the world are you?"

It was Magnolia calling. "I know we need to catch up, Maggie, but I'm really busy."

"No, no. Listen, Reba finally confided in me what happened with her crazy husband and has to get away from here. I'm sending her to Charlotte, Nina. Can she dance in your company?"

"Of course I can use her, but I'm not in production right now, so I can't pay her."

"Let her do lessons. Whatever, dear. She will figure it out. She simply must leave The City."

Two days later, Nina picked up Reba from the airport, and checked her into an extended stay hotel. The next morning, Reba and Nina met at the clinic, and explained the situation to Erica. For the next few days, Erica and Reba worked together and found Reba a teacher assistant position in physical education at a middle school.

The pain in the side of her head came from absolutely nowhere. Reba fell into the brick wall. Before she could get her bearings, the second punch came. This time to her stomach. "Did you really think you could get away from me?" He laughed, and left her on the ground.

It took a few minutes for Reba to gather herself. Fortunately, Erica was picking her up from work, and it wasn't long before she arrived to find Reba sitting on the ground against the wall. She couldn't move. Erica finally got Reba in the car, took her straight to the emergency room and called Nina.

"How the hell did he find her?" Wilson asked, after Nina explained to him what happened.

"We just don't know. She won't admit to telling anyone but her mother and sister. Unless one of them told him."

Reba had only stayed in the hospital a few hours, and went home with Erica. She didn't have any broken bones. The doctor diagnosed maybe a mild concussion, but Reba had refused the CT scan. Her insurance hadn't started yet.

A week after the incident, Reba moved in with one of the Safety Alliance volunteers, Jackie. They hit it off quickly. Reba was content and more at ease than she had been in years. They didn't venture out much, but tonight was Jackie's birthday. They walked to a restaurant, had dinner and drinks. On the way back, two blocks from the house, a man approached them. "Well Reba. We meet again." Jackie knew immediately he was Reba's husband, and her training kicked in. Jackie looked him over from head to toe. Hair color, eye color, height, weight, scars, tattoos-anything that wouldn't change. She looked for something to use as a weapon. A split second later, she heard a blast. Reba had shot him. One shot to his chest. He hit the ground hard. Reba laid the gun down slowly and kicked it away. "Call 911," she said to Jackie.

It took Jackie a minute to realize what Reba did. The man was lying on the ground, bleeding. Reba was standing perfectly still.

"911. Do you need police, fire or medic?"

"Police and medic."

In about five minutes, the fire truck and ambulance arrived. The man was pronounced dead at the scene. Reba was arrested.

"Reba, say nothing to anybody. I will meet you at the station." Jackie sounded nervous.

Reba nodded.

Nina couldn't believe her ears. Erica was telling her what Reba did the night before. "What do I need to do?" Nina asked.

"Reba needs a lawyer. I called Ms. Motley, but she said 'no.'"

Nina didn't immediately respond.

"She has to appear in court this afternoon."

"Does Safety Alliance have another attorney?"

"Yes, but he's just a regular lawyer."

"He can get her through the arraignment."

"Reba Evans Jones, you are charged with first degree premeditated murder. How do you plead?"

"Not guilty," Reba replied. Her voice was strong. Her back was straight. Her demeanor was calm.

"The people on bail?" The judge asked.

"We oppose bail, Your Honor. Mrs. Jones has no long-term ties to this community."

"Judge, she moved here to get away from Mr. Jones."

Jackie thought, "is that all he's going to say?"

Before the judge could respond, the prosecutor said, "She killed a man in cold blood."

The judge paused for just a few seconds. "Bail is set at $500,000.00. Cash or bond."

Reba looked back at Jackie. They both knew she couldn't make bail, and was headed to jail. Jackie mouthed to Reba, "I will be back."

CHAPTER 60

It was two days before Nina called Magnolia to let her know what happened.

"Oh, my stars! How is she managing?"

"She's okay, but her bail is $500,000.00. She's still in lockup."

"Dahling, you should have called me right away. I can arrange bond for her." It was exactly what Nina wanted her to say.

"We tried to work it out here first." That was a mild exaggeration. She knew Wilson would have arranged bail for Reba too. She didn't ask him. Because Nina knew he wouldn't approve of her plan.

Nina gave Magnolia the details and then let Jackie know to expect a call to get Reba.

"Who?"

"Nina Joyner."

"Is Wilson with her?"

"No."

"Give me a minute."

Paris needed time to get herself together. Why was Nina here to see her?

"Oh my God, maybe something happened to Wilson."

She walked to the reception area. Nina's body language didn't look like Paris would expect if something was going on with Wilson.

"Nina."

"Thanks for seeing me without an appointment."

"Let's go to the conference room."

For a split second, Nina questioned her decision to ask Paris for help.

"What is it, Nina?" Offense.

Deep breath. "I know Jackie Chaney asked you to represent Reba Jones, and you said no. I'm here asking you to reconsider. Please," she added.

Paris had the upper hand and knew it, but had to decide what to do with it. Smiling slightly, she folded her hands on the table in front of her. Nina waited. She had no choice.

"Does Wilson know you're here?" The minute it came out of her mouth, she wanted to take it back. That was her heart talking. This situation had to be handled with her head.

"No, he doesn't. And he won't be happy when I tell him."

Paris knew then the time since his blow up had not mellowed his attitude.

"Why do you think I can help Reba? The odds are against her."

"Yes, she shot him, but didn't mean to kill him." For the next few minutes, Nina told Paris everything she knew about Reba. All the way back to the dancer's rumors in New York. Nina recounted what Jackie told her Reba shared.

As she listened, Paris thought this was exactly the type of case she would take and win–under other circumstances.

"Will you at least talk with Reba?"

"Where is she?"

"Back at the apartment."

Paris exhaled loudly. "Bring her here tomorrow. And understand Nina, no promises. My case load is hectic, and this sounds like it's going to be a lot."

"Thank you, Paris."

"By the way, if I take this on, who's paying me?" Paris was hoping Nina would say Wilson.

"She has a sponsor."

"Sweetie, why would you do that?" Wilson had a mouthful of spaghetti, and piping hot fried tilapia on his fork. Nina didn't get it, but a friend from Memphis introduced him to spaghetti, fish and a "side of slaw." It was one of his favorite meals. She cooked it from time to time. Today was one of those times. He needed to be in a good mood.

"Paris is a good… great, even attorney with experience in cases like this. Reba is in a lot of trouble. She needs the best to be acquitted."

"I would have preferred we talked about this before you met with her." He said between bites. "I don't trust Paris."

"You don't think she will throw the case, do you?"

"No, not at all. Paris loves to win and thrives on power, but wants to get back at me. She may send Reba away and not even go through the trial. She has no idea about our process."

"I pray not. Maggie will lose her money, and Paris could lose her license."

"Not if she can convince the judge her client left on her own. Paris has a command of words and can make a compelling argument."

"We can't undo it, but you stay out of it as much as you can. I know Paris. Don't trust her, but don't underestimate her."

Jackie took Reba to meet Paris. Nina took Wilson's advice and decided not to go with them. The meeting was intense, but ultimately Paris took Reba as a client. The same day, Reba was informed she lost her new job at the school because of the incident. She was able to take over a few of Nina's private students to earn some money. Erica and Jackie stayed close, but it was a trying time for them all.

Paris was still holding out for some involvement from Wilson, but when the certified check arrived from Magnolia, she knew he really meant what he said. Months passed, but the trial finally started on a rainy Wednesday morning. Jury selection took only one day and Paris felt good about the make-up of it. There were eight women ranging in age from 26 to 67. Five of them were married.

The prosecutor's opening statement was simple. Reba planned to kill her husband and at the first opportunity, she did.

"Mrs. Jones didn't seek help from law enforcement. She took the law into her own hands."

Paris' opening statement countered. She painted a picture of a ballerina who was battered and beaten to the point of being unable to perform. "She didn't intend to kill him, just to protect herself, after being attacked two weeks before."

The prosecutor's first witness was Jackie. "State your full name, please."

"Jacklyn Adair Chaney."

"What is your relationship to Reba Jones?" The prosecutor asked.

"She is my roommate."

"Do you legally own a nine millimeter handgun?"

"Yes."

"Where is that gun now?"

"In police custody."

"Why?"

"Your Honor! The defense has already stipulated to the weapon," Paris said.

"Move on," the judge told the Prosecutor.

He questioned Jackie about how Reba came into possession of her gun.

"I kept it on the top shelf of the hall closet."

The prosecutor tried to show that Reba searched for the gun as part of her plan to kill her husband.

"Ms. Chaney, was the gun hidden?" Paris asked on cross examination.

"No. It was on a shelf in plain view."

"Should you have secured it differently?"

"I don't think so. I don't have children. Until Reba moved in, I lived alone. I wasn't trying to hide it from anybody."

Paris had determined Mr. Jones tracked Reba's transaction at a local restaurant on her debit card and that's how he found her. He had to have followed her for a few days to know where she worked. She hadn't been paid yet, so if the debit card theory was accurate, he couldn't see her employer.

The prosecution rested in two days, just the way they started; premeditated murder. They had nothing, and Paris knew it. The defense had evidence of past violence Reba suffered at the hands of Mr. Jones over several years. All of it was compelling and supported her statement that Reba was a victim of domestic abuse and had to protect herself. In doing so, she shot Mr. Jones and, because of her inexperience with a firearm, landed a fatal blow. The final expert defense witness was a counselor from Safety Alliance. "In your expert opinion, what is Mrs. Jones' condition?"

"Mrs. Jones is suffering from Battered Woman Syndrome."

"Is her behavior unusual?"

"Not at all. Her behavior before the incident and after is indicative of the disease."

In a move most attorneys wouldn't make, Paris put Reba on the stand. They were both fully aware the prosecutors would cross-examine her. Reba recounted the four and a half years with her husband. All the broken bones, days missed from work, busted lips, black eyes.

"Mrs. Jones, will you explain how you came to be in possession of Ms. Chaney's gun?"

"I found it on the top shelf of the linen closet when I was looking for a pillow."

"Why did you take it?"

"When I saw it; my thought was I could scare him away from me if he tried to jump me again."

"Explain 'jump you again.'"

"I was looking for a second pillow the day after he jumped me at work. I had a concussion and I couldn't sleep flat on my back."

"Did you tell Ms. Chaney you had the weapon?"

"No, Ms. Motley. I did not."

The questions and answers went on a while longer. Reba making her case again and again that she did not intend to use the gun, but when she had to, did not intend to kill her husband.

The prosecution repeated their same line of questioning; trying to trap Reba into admitting she wanted her husband dead. They were unsuccessful.

"Your Honor, the defense rests." The next day, the judge gave instructions to the jury and sent them to deliberate.

During the week of the trial, Paris noticed Erica and Jackie in the gallery and Nina a couple of days but no Wilson. He really was a no show. He had not come to her trials but a few times over the years, but thought he would at least come this time because Nina was so invested in it.

Paris couldn't believe her ears. She and the prosecutor were called into the judge's chambers to be told the jury was deadlocked. The prosecutor knew his case was weak and he didn't want to try it again. He asked the judge to compel the jury to continue deliberating. In Paris' mind, this was a slam dunk. The jury should have unanimously acquitted. She didn't want to retry the case either.

"Ms. Motley?"

"I agree, Your Honor." Paris wanted to know what the question was, who the hold out was and why, but couldn't ask.

Another full day and they were in the same place. This time, the judge called all parties into the courtroom. "Madam Foreperson, has the jury reached a verdict?"

"No, Your Honor. We are still deadlocked."

"What is the dissenting number?"

"We are fifty fifty, sir."

Paris and the Prosecutor were stunned.

"Would more time make a difference?"

Paris quickly scanned the jury's faces, knowing the answer before she heard it.

"No, Judge."

"Thank you." The foreperson took her seat.

“Your Honor.” The prosecutor and Paris said at the same time. The judge acknowledged Paris. “May we poll the jury?” Before answering, he looked at the other table.

“No objection.”

One by one, the jurors were asked if their vote was acquit or not acquit. Two of the four men were on the side to acquit, as were the twenty-six-year-old single woman, a fifty-five-year-old widow, the sixty and sixty-seven-year-old married women. The judge sat quietly.

“Thank you. We will take a fifteen-minute recess,” he said and left the bench.

“What does this even mean?” Reba asked Paris.

“Honestly, I don’t know. The prosecutor’s case is trash, and he knows it. But I’m surprised by the judge’s response.”

“Will we have to go through another trial?”

“That’s a good possibility, but I expect this judge will advise us to work it out with the prosecutor.” Paris stood to stretch her legs, looking over her shoulder briefly. There was Nina, Natalie and Erik, Natasha, Erica and Jackie. No Wilson. As she sat, Paris glanced over at the Prosecutor’s table. He looked puzzled and a little anxious too.

The judge came back, and with no fanfare, declared a mistrial. “Counselors, my chamber please. We are dismissed.” In chambers, the judge did exactly as Paris predicted. He admonished them to “work it out.” After about thirty minutes of back and forth, the prosecutor offered Reba five years. He was relentless against Paris’ argument for no jail time.

“You have nothing and you know it.”

"I had six jurors who believed your client planned to kill him."

"That you did," she thought.

"Five years or we retry the case."

"See you in court," Paris said, grabbing her bag. She knew he would call back.

CHAPTER 61

After the episode with Paris, Nina convinced Wilson to talk with his sisters about the situation surrounding the legalities of The Fine Companies. Whatever questions he had, the oldest sister cleared up. Jeanette assured him the original deed to Fine China was in a safe deposit box along with the original will Pansy signed documenting the company remains in her lineage. "I found it in some of Daddy's stuff when we cleaned out the house and I put it away."

"How would you like to be out of the clinic and in the studio full time?"

Wilson and Nina were driving to Edisto Island for a long weekend getaway. They hadn't had any real downtime in months. They had worked closely with Mrs. Rasmus to get the network established.

Their pact, no work or work talk this weekend. She was driving and looking straight ahead. He was looking at her. "I would love it, but the clinic can't afford it, and the timing would have to be optimum."

She glanced at him.

"According to my sister Robin, we can outsource those functions for about the same as they're paying you. The timing can be whatever it needs to be."

"I definitely would like to investigate it further."

"I will connect you and Rob next week."

"Thanks babe. What made you start the conversation with her?"

"You deserve to be in the studio full-time. Dancing is obviously your thing. You can build the dance business if you can set your own schedule and manage the distractions."

"You can have the conversation with Natalie."

"I will. I'm the board chairman who never says no, and I never make any demands. I don't expect any push back. This time, I intend to get what I want."

"What do you want, Mr. Board Chairman?" Nina looked at Wilson and winked.

Wilson took a breath. "Over this weekend, I want us to talk about starting a family."

CHAPTER 62

Charlotte, North Carolina

Reba wore a polo shirt with the Fine Company logo, jeans, and tennis shoes, and carried a box with the same logo.

"Hey Reba. You can sit that in the back," said the owner of the gift shop in the Dilworth area of Charlotte. Reba walked through the shop and into the storage area. She changed her clothes, leaving the shirt in the employee bathroom. She pulled her hair into a ponytail, put on a baseball cap and sunglasses. Driving to the airport, Reba took the carry-on bag from the trunk and left the keys inside.

One call on the burner phone walking through the airport. "Hi Mom."

"You doing alright?"

"Yep! Headed to the gate. I'll call you tomorrow."

"Be careful, sweetie. I love you."

"For sure. I love you too. And, Mom, thanks for making sure he knew where I was."

EPILOGUE

From time-to-time Adam Fine would accompany his parents to a neighboring plantation owned by the Greene Family. He went under the pretense of keeping company with their daughter, Eve. The truth: he wanted to see her maid, Miriam.

Adam hadn't ever seen a woman white or colored, he thought, more beautiful than Miriam. Her hair was thick and black. She wore it pulled back in a bun most of the time, which allowed her facial features to be seen. Her lashes were long; her lips were full. She had an ample bosom and curvy hips. Miriam aroused his curiosity and his anatomy.

On Sundays, Miriam could accompany her brother, George, who was a preacher, to visit the Fine Plantation when he came to preach to the servants and share an afternoon meal with them.

One Sunday, when she was preparing to leave, Adam approached her heading to the wagon. He had been watching her from his porch. "Miriam, a word, please."

"Yes sir, Mr. Fine," she smiled, but didn't look directly into his eyes.

Adam hesitated.

"Can I get you a slice of cake or some tea?" She asked.

"Yes, thank you."

Walking into the kitchen, she sliced the cake and laid it on the table before him. He touched her hand and lingered there for a long while. When he finally moved his hand, she turned to walk away.

"Come next Sunday, please."

Miriam nodded but didn't look back.

When Adam would visit Eve, Miriam was usually in the room with them or close by. He watched her closely when she served them tea or brought his coat. More than once, she caught him staring at her while Eve was chattering on about something.

On the Fourth of July, the servants were allowed to have a big celebration. This year the holiday was on Sunday. There was church in the morning and a huge picnic in the afternoon. There was plenty of food and each family was gifted with a watermelon and extra sugar and milk to make ice cream.

Adam volunteered to go to the servants' quarters to make the annual speech. Cornelius agreed. Glad he didn't have to do it. After Adam reminded the servants of the significance of Independence Day, he stayed briefly to have a cup of ice cream and get Miriam's attention.

As the months passed, on the Sundays she visited the Fine Plantation, Miriam would sneak away from the group and meet Adam in the woods by the lake or in the basement of the main house.

"Adam, I need to tell you, Miss Eve bein' courted by Mr. Stephens, and I 'spect they be gettin' married.

"You moving away with them?"

"No, I doubt it. He got many servants. Most likely I be sold."

"Oh no. I can't let that happen." That was exactly what she wanted him to say and snuggled closer.

"You get dressed. Don't want George looking for you. Let me think on it. I will come up with a plan."

Adam was pre-occupied for the next two weeks, trying to think of a way to keep Miriam close. He couldn't justify adding a servant to their household staff. They didn't need one. He finally told his father he wanted to buy her from the Greenes, but only to let her leave by making a delivery for Fine China. He explained the situation as best he could, leaving out many details. Specifically, that he was in love with her.

Cornelius was not supportive of the idea. He didn't understand why Adam thought Mr. Greene would sell her, and he thought it too risky to attach Fine China's name to someone they hardly knew. "You hardly know," Adam thought. Interestingly, Cornelius didn't ask Adam how he knew all this.

Determined to make this work, Adam knew he would have to make a harsh decision. There were people outside his faith community who could be bought. In their world, everything had a price. For a couple of days, Adam contemplated how to accomplish what he needed to, getting Miriam away from the Greenes and onto his property. And if he could do it without his father's knowledge, that would be even better. Finally deciding, he resolved to find a broker who could persuade Mr. Greene to sell George and Miriam.

"My brother wants to court yo Ora."

"Do you trust her?"

"Don't know her much, but trust my brother."

"I'm fine with that."

And of course George could marry Ora. He didn't tell Miriam in case things didn't work out. She would be disappointed, and he couldn't bear to see her unhappy.

Through an acquaintance at a bar, Adam met a man who assured him he could make a deal with Greene, Jr. who would persuade his father. After a month of negotiating, a trade was made. George and Miriam came to Fine's plantation and two servants of "equal value" went to work for the Greenes. That wasn't exactly what Adam wanted because he had to involve Cornelius, but in the end, he accomplished his goal of having access to Miriam. Also, through the broker's contacts, Adam could get a small four-room house built on the back edge of the Fine property for George, Ora and Miriam.

Miriam knew everything about the Fine family and what went on in their household. Adam told her about James and Grace and about everything that was happening in New York.

"Adam, you ain't that different from him. I'm the same for you, Grace was for him."

One afternoon, while they were together, Adam told Miriam about the telegram and the fire on his brother's property. "I understand there is a lot of damage. My father received a post asking him to come to New Amsterdam and help find out what happened."

"Adam, I think you outta go with yo daddy and see about yo brother. Help him if ya can. See about who set that fire. Make them pay. Buy James the equipment he need to start again."

When he was home from New Amsterdam, Adam was really glad to see Miriam and report that he and Cornelius were able to make Sullivan pay.

"I'm glad you back. Need to tell you I missed my monthly, second time."

As Miriam's time got closer to having the baby, she was worried about how to get the news to Adam. He told her to have Ora bring flowers to the house when the baby came and leave them at the back door.

"We needa decide on a name 'case you not here when it's born."

They decided on Daniel for a boy and Lydia for a girl.

Adam checked often and a few weeks later on a Saturday morning, he looked outside and saw a big bouquet of hydrangeas on the back steps. As quickly as he could get away, Adam went to see Miriam.

"This yo son Daniel and yo daughter Lydia," Miriam said with a big smile. Adam had a stunned look on his face.

Adam and Miriam's first bad day together was the day he told her he was getting married. She cried. Her sobs were hard and raw. For days, she wouldn't talk to him, but let him see the twins.

"I don't love her like I love you, but it's what I have to do."

"'Cause yo mama say ya need to marry her?"

"Please try to understand." Adam was almost begging her.

"I understand ya gone be havin' babies' with her, too." Miriam screamed at him.

"That doesn't change anything between us. I'm still coming to see you and taking care of our children, and you. Have you ever asked me for anything that I didn't give you?"

"No."

"And that won't change."

After one trip to New Amsterdam to see James and his family, Adam admitted to Miriam that he took Dove with him. She wasn't happy, but he brought some gifts back for her and the children, so she didn't say much. He told her about Pansy playing the piano and about how smart she was.

"Ain't they got white teachers there you can find to help teach Pansy? She smart and need extra lessons."

Adam was surprised when Miriam told him, "George and Ora movin' to Greensboro. He got a job at a college over there." Adam wasn't sure he liked Miriam and the children being out there by themselves, but there wasn't much he could do about it. "We be fine!"

During their visit, they talked about Pansy. "She needa come to college in North Carolina. Bennett College. You can pay for her, right?"

"If it's a good school."

"George say it is. Smart colored women go there."

"I'll look into it. If she wants to go, I will send the money."

"You jus' tell her mama and daddy you know somebody who work there.

Adam and Miriam's second bad day together turned into months of bad days. When his sons died. The first one was bad. The second one was pure devastation. She held him in her arms for hours and let him cry. Most days he was drunk, and just wanted to hold the children. Every night, Miriam had to send him home. Finally, on a day when he was sober, he told her Pansy had taken over the business. Miriam told him she was going to have another baby.

"Are you listening to me? We havin' another baby?"

"I hope it's twins again."

Ora came back to stay with Miriam when the time was close to her having the baby. When the mums appeared on the back porch, Adam went to see Miriam.

"One boy. His name Matthew, like you say."

When Adam was finally better, Miriam asked him, "What you gone do for Pansy? She saved the business."

"What do you want me to do?" He didn't expect her answer.

"Give Fine China to her."

"A colored woman can't own a business in this state."

"You can fix it."

"Miriam, you're using me to get what you want for your people."

"Adam, you usin' me to get yo pleasure."

Miriam was happy to hear that Pansy was getting married, and excited when Adam shared that she and her husband were having a baby and even gathered some of her baby's things and sent to her.

"I need your help."

"If I can." Miriam said.

"Pansy needs someone to care for her daughter while she's at the store. I trust only you."

"Do she know about me?"

"No, but she will be fine knowing I asked you."

"I'm glad to help."

"She will want to pay you. Just accept it." Adam knew he needed to say that because Miriam wouldn't want to accept any pay.

"I understand."

Over the years, Miriam and Adam and their children were a family. Because of them, he was able to live. Dove was never completely well again.

"I want Lydia to go to Bennett College, too." Adam was serious.

“I been ‘specting you to say that.”

“Mim, you know me better than anybody. Better than my wife. I love you so much. In a perfect world, it would be us.”

A NEW SONG

Cheryl J. McCullough

PROLOGUE

It was literally love at first sight. When she walked into the conference room for the interview, he knew this was the one. Maybe not for the job, but for him. If this was the right person for the job, he would soon move her to another department. If another candidate was best for the job, he would hire her anyway. What if she wasn't single? He would have to work around that.

As he interviewed her, he became more smitten. This young lady was sharp and articulate, but a little unkempt. Her hair needed to be done. There was a small pin in her blouse where a button should have been, and her shoes were old. But her smile lit up the room, and his heart. Being twenty-four years old, fresh out of graduate school and ambitious, why would she be attracted to him?

At the end of the interview, they shook hands, and he told her he had one other person to interview, and his assistant would be in touch with her the following day. He had already decided to hire her and pay her more than the minimum in the job description. As soon as she left, he sent a message to Human Resources that he wanted to hire her. He was courteous and interviewed the other person.

Chapter 1

"What's up, big guy?"

"Lawrence Cooper, II said as he walked into his father's office." The door was open, so he didn't expect anyone to be in the office but his dad.

"Oh, my bad." He extended his hand to the young lady sitting across from his dad.

"Lawrence Cooper. Nice to meet you."

"Perri Winters, nice to meet you too." She smiled at Lawrence, II and then looked at Lawrence, Sr. All along thinking how fine the younger Lawrence was.

"This is my son, Deuce." Lawrence chuckled. "Perri is our newest associate. Today is her first day."

"Oh, okay, cool. I came by to take you to lunch."

"Rain check. I'm taking Perri to lunch."

Perri smiled. She didn't know that, but was glad. A decent lunch would be enough to eat for the day.

Lawrence got up from the table where they were working and chatted with his son for a few minutes, including asking about "my beautiful daughter-in-law."

"Oh well," Perri thought, looking at Deuce and noticing the wedding band.

Deuce left and Lawrence came back to his seat across from Perri at the round table in his office. "Do you have other children?"

"Nope. He is my only child. We planned to have two or four." He laughed. "My late wife didn't want a middle child. She had medical problems, and we were advised we shouldn't have more children. So, Deuce was the center of our universe."

"What does he do?"

"He is a commercial airline pilot. My daughter-in-law is a teacher; middle school science."

"If I had become a teacher, I would have taught history, civics, government, something like that." Perri continued talking and Lawrence was thinking how glad he was she didn't teach, and came to work with him.

Since it was lunchtime, they took a break. "What would you like to eat?" Lawrence asked Perri as he held her chair while she stood. "Since I'm not familiar with what's in the area, I will let you decide."

The weather was 65 degrees, sunny, no clouds at all. They walked across Fairview Road. Perri remarked how much she enjoyed walking in Charlotte. "The weather here is so nice most of the year."

"The weather is one reason we moved here. I like experiencing all four seasons, being within driving distance of the mountains and the beach."

They walked into the Hilton, across the lobby and into the restaurant. Perri was impressed when the hostess greeted Lawrence by name.

"Good afternoon Mr. Cooper. Two for lunch?"

"Yes, thank you."

As they ate, they continued to talk. Lawrence asked Perri about her family.

"My parents are from Alabama. My dad got a job in Florida and that's how we ended up there. My sister is in college in Florida. I'm the only one away from home."

Their conversation was easy. He made her laugh, and he was easily falling for her. Walking back to their office, Perri told him about her daily workout routine and asked about his.

"You are obviously in good shape, and you look great for a man your age." The comment stung. At that moment, he became determined to show her he wasn't an old man but a forty-seven-year-old man who wanted her.

Chapter 2

Over the next few weeks, Lawrence spent as much time with Perri as he could. At some point, he realized he was creating reasons to work with her or call her in for a meeting. It had been over a year since he had a new hire in his department, but he hadn't taken this much personal attention with her, and he knew he needed to back off. Perri didn't seem to mind the attention.

On Friday, the company volunteered at the local food bank. Each department had a designated time to go. The following Friday, their department was going. Lawrence overheard one of the young ladies on his team telling Perri about it and advising her to dress comfortably.

"You can wear jeans or sweats, your choice, and we wear these company t-shirts." She gave Perri two. "I guessed your size."

"Thanks, medium is exactly right."

"And the big guy usually springs for a late lunch."

"You call him that?" Perri asked her co-worker, laughing and stretching her eyes wide.

"Not to his face! That's what his son calls him, so we do too. We all think it's pretty funny."

"What happened to his wife? He referred to her as his 'late wife.'"

"It was unreal. We have the company outing at a baseball game on Friday night. She was there. We all had a good time. Big Guy goes to play golf Saturday morning. He leaves her in bed. When he gets home, she's dead. Had a heart attack!"

"Are you serious?" Perri asked, sitting at the co-worker's desk.

"Yes, very serious."

"How long ago? When did it happen?" Perri was stunned.

"It was six years ago. I had been here about a year. Deuce was still in college."

They heard him coming and changed the subject. "Be sure to wear comfortable shoes. There's a lot of walking on the cement floor," the co-worker said.

Lawrence had come out of his office on purpose. He didn't want the co-worker to tell Perri anymore about the situation surrounding his wife's passing. He had been devastated, and it took a long time to find peace.

The next morning, Perri and Lawrence pulled into the Food Bank parking lot at the same time. He parked beside her and got out of his car quickly to open her door.

"Love you too," she was saying, getting out of her car. Lawrence wanted to know who was on the phone, but he couldn't ask. He really wanted to know if that 'love you' was to the man in her life.

"Good morning!" Perri sounded excited.

"Good morning." He responded evenly. She was dressed in sweats and tennis shoes, the company T-shirt and smelled incredible. The door to the warehouse opened automatically, and he placed his hand on the small of her back as they walked in.

There was a coffee station set up right inside the check in area and pastries on another table across from the coffee.

"Can I get you something?"

"Yes, coffee, one sugar, no cream."

Perri went to get the coffee, and he went to see what was on the other table. They met in the aisle and walked to a small high-top table. "Brought blueberry and apple cinnamon. Your choice."

"Blueberry. Thank you."

They ate and chatted about nothing in particular. A few minutes passed, and they went to the staging area to get their assignments. Although he was the manager, he wouldn't accept the leader's role. One of the other analysts gave instructions.

"Next time we come, I want you to be in charge," Lawrence whispered in Perri's ear. His hand on her shoulder. She looked up at him, raising one eyebrow and laughed.

As they worked, she watched him, but didn't want him to notice. He looked amazing in the sweat suit. His abs were not quite a six-pack, but nice, and his butt was nice too!

At the end of the shift, Lawrence invited the team to join him for lunch. He wanted to sit close to Perri, but usually the men gathered at one end of the table and the ladies at the other. He didn't change it. But it was Friday, and he wouldn't see her over the weekend. He wanted to see her.

"Hey Big Guy, what's up?"

"Nothing. Is Bridget home tonight?"

"No, she's going to book club."

"Come, hang out with your old man."

"I can do that." Lawrence and Deuce made plans to get pizza and watch the fight on television.

"I'll come over there. That way, I can drop Bridget off at her friend's house."

The time spent with Deuce Friday night took his mind off Perri for a while, but Lawrence woke up Saturday morning thinking about her. He got up and washed his car and decided he would bite the bullet and call her. If the answer was no, he would lick his wounds and keep moving.

Perri was doing laundry but thought her phone was ringing. She guessed it was her sister. They talked a couple of times a day, but was surprised to see Lawrence's name on the screen. It was Saturday morning. What could be wrong?

"Good morning, Lawrence."

"Good morning Perri, how are you?"

"I'm good. Are you okay?"

He wanted to say no. He wanted to tell her he was totally falling for her.

"Yes, I'm fine."

"Yes, you are," she thought to herself.

"Are you free for lunch today?"

Perri was surprised at the question and hesitated before answering.

"Yes, I'm free. Do you want me to come into the office?"

"No, this is a social call, not work related." His heart was beating faster than normal.

They were both quiet for a moment.

"I can have lunch with you," she said softly. Her business tone was gone.

He looked at the clock on the microwave. "Is 12:30 good?"

"Sure."

"Text me your address and I will pick you up."

The thought went through her mind quickly. "I don't know this guy well enough for him to know where I live. He's a good boss, but for all I know, he's a maniac away from the office."

"I will meet you somewhere." Her tone was firm.

They made plans and hung up.

Separately, they both exhaled.

Perri dressed in a long sundress and high-heeled sandals. She loved jewelry and added necklaces, earrings, and bracelets, but tried to avoid thinking about her lunch date with her boss. A man who was at least twenty years older than her, tall, dark, handsome, very intelligent and funny.

"Oh my gosh! He asked me out!" Perri sat down at the foot of her bed, then called her sister. Lacey didn't answer, so she left a quick message.

"Going out with this guy from work. Call me. If I say something crazy, call back ten minutes later. If I'm good, I'll tell you."

Lawrence drove to the restaurant in Pineville early. They determined that was halfway between his house in Ballantyne and her apartment in Steele Creek. He wanted to wait for her.

"This is insane," he thought. "My son is older than she is. What would he say if I told him?" He looked up and saw her car turning into a parking space down the row from him. He got out of his car quickly to open her door. As soon as he did, he caught a whiff of her perfume. His body reacted. They were both wearing sunglasses, so neither could tell the other was looking. Again, he placed his hand on the small of her back, right above her hips, as they walked up the four steps to the restaurant door. She shivered slightly when he touched her, and he became aroused. He hoped it wasn't noticeable.

Perri hoped Lawrence didn't notice she was blushing. When he touched her back, she felt a sensation between her legs.

They were seated right away. For a Saturday at lunch, the restaurant wasn't very busy. Perri looked at the menu while Lawrence ordered an appetizer, a beer and iced tea for her. Just as the waiter walked away, Perri's phone rang.

"Hey Lacey."

Lawrence looked at her with a blank expression on his face.

"I'm good, at lunch with a co-worker. I'll call you later."

"Was that the call to get you out of here if you didn't want to stay?" Lawrence laughed.

"No! That was my sister."

"Likely story." They both laughed.

They talked, ate and laughed a lot. "You are funny. I never would have thought that from the way you are at work."

"Work is work. This is a date," he responded and waited for her to say something.

But she didn't, just smiled and held his gaze.

Lawrence rarely ate dessert, but he wasn't ready to leave. He talked Perri into sharing a slice of cheesecake. When the cheesecake was gone and he paid the check, they left the table, both silent, probably considering their own feelings. The sun was bright and Perri pulled her sunglasses down from on top of her head, just as Lawrence reached for her hand to go down the steps.

"We should go for a walk!" Perri said bubbly.

He exhaled; glad she brought it up. He looked down at her feet. "Those don't look like walking shoes to me."

"I have flats in my car."

He chuckled.

"Belle Johnston Park is a few minutes away. That's a good place to walk. There is a lake…" Perri interrupted him.
"Sounds good. I'll follow you."

In their cars, they both had a few minutes to re-group. Perri let it all just wash over her. She was enjoying his company, didn't want to read too much into it, but intended to ask him why he invited her to lunch.

He was falling hard, literally, and fast. Perri was smart, witty, and beautiful to top it all off. And he wanted her.

At the park, Perri put her purse in the trunk and changed her shoes. They walked leisurely around the water, chatting and stopping to watch some guys racing remote-controlled sail boats. After the second lap around, Lawrence suggested they take a seat on a lakeside swing.

There were two ducks in the water who appeared to be fighting. One was on top of the other. The one on top was pushing the other one under water. "Why is he trying to drown that other duck?" He laughed at her question. Before he could answer, she continued. "He's abusing her!" Lawrence really laughed now. "Why is that funny?"

"Sweetie, they aren't fighting. They're mating."

"Mating? By pushing her under the water?" Perri was exasperated.

"Come here." She leaned against the back of the swing. Her eyes were still on the ducks.

"Look at me." He took both her hands and kissed the back of the left, then the right. Now her focus was totally on what he was doing. "The ducks are fine. They are making love. It may seem bizarre, but that's how they do it." He was half smiling.

"I guess."

"Now, let's talk about us."

Lawrence decided on the drive from the restaurant to the park he was going for broke. If she embraced them being a couple, they would have to work hard to compartmentalize their relationships. If not, it was going to be tough. Either way, from a professional standpoint, he was soon going to lose one of his best analysts and best employees.

"You called this meeting Mr. Cooper. What's on your mind?" Perri was wearing her sunglasses, but he knew she was looking directly into his eyes. Her tone was playful. He hesitated.

"Perri, the day you walked into the conference room for the interview, I knew you were the woman for me." Her facial expression didn't change. He wished he could see her eyes. "Over the four months we've worked together, and I've gotten to know you, I'm even more convinced." Perri took a deep breath but didn't say anything, just blew it out slowly as he talked. "I know the obvious question, comment, or concern is the difference in our age." She nodded yes, the first real response.

"I don't care about that, Perri." He put his arm around her, pulled her to him, and kissed her lightly on the lips. They were both quiet.

"Lawrence, we are at different places in our lives. I'm just getting my career started. I've never been in a real relationship, and I'm not sure I want to be." He started to say something, but she kept talking. "I admit I'm attracted to you, and I can tell you are attracted to me."

"It's more than attraction, Perri."

"You are twenty years older than me."

"Twenty-three actually."

"At some point, I want a husband and children. I'm sure you don't want to start over." Lawrence pulled his sunglasses up on his head and looked at her.

"Everything you said is true. I am older. We are at different points in our lives. I expect you to want a family, but I want those things with you." Lawrence then pulled her into his arms. He held her for a while, neither of them saying anything again. She felt good to him and smelled good. Her breasts were against his chest. He closed his eyes for a couple of seconds. He was aroused.

"Is that it?" He thought. *"Am I just attracted to her physically?"* He felt bad at the thought. As if reading his mind, she leaned away.

"Are you sure your interest in me isn't just physical?"

"Yes, I'm sure." But he wasn't.

For an hour, they sat and talked. For another thirty minutes, they walked and talked. Finally, they decided, at her suggestion, that they take the rest of the day and Sunday to consider everything they discussed.

"I don't think we can go to work Monday without some kind of resolve."

The comment made Perri uneasy. "What do you consider a 'resolve'?" She made the quotations sign with her fingers. He could tell by her body language that word didn't work for her.

"Don't overreact, Perri, please. I only meant we need to know if we move forward and establish a relationship or if we just stay colleagues and friends."

"And what that looks like?" Perri added.

Sunday night Lawrence called Perri. The conversation was relatively short. She knew how he felt, so it was her decision.

Chapter 3

Two months passed, and Perri and Lawrence settled into their routine. A couple of days a week, they would go to lunch together. Most evenings, they had dinner, and they saw each other regularly on the weekends. Their co-workers suspected something was going on, but nobody asked. The morning they arrived together for the volunteer project at the food bank, the whispers and gossip increased.

Lawrence finally told Deuce and Bridget. She didn't say much, but Deuce told him he was having a mid-life crisis. Lawrence was in love, and for the first time, he didn't take his son's warning or advice.

The conversation Perri had with her sister Lacey didn't go well at all. "Why would you get involved with your boss?"

"You say 'involved' like we're having a sordid affair. We are in a relationship, Lacey!"

"Okay, it's a relationship, but it's still not good. He's almost as old as daddy. I know you want to be in a relationship, but dang!"

Perri knew everything her sister said was right, but they wanted each other. They enjoyed each other's company, and as far as they were concerned, the negative opinions of others were just that, other people's opinions.

"Let's go to the beach for the long weekend," Lawrence suggested to Perri over dinner.

"I love the beach. Do you think we can get a reservation on such short notice?"

"Yep, your man has the hook-up!"

"Does my man care to share?"

"No, just trust me on this one." He winked at her. "Be right back." Lawrence excused himself and as he headed to the restroom, he saw their waitress. "You can bring the check."

"Yes, sir."

Returning to the table, Lawrence heard the waitress make a comment he hated. "Your dad asked me to drop off the check."

"My dad? My dad is certainly not here. If you are referring to the amazing gentleman, I just had dinner with, he's, my man." The waitress looked embarrassed. She walked away, saying nothing. Lawrence left cash on the table, and they walked out.

The first time Perri went to Lawrence's house, he showed her his music room. He had shelves and shelves of CDs and music he had downloaded, cataloged according to genre. There was great artwork on the walls, and there were speakers and headphones, a recliner, a sofa, and a desk with a computer. He explained that there were only two uses for that computer: downloading more music and keeping track of it all. Perri was amused by the turntable. He told her he kept it for the collections of albums he had. She was also amused by the albums. Lawrence was a jazz enthusiast and scholar. He had R & B, gospel, classical and some country, but of the 2640 CDs ninety percent of it was jazz.

He would tell Perri about the music and the artists and show her documentaries. She was totally awed by his knowledge. Some artists he mentioned she was familiar with from music history classes. He told her over half of his collection was recorded in the 1960s.

"That was before I was born!" They laughed.

There was usually a jazz CD playing in his car or on the satellite radio station. Becoming familiar with the music, Perri determined what she liked a lot and liked less. The saxophone featured music was definitely her favorite.

"Do you want the CDs out of the car?"

"No, I have the ones I want."

They were packing the SUV for the drive to Hilton Head Island. He decided he wanted to leave Friday rather than Saturday. That gave them more time together. He gave his department the afternoon off, and he and Perri were on the road by 3:00.

The three-hour drive seemed to go quickly. As they crossed the bridge onto the island, Lawrence asked Perri to get an address from his phone. She found it and typed it into the GPS. A short while later, they turned into the driveway of a massive house. "I thought we were going to a hotel," Perri commented, smiling.

"No ma'am. Private residence, with golf course over there and the beach behind us."

"Whose house is this?"

"A college buddy of mine."

They looked around and Lawrence let Perri decide about the sleeping arrangements. "We can sleep in here. Waking up to the water will be amazing," she said, looking out the balcony door. It was dusk and there was just enough daylight left to see the tide coming in. He walked up behind her and put his arms around her waist. Leaning against him, she could hear him breathing, feel his heart beating, and feel his erection against her body. He felt her shiver slightly and held her more tightly.

"Let's go for a walk," he suggested.

"Let's unpack first."

They played around so long while they were unpacking; they forwent their walk and went to dinner. Lawrence left one bag in the truck and as they were leaving for dinner, he took it in. Perri was waiting, but it seemed to take him so long, she went back into the house.

"What are you doing?"

He didn't look back. "I don't need any help!" He closed the refrigerator, took her by the hand, set the alarm and they left.

Chapter 4

This was the most awkward, most anticipated, and most awaited occasion either of them had in a long time. Instead of stopping at the sofa, he led her to the bed. Perri sat, and Lawrence went to get them a glass of wine. The bottle had been chilling while they went to dinner. Riesling was one of her favorites. Lawrence started the music and poured the wine, joining Perri on the bed. Leaning back on the headboard, he pulled her into his arms, between his legs. It was better than her vision. Neither said anything. They were caught up in the moment. Moving her hair to gently kiss her neck, she squirmed. He laughed. By the sixth kiss, Lawrence had found her "spot." Her body reacted immediately. She took a big sip of wine, leaving very little in the glass, handing him the glass to sit on the nightstand.

Najee was playing. He reached over to turn out the light, and nibbled on her earlobe, unzipping her dress, planting kisses on her back. Perri looked back for a kiss, but he shook his head no.

"Why?"

"I'll give it to you when I want you to have it."

Lawrence slipped Perri's dress from her shoulders and unhooked her bra. Holding her hand for her to get up from the bed, the dress dropped to the floor. He reached to slide the bra straps off her arms, then pulled his shirt over his head, joined Perri, and stepped out of his pants. She picked up the clothes from the floor and put them on the chair to have a couple of seconds to breathe. Her head was spinning. Was it him or the wine?

Perri was only wearing panties; Lawrence was wearing only briefs. He pulled her to him, sat on the bed, and caressed her breasts. She leaned in again for a kiss, but he said no again.

"Do you want me to beg for it?"

"No, I'll give it to you when I want you to have it."

Gradually, they rolled around on the bed, chasing each other and constantly changing positions. The music had started over. He was humming in her ear. With no warning, he kissed her hard and long. She could hardly breathe.

Perri's body was screaming for him. Lawrence was controlling how she could connect with his body. They both were ready, but he wouldn't give it to her; not tonight. He wanted her too; badly, but he wanted to wait. There could only be one first time.

Lawrence's intention was to wait until morning, when the sun came up, wake her with a kiss and slowly work his way back to where they were the night before.

They snuggled and cuddled. He played with her fingers and toes, looked her in the eye and talked to her softly between the hugs and kisses. They held each other tight. Perri felt absolutely comfortable, absolutely secure in his arms. They danced a while, kissed, held each other, and he slid his hands over the satin nightgown.

"Put a little more in my glass. I'll be right back."

She refreshed their drinks and set both glasses on the

nightstand, on his side of the bed. He came back and skipped a few songs to get to "Sweet and Saxy" by Kim Waters.

Lawrence ran his tongue across Perri's lips, but when she responded, he pulled away. He was teasing her. She smiled, but her eyes were saying something else. For a few seconds, they concentrated on the music. Kim Waters and his sax were well into "Love Mode."

Laying on his back and pulling her on top of him, she opened her legs and their bodies connected naturally. It was magical. All their senses were engaged. Kim Waters and his saxophone were in the middle of "Don't Stop Now." He could smell her scent. They were satisfying each other, and they were unwinding and unwrapping all the layers. They gave affectionate attention to every detail lovingly. It was an incredible night. They came together over and over, off and on all night long.

Perri was dozing, but Lawrence was wide awake. Easing out of bed, putting on his boxers, and walking into the loft area, he looked at the golf course in the distance. It occurred to him they had not had a conversation about birth control. He didn't use a condom and didn't know if Perri was on the pill. That fact showed their age difference. The last relationship he was in; the woman's tubes were tied. She was in her mid-forties with adult children and no desire to get pregnant. "Damn," he thought. They needed to discuss it, but he didn't want anything to spoil their weekend. The night before had been incredible, and making love to her that morning while the sun rose was even more extraordinary.

Perri was inexperienced, but teachable, doing what he asked. Being very verbal, he knew how she felt, what she wanted, and her energy level was high. Lawrence couldn't wait to be with her again. Why did he have to wait? Just go to the other side of the wall!

Going back to bed and snuggling close to her, his arms wrapped around her. Just as he kissed the back of her neck, Perri turned over and faced him. In one motion, was on top of him. Their eyes met and held.

<h1 style="text-align:center;">*Chapter 5*</h1>

"I accepted the position in legal," Lawrence told Perri at lunch.

"When do you start?"

"Next Monday."

"Lawrence, I told you I would transfer. You built our department. It's not fair for you to have to move."

"I want you to stay where you are. I was the director in legal some years ago. It will be an easier transition for me."

"You act like I can't do hard; change is necessary sometime."

"Perri, this isn't open for discussion. I made the decision, and that's final."

She hated it when Lawrence talked down to her like a kid. "Lawrence, you did it again. You made a decision without discussing it with me. I'm not your daughter, I'm your partner. We are in a relationship. People in relationships discuss things like this." The discussion became an argument. Perri wanted him to understand. It wasn't about the job, it was his failure to respect her position in his life. He did the same thing about her apartment. He negotiated her being able to get out of her lease without talking to her, after she was at his house for a month, only going to her apartment for clothes.

"Sweetie, I know how this works. I've been at this a long time.

This is the better plan."

"Better, but not best." Perri left the table.

They rode back to work in silence. Before they got out of the car, Lawrence leaned over to kiss Perri, but she didn't respond, just got out of the car and walked into the office. By the time they were at home and sitting down to dinner, the argument had blown over.

Lacey and Perri talked now at least once a day, and Saturday morning was their long conversation.

"When are you coming in for the party?" Lacey asked.

Perri sighed before she answered. "I don't know. I'm still deciding what to do."

"What to do about what? I know you're not trying to decide if you're coming home for your daddy's fiftieth birthday party!" Lacey said indignantly.

"No girl. I'm coming home for the party; I just haven't told Lawrence anything about it."

"Why?"

"Because I'm not inviting him." Perri uttered quietly.

"Again, I ask, why?" Lacey folded her arms, waiting for Perri to say something. There was a noticeable silence.

Finally, Perri answered. "Mama and Daddy are going to have a fit, and I don't want to ruin the weekend."

"My, my. So, you admit this May to December romance you're

involved in is a problem."

"It's not a problem, Lacey. But I know Mama and Daddy won't understand. Daddy will not be okay knowing I'm in love with and living with a man almost twice my age!"

"I'm sure I told you this a few months ago."

"I'm sure you did too, Lacey."

After another ten minutes of back and forth, they started talking about something else. When they hung up, Perri walked around the house, contemplating her life. Bottom line, she had to come clean with Lawrence, and prayed it wouldn't end their relationship.

The conversation didn't go well. "Are you serious? You are going to do this again. It's been a year, honey. How long are you going to wait?" Lawrence asked. He was angry. Perri was standing there with tears in her eyes. "I let it go when you went to Florida the last time, and now you're telling me you don't want to include me again."

"Please try to see it from my perspective. I don't want controversy to surround my dad's fiftieth birthday celebration."

"So, I'm controversial! Wow Perri."

"Lawrence, you know what I mean."

"Yeah, I know," Lawrence replied and walked out of the room. A few minutes later, she heard the garage door. Looking out, Perri watched Lawrence back out of the driveway.

Chapter 6

Perri was right, and Lawrence knew it. If he were in her father's place, he wouldn't want his daughter telling him she was in love with a man his age, either. This was an ongoing issue for them. Perri didn't fit in well with his friends; he didn't fit in well with hers. Deuce, Bridget, and Lacey dealt with the situation, but neither of them particularly cared for it. Bridget remarked to Deuce once that she understood why Perri would be "crushing" on his dad. "He's a good-looking man with swag. He has money and stature, but they don't have a lot in common."

Lawrence's friends' wives shunned Perri. She was their daughter's age, and they didn't include her in their social activities. Perri didn't care. Who wants to go to lunch at the club, anyway? But it bothered Lawrence.

Perri went to Florida for her dad's celebration, and Lawrence was miserable. He made one decision, though; things were going to change when she got back. Perri missed Lawrence, missed seeing him and being with him. But Lawrence was furious. More than anything, he was hurt. He couldn't fathom Perri not including him in the plans with her family, nor did he understand not telling her parents about their relationship. They didn't communicate for two days. She had deceived him, hurt his feelings, and minimized their relationship, but wasn't sure how to fix it. If he wanted to end their relationship, she would ask him to give her time to get an apartment. "He will. He's a reasonable man." And Perri had plenty of money in the bank. Her personal things, like hair, nails, book club books, lunch when they didn't go together, were her responsibility. From time to time Perri would buy dinner, or clothes. But if she used her credit card, he paid those bills, too. He even added her to his gym membership, and he was paying for the new car he bought her a week after they started living together.

The third night, he called her at two o'clock in the morning on Face Time and told her he needed to see her naked body. She pulled her T-shirt over her head. As soon as he saw her breasts, he was aroused. When he let her see his erection, the pleasure between her legs pulsated. Perri wanted to go home. The party was the next day. One more night without him and Sunday night would be amazing for them.

The birthday party was wonderful, and everything went off without a hitch. Sunday before Perri was leaving to go back to Charlotte, she, Lacey, and their parents were to have brunch. They were planning to go out, but Perri said she and Lacey wanted to cook so they could talk. Perri had her speech planned, but forgot it all when the time came.

"Daddy, Mama, I want to tell you something." Perri told them she's dating, his name, what he does for a living, and that they live together. That precipitated a long dialogue. She didn't reveal his age directly, just showed them a picture of him.

"How old is Lawrence?" Her mother asked very matter-of-factly.

"He's almost 48," Perri stated just as matter-of-factly. Her mother laughed, leaned back in her chair, and looked at her husband. She couldn't wait to hear what he was going to say. There was a long silence. Finally, Lacey spoke up.

"He's a wonderful man, and he really loves Perri." Perri just looked at Lacey. They both knew their parents were going to come down on Lacey for supporting this.

"How long have you known Lacey?" Their mother asked.

"Since their first date; almost a year."

"So, you were seeing him when you were here the last time?" Her mother asked again.

"Yes, but we weren't living together then."

Perri's dad still had said nothing. Just as Lacey spoke, he interrupted her.

"Perri, what in the world is going on in that head of yours? There is only one thing a man his age, a man old enough to be your father, wants you for, and that's sex. Plain and simple."

"That's not true Daddy."

"Of course, in your eyes, it's not true. You don't know men. How long has he been divorced?"

"He's not divorced. He's a widower. His wife died six years ago." Perri answered firmly.

"So, he's lonely and looking for companionship."

They went back and forth for a while. Perri cried, and Lacey defended her. "How would you feel if something happened to your mother, and I brought a girl in here half my age?" Her dad leaned forward on the table, waiting for her to answer.

"I may not like it, but I would respect your right to make that decision; to decide for yourself who you want in your life. I wouldn't tell you who to love."

Perri was done having this conversation with her parents. She looked at the clock. "I need to get my things together, so I won't miss my flight." She walked out of the kitchen.

"Lacey, why didn't you say something about this?" Her mother asked.

"'Cause it wasn't my story to tell." Lacey then walked out of the room.

Perri was sitting at the foot of the bed, crying, having held the tears as long as she could. Lacey sat beside her. "Perri, you knew how this was going to go. It's behind you now."

"Yeah, but Mama and Daddy are angry at me. Lawrence is hurt and disappointed. It's all just too much."

Lacey chuckled. "The bottom line is, you came clean with the parents, and when you get back, you and Lawrence will talk, and it will be fine. That man would drink your bath water!"

Perri laughed.

Chapter 7

Lawrence walked out to the garage when he heard the door go up. He was standing there when Perri got out of the car. It was awkward. They hugged, but didn't linger. He took her luggage out of the car in silence. Once they were inside, he told her about the call he received the day before from Deuce. "He and Bridget are having a baby!"

"That's exciting!" Perry was genuinely happy for Lawrence.

For a few minutes, they talked, and he shared the details.

Once the baby conversation was over, Perri needed to be on offense; to apologize, and to tell Lawrence about the conversation with her parents. He carried her luggage upstairs and then went back down without saying anything. After unpacking her things, freshening up, changing into a T-shirt and thong, Perri went downstairs. She sat on the sofa with both legs under her body. He looked at her with no make-up, and her hair on top of her head in a ponytail, which made her look young.

"May I interrupt you for a few minutes?" He didn't respond, just reached for the remote and turned down the volume on the television. She started by apologizing for not telling him about going to Pensacola, not telling him about the birthday party and not including him in her plans. Then told him about her parents' reactions. "I feel terrible. I've never left home unhappy, and I know they're unhappy with me." Tears rolled down her cheeks.

They talked for an hour; he accepted her apology, and they made love on the sofa. After a bit, he left her there and went to his study. "I have something for you," he said from behind her. He came around the sofa, kneeled in front of her and, with no fanfare, asked, "Will you marry me?"

"Yes."

He slipped the ring on her finger, got up off his knee, and carried her upstairs. Just as she thought it would be, the night was amazing.

Chapter 8

It took two days for the news of Perri and Lawrence's engagement to circulate through the company. The sentiment was mixed, but neither of them cared. The ladies were thoroughly impressed with the ring. The guys were impressed that the "Big Guy" could pull like that. It was more ring than she would have chosen, but was fine with it. Perri took a picture and sent it to Lacey. "Damn girl," had been her response.

"I have to go to Atlanta Thursday, be back Friday," Lawrence told Perri at lunch.

"How can you leave your fiancée after only three days?" She pouted and then smiled.

"You can go with me if you want to." He was hoping she would say no.

"Naw, I have work to do. I will just suffer through my night without you. I guess I can sleep alone for one night."

"I'll let you show me how much you missed me when I get back," he was gazing into her eyes.

Lawrence had just lied to Perri. He decided it was better to ask for forgiveness than ask for permission. He wasn't going to Atlanta, but to Pensacola. He had looked in her phone and found her parents' address and phone numbers. The only thing he hadn't considered was if Lacey was at home. She would call Perri immediately, and he preferred to tell her himself. But that was a chance he was willing to take.

Perri spent the evening making plans to get married. She had always imagined a big formal wedding, a gown complete with a train, flowers and bridesmaids. But that was not to be. The relationship with Lawrence had alienated Perri from her friends, so no bridesmaids, and there was no way her parents would come. Reality check: a wedding was off the table. Lacey suggested a destination wedding, and that seemed like a good idea at this point.

Lawrence checked into the hotel, did some work, and then called Perri's father a little after six o'clock. Once her father knew that there was no emergency, and Perri was fine, he wanted to know why Lawrence was calling. He invited both parents to meet him in the hotel restaurant. He told them he wanted to talk with them and asked them not to call Perri. "She doesn't know I'm here," he said, before asking about Lacey. Perri's father did not answer directly whether Lacey was expected at home, but he agreed not to alert Perri that Lawrence was there.

"Give me a few minutes to talk with my wife and I will call you back."

Lawrence agreed, but had already decided he would call back if he thought it was taking too long.

In about thirty minutes, Steven Winters called back. "We would prefer you to come to our house." He gave Lawrence the address, not knowing he already had it. Lawrence left immediately and was there in about twenty minutes.

Steven opened the door, and Perri's mother was standing a few feet behind him. Lawrence extended his hand and Steven shook it. "This is my wife, Patricia."

"Pleasure to meet you," Lawrence said, looking at her closely. Lacey looked more like their mother. Perri was a good mix of both parents. As they walked into the living room, Lawrence noticed a picture of Perri and Lacey as little girls on the wall in the hall. He wanted to see more pictures, but he didn't ask.

It was an awkward time. "May I get you something to drink?" Patricia asked. She knew why Perri was attracted to Lawrence. He was very handsome, with an athletic physique. He was well dressed, well-spoken and obviously very sophisticated.

Perri sounds like her mother, he thought. "No, thank you…"

Before Lawrence could finish his sentence, Steven spoke. "What's up, man? Why are you here?"

"Perri told me about your conversation when she was here for your birthday. I know you don't like our relationship, but I hope for her sake you can accept it and not alienate your daughter."

"Alienate our daughter? That child is my flesh and blood; I gave birth to her. You can't compete with that." Patricia responded.

"My intention is certainly not to compete. You are her parents. You love her and so do I."

"You love my daughter, who is young enough to be your daughter?"

"Yes, Steven, I do, and she loves me."

Steven interrupted him again. "My daughter may think she loves you, but this is a phase. I guarantee it. I just hate her decision to live with you, and waste her youth on you, rather than being with a man her age."

Lawrence was trying to maintain his composure. "If it's a phase, it's going to last a lifetime. Perri accepted my proposal. We are getting married." Lawrence made the statement boldly. He was very direct. There was a thick silence for a long moment. Patricia got up from the sofa and walked to the window. She fingered the drape for a few seconds.

"My daughter is engaged, and didn't tell me."

Nobody said anything for a while, and then Lawrence seized the opportunity. "Your daughter is engaged and didn't tell you because you closed that door. You told her she's not capable of making a good decision about her life. If I was twenty-seven instead of forty-seven, you would encourage her to pursue this relationship."

"The reverse psychology ain't working," Steven said.

That's when the argument started. Steven and Lawrence went back and forth. Patricia interjected periodically. Finally, having had enough, she made them both shut up.

"Nothing is coming out of this! Perri is in Charlotte, living with Lawrence, apparently intends to marry him, and there's not a lot we can do about it." Patricia was looking at her husband. Tears were rolling down her cheeks.

"There may be nothing *you* can do about it," he responded. "I am going to call Perri and forbid her to marry this man," he gestured toward Lawrence, "and advise her to move out of his house and live the way she was raised.”

Lawrence stood to leave. He looked at Steven. “If you lose her, you will never get her back.”

He turned toward the door and across the foyer on the dining room wall he could see a picture of Perri; her debutante picture, in a beautiful white gown. He smiled as he walked out the front door.

“The next beautiful white gown will be a wedding gown,” he thought.

Chapter 9

Lawrence was at home before Perri left work. On the flight, he contemplated cooking dinner, taking her out, buying flowers, buying her a gift, and various combinations of those things. He was in big trouble with her. More than he expected to be. He knew she would be angry, but not to this magnitude. He hadn't ever heard her curse. She had cursed several times during their conversation. He decided on flowers. He knew overdoing it wouldn't help. Lacey had called her on three-way to help manage her parents.

Her mother called as soon as Lawrence left. By the time Perri talked to him, she was borderline hysterical. Her mother had cried; her father had yelled. The only sane person in the situation was Lacey. Despite all her diplomacy, the whole encounter went terribly wrong. Steven gave Perri an ultimatum; "I demand you move out of that man's house, and live like a decent young woman, or…"

"Or what Daddy?"

"Or we are going to have a problem."

"Well, we definitely have a problem, because you won't 'demand' that I do anything."

Perri should have been home an hour ago, but wasn't. Lawrence called her. He wanted to face the music. She texted back; "at the gym." Another hour passed. Lawrence was upstairs when she came in and saw the flowers in the foyer. He was waiting at the top of the stairs. Perri walked past, spoke and went straight to the bathroom. Lawrence waited until he heard the water running to go in. He leaned against the counter, arms folded, and watched her for a minute. His gesture didn't faze her like it usually did when he came in to watch her shower. He went to the dressing room and came back naked. He opened the door and stepped into the shower. Her back was turned. She didn't acknowledge him. He put his arms around her waist and pushed her against the wall, but Perri willed herself not to respond. He kissed the back of her neck. She still didn't respond. He took his hands off her and stepped out.

They rarely used the sitting area in their bedroom. There was a sofa, a recliner, an armchair, a coffee table and a television. When Perri came out of the bathroom, Lawrence was sitting in the recliner. That wasn't what she expected, but walked over and sat across from him in the other chair. He immediately looked for her ring. It was still on her finger.

"That was quite a stunt you pulled, and don't compare it to my trip to Florida without you. I did not lie to you about where I was going. What if something happened? I thought you were in Atlanta." Perri did not raise her voice. "I don't know if I'm angrier about you going to talk to my parents and not telling me, especially considering the circumstances, or if I'm angrier about your continued and blatant disrespect…"

"Perri!"

"Lawrence!" She made a face. "First, you move to the legal department and decided for me to stay where I am without discussing it with me. Next you negotiate me out of my lease and moved my things, again unbeknownst to me. Then you buy the car and now you take it upon yourself to confront my parents, which makes my situation with them worse."

"You know that is not what I intended," Lawrence said in his own defense.

"I don't, for one-minute, question your intent. I question your approach. How many times have we discussed your inability to include me in making decisions about us? And your inability to see me as equal in this relationship. For the hundredth time, I am not your daughter! I am your fiancée. But I will not marry you if we can't work this out!" Her voice was forceful, firm, but not angry.

As he listened, he realized he wanted and needed her more than she wanted or needed him. He was approaching the third quarter of life; she was approaching her second quarter. He had more years behind him than she had even lived. He couldn't lose her; he loved her too much.

Lawrence didn't argue, he didn't debate her points; he didn't defend his decisions or his actions. Perri was right, and he told her so. He asked her to accept his apology.

Chapter 10

The tension between Lawrence and Perri eased over the weekend. Sunday afternoon, Deuce and Bridget came over for a while. Lawrence and Deuce went to play golf while the ladies went shopping for the baby. Bridget's sister was meeting them later to talk about planning a baby shower.

"That should be fun! I haven't ever been to a baby shower," Perri remarked to Bridget.

Bridget's sister made all the plans. Perri had two assignments, to mail the invitations and provide a party favor for each guest to take home.

The seven months of Bridget's pregnancy seemed to go by quickly. That was partly true because they didn't tell anybody until the end of the first trimester. She agreed now was time to plan the shower. It was being held a month later at the clubhouse in Deuce and Bridget's subdivision. Lawrence helped Perri carry in the gifts she bought. She was a little uncomfortable. Bridget and her sister were the only people there she knew, but they were all very nice.

The games were fun, and then they ate before Bridget opened her gifts. As she was fixing her plate, one of Bridget's cousins noticed Perri's engagement ring, and commented on how beautiful it was. A little later, the same cousin asked if Perri was Deuce's sister.

"I saw you come in with his dad."

"No, Deuce is an only child!" Bridget did not explain further who Perri was. Perri waited two seconds for Bridget to answer the question. She didn't.

"I am Lawrence's fiancé." Perri rolled her eyes at Bridget.

"Are you serious?" The cousin asked, frowning.

"Very serious." Perri looked at the ring for emphasis.

"It's your business, but he's too old for you," the cousin continued.

"You're right, it's my business." Perri picked up a cup of punch and walked away.

When the other guests left, Bridget knew she had to say something to Perri about her cousin's comment. "I'm sorry my cousin said that about you and Lawrence," Bridget told Perri, as they were putting a few gifts in the car. They were leaving the big items for the men.

"What I'm sorry about is you not telling her about Lawrence and me. I don't know how we are going to be a family when you can't accept our relationship."

"You have to admit it's awkward, Perri."

"Awkward. Really! We are in love and we're getting married. What's awkward about that?" Perri was looking her directly in the eye.

Bridget laughed. "I think it's foolish, and Deuce does too!" As soon as it was out of her mouth, she wanted to take it back. The look on Perri's face was hurt. Bridget was sure the hurt was because she said Deuce thought their relationship was foolish. Perri closed the car trunk and walked away.

For the first time, Perri cried. None of the previous negative comments had bothered her. But this was her limit, and she was tired of hearing it. If Deuce thought their relationship showed a lack of good judgement, that would wound Lawrence deeply. He wanted them to be a family, a happy family.

When Lawrence and Deuce walked into the clubhouse, the tension was obviously heavy. They looked at each other, and Deuce spoke up. "How was the shower? From the looks of things…"

"It was great! We had a good time. This isn't all the gifts. We put some in the car already," Bridget said, really bubbly. She took Deuce by the hand, and they walked over to where the stroller, high chair and other big items were. Perri was just standing there, not saying anything.

"Sweetheart, what's wrong?" He didn't get a response, so he looked to see if Bridget was going to say anything. Still no response. "Perri, what is it?" She told Lawrence what happened at the shower and told him about his daughter-in-law's comment. Bridget dropped her head. Deuce just looked at his dad and Perri.

"Is that what you really think? That my relationship with Perri is crazy?"

Deuce looked at Bridget again and walked toward his dad. "Yeah, Big Guy, I do. I clearly understand why you are attracted to her beauty and intellect, but I don't understand why you want to be with someone so young. My thought when you told me about her was he's having a mid-life crisis, he wants to sleep with her and then he'll be over this phase. Real talk."

"But you never said anything. You let me believe you supported me in this."

"When I realized you were serious, everything was moving so fast, I didn't know what to say."

Lawrence sighed loudly. "Let's get this stuff to your house, so Perri and I can go home."

Chapter 11

Two days after the shower, Bridget got really sick. She had a terrible headache and couldn't lift her head from the pillow. Deuce called the medics, who took her straight to the hospital. She was admitted with preeclampsia.

When the Obstetrics team finally got Bridget's blood pressure under control, they recommended inducing her labor and taking the baby. Deuce and Bridget were both nervous about it, because she was several weeks early. Deuce called Lawrence, who encouraged them to take the doctor's advice.

After 12 hours of labor, and Bridget trying her best to have the baby naturally, the doctors finally performed a Cesarean Section, and Lawrence Simon Cooper, III "Trey," was born. Deuce and Lawrence were ecstatic. Perri was happy for Lawrence, but glad they would leave town soon.

Perri and Lawrence were married in Honolulu, Hawaii. Lacey and Deuce were there. Deuce only stayed for two days because Bridget couldn't come. Lacey took advantage of her free trip and stayed for a week. Steve and Patricia were invited but didn't come. It was a beautiful wedding, complete with Hula dancers and flowers galore. The ceremony was held in a gazebo on the beach, with the ocean as a backdrop. They stayed in Hawaii for ten days.

Deuce and Lawrence talked a few days after the shower. Deuce apologized, and they talked through it. Lawrence knew Deuce wasn't one hundred percent on board, but he respected his decision. Perri and Bridget were not talking.

Perri was glad they were away. She didn't want to share the attention with Trey or Bridget. She was thoroughly enjoying being the center of his universe. Everybody was catering to her, especially Lawrence. That night when they were in bed, Lawrence asked Perri how she liked making love to a grandfather.

"Amazing!"

Their last morning there, they made love in the bed, then the shower, and afterwards had a leisurely breakfast. The limousine got them to the airport in plenty of time. They strolled through the shops as they headed to their gate. Lawrence bought a couple of things for Trey. As they exited the toy store, they heard someone call Lawrence.

"Big guy!" Perri and Lawrence stopped and turned around.

"What's up, man?"

Lawrence laughed a deep belly laugh. A tall, handsome, very muscular young man approached them, and he and Lawrence hugged. "What are you doing in Honolulu?"

"I literally just landed. I'm reporting for duty at Pearl Harbor."

"Babe, this is Carlton Gresham. He was Deuce's college roommate. This is my bride, Perri Winters Cooper!"

Perri smiled and shook Carlton's hand. He held her hand a few seconds longer than he should have.

"Damn Big Guy! Congrats! Deuce told me you were getting married. Man, you know you got more than you qualify for!" They laughed. Perri blushed.

Carlton hadn't returned Deuce's call from the day before, so he didn't know about the baby. They talked a few more minutes and Lawrence knew he and Perri needed to get to the gate.

"It was a pleasure to meet you, Perri." Carlton hugged her and whispered n her ear, "You are too young and too fine to be married to a man his age." He shook hands and hugged Lawrence.

Chapter 12

For their first anniversary, Perri gave Lawrence a beautifully wrapped long, flat box. He had asked for a Rolex. He opened it, and for a split second, didn't know what it was. Then it dawned on him. It was a pregnancy test; a positive pregnancy test.

On the fourth of July, Lauren Winters Cooper was born. Lawrence was in love immediately. She changed everything. Lawrence loved Deuce, and he loved Trey, but that little girl became the center of his world immediately when the nurse laid her in his arms.

Fifteen months later, Langston Winters Cooper was born. Perri had her hands full, but Lawrence couldn't have been happier. As much as she loved her children, after a few months, Perri wanted to go back to work. But Lawrence wanted her at home with Langston and Lauren. He promised her he would retire early, and she could go back to work when Langston went to school, and he would be home with the children. Perri agreed, thinking that was a pretty progressive attitude for her very traditional husband.

During her marriage and children being born, Perri's relationship with her parents remained strained, particularly with her father. She and Lawrence took the children to Florida once a year, stayed in a hotel, and Lauren and Langston visited their grandparents. The summer before Langston went to first grade, Perri talked Lawrence into leaving the children with their grandparents and they went to Jamaica. When they returned, Lawrence planned to retire and Perri planned to go back to work.

The transition was smooth for everybody but Langston. He didn't like being in school all day. He wanted to go three days a week, get out early, spend the afternoon with his mom, and go back to get Lauren.

Steven Winters loved his grandchildren, and deep inside, he knew Perri was very happy. Lawrence took good care of her, and being able to stay at home with the kids was great. She had a good life, and that's what he wanted for her. But he and Lawrence were only civil towards each other. They had an unspoken rule to be cordial in the presence of the kids. Patricia made peace with the situation and longed for the relationship they had before Lawrence became part of the equation. But she sided with Steven and had not supported Perri. That was a decision that came back to haunt her.

Chapter 13

Perri missed Langston and Lauren, but was glad to be working again. After a few months, she moved to senior analyst and then to manager in a year. The children were doing well in school. Langston eventually got on board. He was playing soccer and basketball. Lauren was running track, swimming, and learning to play the flute.

The role reversal was working more for Perri than for Lawrence. He wasn't saying much because he promised her he would do it. But the truth be told, this wasn't how he wanted to spend his retirement. He could hardly get in eighteen holes before he had to jump in the car and pick up somebody. The second year in, he made a decision, and it precipitated a big fight.

"I hired a nanny."

"You did what?" Perri asked, looking at Lawrence puzzled.

"I hired a nanny. She's a student at Johnson C. Smith, has good grades, excellent driving record, has a car, experienced, CPR certified…" He listed her credentials, but Perri wasn't listening. He did it again; made a decision that affected the family, without consulting her. It was obvious; he was oblivious to what she wanted! Finally, he realized Perri wasn't saying anything. She was just staring at him, and not smiling.

"In all the years we have known each other and all the years we have been married, you have consistently done one thing that absolutely ticks me off!"

Lawrence was looking at her like a deer caught in headlights. He had no idea what was bothering her.

"You really don't have a clue, do you?

He shrugged.

"Lawrence, you are just not that dumb! How many times have we talked about you making decisions for me, for the children, for the household without us talking about it?"

"Running the kids around was my responsibility. I needed to do something different, and I handled it!" He explained why he thought it was necessary. Two things dawned on Perri. He didn't think he had done anything wrong, but her husband was sixty-two years old in every sense of the word. She decided not to go any further with it.

"When do we get to meet her?" Perri asked.

"I will ask her to come out here tomorrow."

"Be sure to tell Langston and especially Lauren you hired them a 'nanny.'" Perri chuckled, rolled her eyes and walked out of the room.

Chapter 14

It had been a very long day. The whole family spent the day outside together. It was Trey's sixteenth birthday, and the high school championship baseball game. It was eighty degrees and sunny at game time, but there was a dark cloud to the west of the stadium.

The Coopers arrived early. Lawrence liked to sit up top, so his back would be against the fence. Perri sat in front of him, between his legs. Bridget would sit with them, but Deuce would stand at the fence behind the batter's box. Bridget called him "that parent." Lauren, Langston, Trey and Deuce and Bridget's younger son, Brandon, sat away from the rest of the group. Langston and Brandon sat with their friends, and Lauren sat with her friends. Trey's team won 9- 8 in an extra inning. He had one home run and four outs at first base.

At dinner, Lawrence gave Trey a check to start his savings for a car. "The next car will be mine!" Lauren announced to the table. They all laughed. Perri noticed Lawrence was relatively quiet during dinner. She chalked it up to him being so proud of his family and loved having all of them together.

Later that night when they were alone, Lawrence told Perri how much he loved her, and how proud he was to be her husband, and the father of their incredible children. He had tears in his eyes. Perri put both arms around her husband and held him tightly. When she leaned away, she looked deep into his eyes and then kissed him passionately. His body responded immediately. The last few times they made love, they had to work a little harder. Rolling over, so she was on top, in one motion, he was deep inside her. This was the

Lawrence of some years ago. The man who she couldn't look at in the office the next day for fear of blushing. The explosions came at the same time, but he didn't stop. He turned her over, and now he was on top. Her eyes were closed. She was enjoying how he made her feel. It had been some time since there had been this level of passion from him. "Look at me," he whispered. Perri opened her eyes. "I love you," he said with every thrust.

"I love you," she responded, gladly receiving each one. Then the second explosion happened, which had become rare for them.

It was pouring rain the next morning when Perri eased out of bed, leaving Lawrence snoring. He didn't even stir when she untangled herself from his arms. Walking through the house, Lauren's bedroom door was closed. Perri peeped in. She was asleep. Langston's door was opened, but he wasn't in his bed. She walked down the hall to the family room. He was on the sofa and Brandon was in the recliner. They were both asleep. The television was on and the video game remotes were on the floor. There were empty juice bottles, water bottles, potato chip bags, and a box with one chicken wing left. They would clean it up. They always did.

Perri was hungry, but waited a while before starting breakfast. She went downstairs and walked onto the sun porch and sat on the brightly colored floral patio sofa, watching as water overflowed out of the birdbath. Lauren's screaming interrupted her daydream. She ran to the bottom of the steps. "Mama! Daddy is having a seizure!" Perri ran up the stairs, two steps at a time. Langston was on the phone. Lauren and Brandon were trying to help Lawrence. He was sitting up in bed, gasping for air. Langston told them what the 911 operator was saying. The boys pulled him out of bed onto the floor and started chest compressions, as he was telling them. Lauren ran downstairs to disarm the alarm and unlock the door. Perri was on her knees beside Lawrence, helping the boys. The paramedics arrived in about five minutes and took over. Lauren was crying, and the boys were talking to Lawrence, trying to keep his attention. Perri got dressed. Just as she stepped into her shoes, the medic said they were taking him to the hospital. She looked at Lauren. "Call Deuce," and walked down the stairs behind the men carrying her husband on a stretcher.

<h1 style="text-align:center">Chapter 15</h1>

Lawrence Simon Cooper, Sr. died of a massive heart attack. Lacey, her husband, and daughters flew in early the next morning. Lacey managed everything. Lauren, Langston, and Brandon were devastated. Lauren had not stopped crying. There wasn't anything anybody could do to console her. She was fifteen years old, and her daddy was dead. There was no way for her to process that. Langston was fourteen, and fatherless. Perri was a forty-year-old widow.

Lacey convinced Perri to plan the funeral as quickly as they could. Prolonging it didn't serve any purpose for anybody. Deuce agreed. "Whoever can't get here, we will just have to understand," he said. Steven and Patricia Winters arrived the night before the funeral. Patricia realized walking into the house she hadn't ever been to her daughter's home.

At the visitation the next morning, Perri couldn't believe how many people she had to speak to, shake hands with and hug. As the funeral director announced that anyone else who wanted to "view the remains should come forward," Perri looked up and saw a familiar face. She couldn't think of his name. He was dressed in a formal navy uniform. He stood over Lawrence's body for a long time and then walked over to Deuce. After speaking to Bridget and the children, he walked toward Perri. His name tag said; "Gresham." It came back to her. They met in Hawaii at the airport when she and Lawrence were coming home from their honeymoon. The tears rolled down her face again. He hugged her tightly. "Perri, I am so sorry you are going through this. Please let me help you. Whatever you need, let me know," Carlton Gresham whispered in her ear. For a split second, she recalled their previous hug and what he said to her.

It was weeks before Perri went a full day without crying. She hadn't gone back to work and hadn't decided to or not. The job, the company, all reminded her of Lawrence. Langston and Lauren vacillated between fighting and not letting the other out of their sight. Deuce went back to work a week after Lawrence passed. Bridget thought he just didn't want to deal with the reality. Brandon was dreaming about the morning he watched his granddad die. Trey got a tattoo on his upper arm, with Lawrence's initials, birth year and death year. Deuce and Bridget didn't like the idea of the tattoo, but they understood that was his way of honoring his grandfather and dealing with his grief.

Perri realized she was alone during the weeks following the funeral. Her parents went back to Pensacola the day after the funeral. Lacey stayed a week, but then left to go home to her family and job. Lawrence's friends and former colleagues were acquaintances of hers, but not friends. None of them had followed up with her. The friends she had prior to meeting Lawrence, she hadn't maintained. The difference in Lawrence's age and her friend's boyfriends and husbands made socializing difficult, and this situation was a result. Perri didn't know how to rebuild her life.

As the months progressed, Perri and the children made peace with their new normal, all of them sharing stories of getting ready to call Lawrence or expecting him to be at home when they got there. Bridget and Lacey finally took Lawrence's things out of the house. His jewelry they put in the safe for Perri to divide later between the children. There were a few other things Perri wanted to keep, too.

Perri was also very surprised to find out how much money Lawrence left her. There was an insurance policy for Deuce and college trust funds for Trey and Brandon.

There were multiple insurance policies for Perri, Langston and Lauren, and college trust funds for them. There were also accounts for Lauren's wedding, for Langston to take his wife on a honeymoon, and for both of them to start their own businesses. There was life insurance on the mortgage and more money in savings than expected, investments and annuities she had no knowledge of. They had nothing to be concerned about financially. As many times as Perri and Lawrence disagreed about him doing things and not discussing them with her, she loved and missed him so much right then.

Chapter 16

It was an unseasonably cool morning. Perri sat on the terrace of her bedroom, day dreaming and letting a cup of coffee get cold. When the phone rang, she didn't recognize the number, but answered anyway. Over the past six months, there had been so many calls. Screening them just meant another one to return.

"Good morning Perri, I hope I'm not disturbing you." She didn't recognize the voice. "This is Carlton Gresham."

This wasn't business. No questions to answer or information to provide. "Hello Carlton. How are you?"

He inquired about Langston and Lauren, and after a few minutes, asked, "How are you, Perri? How are you really?"

She hesitated and wanted to say "horrible" and why did he care? But he was Deuce's friend and there was no need not to be nice. "To be honest, Carlton, today is a pretty good day. I can't say that every day."

"And I can't say I understand, but I'm glad you're good today. I hope tomorrow is even better."

"Thank you." Perri expected the conversation to end, but he kept talking.

"Have you been out, had any time away from the kids?"

"No, I haven't. I need to keep them close."

"For you or for them?"

"Both, I guess." She sighed.

"I'm in town, well, in the area, and I would love to take you all out for a while tomorrow."

"What do you mean in the area?"

"I'm in Columbia for a couple of days." He was upbeat.

"Have you talked to Deuce to see if they're available? Or I can call."

"I talked to Deuce yesterday, but I meant just you, Lauren, and Langston."

"Oh…um…let me see what they're doing tomorrow. May I call you back?" Perri was stumbling over her words.

"That works."

Perri told Langston and Lauren about Carlton's call. "Can we take the boat out?" Langston asked in response to the news. They hadn't touched the boat since Lawrence passed.

"Is the boat ready?"

"Yeah, Ma, you know Daddy always prepped it. Plus, me, Brandon and Trey know what to do."

"But you and Brandon can't drive." Lauren laughed.

"Shut up, girl!"

Perri was a little overwhelmed. "He may not be familiar with boats."

"Ma, he's in the Navy! You know, ships…" Langston said sarcastically. He and Lauren laughed. Perri shook her fist at him.

"If Brandon's going, can I bring someone too?" Lauren asked.

"Yes," Perri shrugged. The realization hit her. Lauren and Langston were ready to move on, but she wasn't.

Perri waited all day to call Carlton back, teetering between sadness and being angry that the world was moving on without her permission. Finally speaking with him, Carlton was cordial and reassured her he could manage the boat. When they hung up, he was delighted they were going out. Having Brandon there made it a little awkward, so he told Deuce before they went. He didn't really care how Deuce felt about it, but he didn't want to put the kids in an uneasy space. Carlton had every intention of pursuing her. Perri was Deuce's stepmother and all, but she was hot and available.

Chapter 17

Trey met them at the boat landing and brought Brandon. Deuce thought Carlton may need a hand, and he and Bridget had plans. When Deuce and Carlton talked, Deuce didn't seem at all alarmed about them going out. He didn't seem to suspect what Carlton was up to, and that worked for Carlton.

It was a beautiful afternoon. There were a lot of boats on the water. The boys and Carlton loaded the coolers onto the boat, and Carlton steered it to the edge of the ramp. The kids climbed in, and Carlton held both Perri's hands while she stepped over the side and into the boat. He noticed how good she looked, wearing a strapless bathing suit and shorts, sunglasses, and a hat. She had on very little make-up and still wore her wedding rings.

Carlton's life vest was on but unbuckled and Perri told him not to move the boat without securing it. "Aye aye, Ma'am!" he said, winking at her. Perri sat up front with Carlton, and felt uncomfortable, like she was betraying Lawrence. She was quiet for the first few minutes. Carlton left her to her thoughts. The kids were taking pictures and Brandon was creating a video on his phone. He walked toward the front. "Uncle C, please explain to the audience the specifications of our trip right now."

"This is Captain Carlton Gresham, Admiral of the USS Perri." They all laughed. Perri looked over at him but didn't say anything. "We are traveling on Lake Wylie in South Carolina, traveling at thirty-five knots, or forty miles per hour. The wind is calm, out of the Southwest at about ten miles per hour." He continued and Brandon and Langston were intrigued by it all.

As they passed some beautiful lakeside homes, Perri could hear Lauren and her friend talking about the ones they liked and the changes they would make from one to the other. She joined their conversation briefly. At that point, Carlton thought she was ready to talk and said something about the boat being a good idea. Perri agreed. They started a general conversation, and as they talked, Lauren came up front and handed Perri her phone. "Is it okay for me to post these?" Perri swiped through several pictures, giving her the phone back.

"Yes."

"Nice!" Carlton remarked.

"What?" Perri asked.

"Lauren gets permission to post on social media. That's good discipline on your part." Perri wanted to tell him she and Lawrence decided together, but didn't. "Can't be too careful with that stuff," was her reply.

Carlton steered the boat into a space beside some other boats. There were people in the water, a guy selling treats on the manmade shore, and another guy selling hot dogs and hamburgers.

"Good look, Uncle C!" Brandon said, jumping out of the boat into about three feet of water. Langston jumped out behind him and then they helped the girls out. Carlton gave Langston some money and then asked Perri if she wanted something. "Some kind of lemonade or lemon slushy please," she answered, looking at the kids, not at Carlton.

"Do you want to get out?" Carlton asked.

"No, thanks."

"Tell me what's on your mind."

Perri took a deep breath and blew it out slowly. "This whole experience, this outing on the boat, it's so surreal. I feel like I'm dreaming. I haven't ever been on this boat without Lawrence. And what's worse, my children seem fine."

"I'm sure they miss their dad, but at their age, they're resilient." She just nodded. He continued. "I've never lost a spouse, but I lost my father when I was thirteen, so I get it. He died in Desert Storm…"

"Is that why you joined the military?"

"Yes. I told my uncle and my mom on the day of the funeral I was going to the Army. But my uncle talked me into Navy ROTC, and like they say, the rest is history."

"How did you manage at that age without him? What did your mother do?" Perri asked quietly.

"My mom went right back to work. She was a teacher and her students asked her to come back. They kept her busy. My uncle stayed on me. I was active in sports, and I had to be accountable to my coaches and teammates. I acted out a little, but it didn't take much to reel me back in. The thought of disappointing my father kept me in line too."

As they talked, the girls came back with the lemonade slush, and a few minutes later the boys came back with cherry for Carlton and a horrific looking mixture for themselves.

The boat outing turned out to be good for everybody. Perri thought about Carlton saying his mother went right back to work. Perri looked for a job. She could go back to her old job, but that would be too painful. Maybe new and different was better. She would take Lauren and Langston to Florida to see Lacey and her parents, and then come back to get on with her life.

<h1 style="text-align:center">Chapter 18</h1>

The night after their outing, Carlton called Perri, and he called the next day too. Perri told him she and the kids were heading to Pensacola to see her family.

Carlton laughed. "Maybe I'll see you."

"What does that mean?"

"I'm in Pensacola at the Naval Station here."

She thought; suddenly, Carlton was always around.

"Carlton, I'm puzzled."

"About what?"

"About why you're paying me so much attention. First, you were in Columbia and came to Charlotte to see us. You've called every day since we went out on the boat, and now you'll see me in Pensacola."

"Pensacola is a coincidence. I didn't know you have family here."

"I'm from Pensacola."

"I didn't know that."

He didn't want to have this conversation on the telephone. "When will you be here?"

"Tomorrow afternoon."

"Can we get together and talk the day after tomorrow?"

"Talk about what, Carlton?" The tone of her voice was annoyed.

"We'll talk when you get here."

What Carlton wanted to tell her was serious. He knew when he met her; all those years ago, she was the one as bizarre as that was. He met her coming back from her honeymoon. Lawrence gave her a good life. Her children were great, and based on what he knew about Lawrence, they were set financially.

Over the years, as he communicated with Deuce, he knew generally what was going on in Perri's life. He was actually surprised she was coming to see her family, or at least her parents. They were majorly opposed to Lawrence marrying their daughter. Carlton wanted Perri to know there was still a lot of living for her to do.

On the flight to Pensacola, Perri reflected on her story; sacrificing family and friends to build a life with the man she loved, and now that was over. Her thoughts were rapid. "How do I rebuild? Do I apologize? Do I try to make new friends?" There had been no contact with any of her friends from college or from her early days in Charlotte. She dozed off thinking about it.

When they landed, there was a text message from Lacey and one from Carlton. Lacey's was answered, but not Carlton's. He was confusing to her. "Why is he so interested in me and my well-being?"

Lacey and her children took Perri, Lauren, and Langston to their parents' home. It was an indescribable feeling for Perri. She had not slept in that house since the conversation with her parents regarding Lawrence all those years ago. Her emotions were high thinking about it. Emotional because of Lawrence, not being in her parents' home. As usual, her parents and the grandchildren had plans that did not include Perri or Lacey.

The next day, Carlton called to ask Perri if they could have a late lunch. Her first response was to say no, but her mouth said yes. After checking for the spare car keys, she agreed to meet him.

They met at an Italian restaurant. Carlton was wearing his work uniform. They hugged slightly. The restaurant was busy, and they had to wait a few minutes, and made small talk while they waited. "Are you coming *from* work or headed *to* work?" Perri asked.

"Going to work in a couple of hours."

"What's your job here at this station?"

"It's top secret!"

Her look was serious. He waited for a few seconds and then laughed. Before he could explain the laughter, the hostess showed them to a table. Once they were seated and ordered beverages, she asked why he laughed.

"My assignment here isn't really top secret. I'm doing some interviewing for the Academy."

"That's interesting. Has Deuce mentioned anything to you about Trey?"

"Yes, he did. I am going to talk with him on campus, though, in a few weeks. There are regional recruiting events."

"Have you always been a recruiter?"

"No," he laughed. "This is all new. I was a chief quartermaster."

"In civilian, please!"

He laughed loudly. "In the retail world, I would be a buyer. I was in charge of buying everything from food to artillery."

"Why the drastic change?"

"I was going to retire. Then I found out about the recruiter position being available. They hired me on the spot. The transfer happened in five weeks, not the usual three months. So as of next month, I have a new assignment."

What Carlton was telling her was intriguing, but didn't know why she had even asked. Carlton noticed her body language. "Did I lose you?"

"Not really, but why are you telling me all this? Why am I even here?"

"Relax Perri. I just wanted to break the ice." She shifted in her seat and took a sip of her drink. He knew time was running out. "Do you remember what I told you the first time we met?" He picked up his drink, leaned back, and smiled.

Perri didn't smile. "Yes, I do, and I thought it was an inappropriate comment."

He smiled again and leaned forward. "If it was so inappropriate, why do you remember?"

Perri didn't answer.

"Did you tell Big Guy what I said?"

"No."

"Why?" he asked.

There was a considerable amount of time before she answered. "Because people were always judging us, saying stupid stuff, so I learned to ignore the comments." Her voice cracked.

"I wasn't judging or making a stupid comment. I was calling it the way I saw it."

"You absolutely were judging us, and you're right, that was the way *YOU* saw it. Lawrence and I didn't care how anybody saw our relationship. I was estranged from my parents for not accepting us, so you know I don't care what you think!" She was looking him directly in the eyes, and he could feel her fury.

"Do you remember what I told you at Big Guy's service?"

"No, what did you say?" She rolled her eyes.

He answered her seriously. "I told you I would help you deal with this."

Looking at him, the anger in her eyes reappeared. "Carlton, there isn't anything you can do to help me."

Carlton decided not to push. They finished eating, talked about Pensacola and how it had changed over the years. He called the next day, but she didn't answer.

Chapter 19

Over the next few weeks, Carlton and Perri talked off and on. He initiated all the calls, and she started to expect them. On one hand, Perri wanted him to call. On the other hand, it was good having someone to talk to, but felt she was betraying Lawrence.

Carlton didn't tell Perri he asked to be assigned to Charlotte. That was actually a little presumptive of him, and he could have been shooting himself in the foot. He wanted her in his life, but she was indifferent toward him. Carlton also didn't tell Deuce he was moving to Charlotte. He would in time. He just wanted Perri to hear it from him, not from Deuce or one of the kids.

Two weeks after Carlton moved to Charlotte, he ran into Trey and a couple of his friends at the gym. Carlton told him he was in town for a meeting and needed a workout. Fortunately, there was a hotel around the corner, so the story didn't seem too farfetched. But he had to call Deuce now. He didn't want to lie, but he still wouldn't tell Deuce the entire story. Through the course of the conversation with Trey, he asked about Langston, Lauren, and Perri.

"They a'ight. Langston seems better than Lauren or Ms. Perri."

Carlton laughed. "You call her Ms. Perri?"

"Yeah, it's awkward. She is technically our grandmother, but my dad's age, so we've always called her Ms. Perri." They changed the subject.

When Trey was gone, Carlton thought about Perri being his grandmother. He shook his head. "Wow!" He thought, laughing, and reached for the phone to call Deuce. After they talked, he called Perri.

He was surprised she had gone back to work. "Did you go back to your old job?"

"No, I couldn't. That would just be too much. This is less pressure, regular hours, and some flexibility to work remotely."

"Sounds like a good fit." He was sincere.

They continued to talk about her new job, and then she asked about his. He didn't want to lie, so he was careful how he answered her. "Actually, I'm in Charlotte for a new job-related meeting. I may be here permanently."

No immediate response from Perri, but then, "Oh, I'm sure Deuce will be excited. The band will be back together!" They laughed.

"Some of the stuff we did in college, we probably don't need to get the band back together!" They laughed again. "What do you think?" he asked.

"Think about what?"

"How do you feel about me being in Charlotte?"

"I don't feel any way about it. Why do you ask?"

"I hope if I'm here, we can spend some time together, get to know each other." She didn't respond, so he kept talking. "You and Deuce are the only people I know in Charlotte. It will be good to have another friend." Perri relaxed her shoulders when Carlton said, "friend."

"Where is your office?" Carlton asked her.

"In Ballantyne, not far from where we live."

"Oh, that's too far for lunch," he laughed.

"Where will you be?"

"Either at South End or University area." He was being truthful about that. At the time, he didn't know where he would be assigned permanently.

"Yep, a little far for lunch."

Carlton recognized the lack of emotion. After a few more minutes, they ended the conversation. He wasn't sure what to make of her indifference, and he was trying not to take it personally.

<h1 style="text-align:center">Chapter 20</h1>

For the third day in a row, and the fifth time in two weeks, Perri's co-worker asked her out. First it was lunch, then dinner, then a drink after work. Today he brought her iced coffee in the afternoon, before getting it herself. It was time to deal with this and stop sidestepping the issue. Her wedding rings were visible. He had to see that. Did he know she was a widow, or did he not care if he thought she was married? Perri discussed it with Lacey, who thought it was hilarious. There wasn't anybody else for her to talk to. There had been no friends. Most days for lunch, Perri went home and shared nothing about her personal life with her co-workers. From time to time, the children and their activities would come up in conversation.

He was waiting at the elevator. She took a deep breath and looked at him, not smiling. Two other people walked up, so Perri didn't say anything until they got off the elevator. "Thank you for the drink, but I don't want you to be misled. I'm not interested in going out."

"Why not?"

Perri looked at her hand and showed him her rings.

He shrugged. "Is that supposed to mean something?"

She didn't know how to respond. There was a thick silence between them.

My husband passed recently, and I don't date."

"Perri, your husband passed over a year ago. It's time for you to move on."

Her anger rose. "I don't know why you know so much about me. I don't like it, and that doesn't change my mind."

"Life goes on, Perri, but I respect your decision. See you tomorrow." He walked away.

The next day at work was awkward for Perri. Her co-worker was his normal self, but it felt like everybody was looking at her, and it seemed like she saw him twice as much that day.

The following day, Perri walked into the break room, and he was standing there. She couldn't walk out. Nobody else was in there. He was fixing a cup of coffee. "Can I get you one?" he asked.

"Yes, thank you," handing him her cup. He filled it and handed it back. She stirred in the sugar and cream, then asked, "How did you know about my husband passing?"

"It's a long story, but we have a mutual friend."

Who could he be talking about? Perri wondered.

"Well, an acquaintance, at least." He didn't give any further details. "Why is it a secret, Perri?" He motioned for her to take a seat. She sat, then sipped her coffee before answering.

"It's tough. My life is very different from anybody else here."

"Why do you think that?"

"I am a widow at forty-one years old and am a single mother."

He chuckled. "Sharon is a widow. Her husband died in combat. She was thirty-three. Carla and Stephanie are single mothers. Carla hasn't ever been married and Steph is divorced. The only difference between you and them, your husband, died. Sharon didn't have a child with her husband before he passed."

Perri just listened. There wasn't anything to say. She worked with these people every day and knew nothing about them.

<h1 style="text-align:center">Chapter 21</h1>

Over the next couple of weeks, Perri had lunch in the break room with her co-workers or went out with them almost every day. She worked remotely less often and engaged more with Sharon. They went to get iced coffee one afternoon, and Perri told her about Lawrence passing. Sharon was very understanding and encouraging. Perri didn't realize how much a compassionate ear was needed until she had one. As they walked out together at the end of the day, there was a car at the curb and a gentleman standing beside the passenger door. Sharon laughed and told Perri to have a good evening. Perri watched as the man and Sharon shared a quick kiss and he opened the car door for her. The scene tugged at Perri's heartstrings and made her miss Lawrence so much.

Perri was sure Sharon missed her late husband too, but was obviously moving on. But Sharon was younger, and didn't have children, Perri surmised. "It's okay for her to move on." As she reached for the car door to close it, her eyes landed specifically on her wedding rings. Closing the car door, she sat for a moment just looking at her hand. Was it time to take the rings off? It had been a year. "I don't have any desire to date. I don't want another man in my life," she said aloud, while backing out of the parking space.

Later that evening, Deuce called, as he did from time to time. He and Perri chatted for a while, and toward the end of the conversation, he mentioned Trey's baseball tournament, graduation and graduation party. Perri wrote all the details and put them on her calendar when they hung up. She thought about Lawrence and how proud he would be of Trey, especially because he was accepted into the Air Force Academy. Before the thought was completely out of her head, she thought about Carlton, and realized there hadn't been any communication from him in several days. Not since the day he invited her to dinner, and she declined. It was strange.

Trey's baseball team won the state championship seven to five. The score was tied at five until the bottom of the sixth inning. It was a good game, and the family was tired from cheering so hard. Not to mention it was hot out there. Trey was celebrating with the team, and Lauren was quickly putting together a plan for the rest of them to go somewhere to eat. As they discussed it, Perri was distracted. Carlton had come into the stands after the game started with three other people: a man and two women. After the game, she noticed him introducing them to Deuce and Bridget. After a few minutes, he came over, spoke to the kids, then to her and left with his friends. He didn't introduce them to her. On the way to the car, Perri heard Brandon ask Deuce about Carlton. "Is Uncle C coming to the house?"

"No, he had other plans."

"Yeah, right! He just didn't want us to scrutinize his new girlfriend!" Brandon and Langston fist bumped in agreement.

Later that evening, when they were home and settled, Perri called Carlton. He didn't answer.

Chapter 22

The first email Perri opened that morning was the details of the company outing at the Carowinds Theme Park. Deciding immediately not to go, she moved on to the next message.

Later that day, someone mentioned the outing and remarked how much fun it was the year before. Everybody in the conversation said they would be there. Perri didn't comment. A few days later, when the email came for all employees to confirm their attendance, Sharon confided in Perri that she wanted to invite her boyfriend and his son.

"What's your hesitation?" Perri asked.

"Bringing him around co-workers is somewhat of a commitment!" They both laughed.

"Have you spent any time with his son?"

"Oh yeah. The three of us do stuff together all the time. I just don't want to take that step first. He will be cool with it, I'm sure. It's me!"

They talked a few more minutes about it, and Perri convinced Sharon to ask her boyfriend and be totally honest with him about her feelings.

"Are you bringing a date? Sharon asked Perri."

"No. I'm not coming." She shook her head and shrugged.

"Why?"

Perri hesitated before responding. Finally, saying to Sharon she still didn't feel comfortable doing family things without Lawrence.

"But you have to. Your children have lives too, and they deserve to have ongoing memories of growing up and having good experiences."

Over the weekend, Perri mentioned the Carowinds outing to Langston, who immediately wanted to go. Lauren said she needed to check her schedule but would go if it was clear. On Monday, Perri told Sharon they were coming, and Sharon told Perri she and her boyfriend and his son were coming too.

Also, over the weekend, Langston brought to Perri's attention they hadn't made any plans for Lauren's birthday. This was the second birthday since Lawrence passed, but the first one was a blur.

"Ma, I think we gotta do something special 'cause she'll be sixteen. You know if Daddy was here, he would be gettin' her a car!"

Perri knew Langston was right, but hadn't decided to get a car. She just didn't feel comfortable.

Monday evening during dinner, Langston brought up the birthday. "Do you want a party?" He asked his sister.

"Yeah, I think so, but I want it on the boat."

"That won't be a party. You can't invite but a few people," he added.

They started arguing, so Perri decided to jump in. "Lauren, how about this? You and a couple of your girlfriends ride the boat to the landing in Mooresville at the park, and I will rent a place on the lake for the party."

"I like it, Mom!"

"The rest of the guests can meet you there."

They worked on party plans for a couple of days, and it all came together. The night before the party, Deuce called to say he couldn't drive the boat. Something came up at work, and he would not get back in time, but had worked it out with Carlton, who was glad to help. Perri was grateful Deuce was proactive and executed Plan B, but wished it wasn't with Carlton. But what could she do?

Perri had not seen Carlton since Trey's game and couldn't help but notice how good he looked. He was cordial toward her, but very loving and playful with Lauren and her friends. Carlton acted like Perri wasn't there. When they reached the docking point, he asked what the plan was from there.

He helped each of them off the boat. Perri was last. As he held her hand for her to step onto the dock, his arm accidentally touched her breast. He didn't notice, but she did, and felt something she hadn't felt in a long time and was angry with herself for feeling it.

The party was a hit. Lauren had the time of her life, in a big way, because Langston made sure of it. When she cut her cake, he whispered something in her ear; they hugged and then both made a gesture toward Heaven. Lauren blew a kiss, and Langston touched his heart and pointed. What they did made Perri emotional. Before Lauren and her friends got back on the boat, she and Langston released sixteen blue balloons. Blue was Lawrence's favorite color.

At the beginning of the boat ride back, Perri sat in the back with the girls, looking at pictures and saying yes or no to what they could post online. After a few minutes, she made her way back to the front, beside Carlton. "Thanks for driving and helping with the party."

"You're welcome. It was my pleasure." He kept his eyes straight ahead. Perri looked at his profile, and again something stirred inside her. Just as she started to say something else to him, his phone rang. He answered, smiled and then told the caller he would call back later.

By the time Perri got home from dropping off Lauren's friends, Carlton and Langston had put the boat up and Carlton was getting ready to leave. Lauren jumped out of the car and hugged him.

"Thank you, Uncle C!"

"You're welcome, beautiful! I hope you had a good day."

"I did. I had a fantastic day!"

Perri walked over and waited for Lauren and Carlton to finish talking. "Thank you, Carlton."

"Sure." He left without waiting to hear the rest of what she had to say.

That night, Perri dreamed about having sex with Carlton. The dream haunted her for the next few days. It was time to at least think about it and to deal with the feelings of missing Lawrence deeply. So much, in fact, there was physical pain.

The ache was not just in her heart, but she missed how he made her feel. The way her body felt when he caressed her breasts or licked her ears. How he talked to her when they made love. Lawrence had been her first, her only. Could she share that level of intimacy with another man? Perri wasn't sure or how to make that decision.

Chapter 23

Perri and Lacey had their regular talk, but Lacey could tell Perri had something on her mind. Finally, Perri told her about Carlton, including the dream, and how much she missed Lawrence physically.

"That's good. I'm glad you finally admitted it to yourself," Lacey told her. "Sis, I think you should go with your feelings."

"I'm not sure how I feel."

"He didn't ask you to marry him, Perri."

"That's what he said."

"Why don't you invite him to the Carowinds thing?"

"Lace, I'm taking the kids."

"So! He's not some stranger."

"Oh my gosh, I don't know."

"I just told you what to do, girl! Call me back in the next two hours and tell me you asked him." Lacey laughed and hung up. Perri didn't laugh.

She couldn't think about it. She hung up with Lacey and dialed Carlton. Voice mail.

"Hi Carlton, it's Perri. Please give me a call. Thanks."

He waited to see if there was a message. Since she didn't say specifically what the call was about, he texted her back. "Can't talk right now. Kids, ok?"

"Dang! A text. I will lose my nerve by the time he calls back." Reading the text, she replied, "Yes, fine. Call when you can." Carlton felt bad about lying to her, but he was tired of Perri.

When they talked the next day, Carlton was surprised Perri invited him to go to the company outing. He didn't want to read much into it, but he said yes.

The park was reserved that day for their company and for one other. There were a couple thousand people in the park, rather than ten thousand. The lines were shorter, and things moved faster. Perri was nervous about being with Carlton, so she was glad not to see anybody from her department for a while. The kids didn't seem to think anything was unusual about Carlton going with them. They knew to meet in the picnic area at lunchtime and took off before Perri could give them too many instructions.

Carlton and Perri started the day by riding The Fury. When they walked off the roller coaster, they were arm in arm, and he was laughing. She was limp. He steered her to the closest empty bench, and they sat.

"I feel like my stomach is turned upside down."

He pulled her close and caught a whiff of her perfume. He was still laughing.

"I told you to work your way up to that one."

"Is 'I told you so' the best you can do?" Perri rolled her eyes and stifled a laugh.

"Maybe you need something to settle your stomach." He nodded toward a concession's kiosk.

"Will you see if they have a ginger ale?"

A few minutes later, he came back with two ginger ales. They sat and watched the crowd for a while and rode the Roaring Rapids before heading to the picnic area to meet the kids. It was bound to happen. Perri ran into her co-worker Sharon. They made introductions, and Sharon's friend suggested they let a couple in front of them so they could ride together. Perri was enjoying herself.

Late that evening when they were back at Perri's house, Carlton thanked her for including him, and told her he hoped they could "hang out" again.

"I'm glad I invited you too, and I'm glad you said yes."

He decided not to overstay his welcome. Perri walked with him to his car, and they shared a long hug. He kissed her forehead and got in.

That night Perri went to sleep thinking about Carlton. It wasn't a dream this time. She wanted him; needed him, and those feelings were real. By the time the next morning came, the decision was made to take off her wedding rings.

Chapter 24

Lauren noticed immediately Perri wasn't wearing her rings but waited until the next day to say anything to her mom. She talked with Langston about it first.

"Is that an important girl thing?" Langston asked.

"I don't know about that, but it means Ma is ready to have a boyfriend," Lauren told him.

Langston thought a minute before saying anything. "A boyfriend would be good. She needs to do stuff without us being around all the time."

Lauren lowered her voice even though Perri wasn't home. "Do you think Uncle C wants to be her boyfriend?"

"Yeah."

"But he was Daddy's friend," Lauren whispered.

"No, he wasn't girl, he is Deuce's friend."

"Is that okay with you?" she asked, still whispering.

"I don't care. I like Uncle C for her, and I won't have to shoot him for doing something stupid."

"Stupid like what?"

"Like putting his hands on her." Langston was serious.

"He wouldn't," Lauren said firmly.

"Whatever! But real talk, you goin' to college in two years, I'm going in three. She needs to have a life."

Lauren told Perri about her talk with Langston, including her brother's threat to shoot Carlton. Perri laughed about that. "Lauren, what prompted that conversation?"

"You took your rings off."

Perri looked down at her hand and then sat on the foot of the bed. "Sweetie, until you fall in love with a man like I fell in love with your dad, there's no way for you to understand how it feels for him to be gone. Taking my rings off was a gesture that shows I am at peace with my marriage being over." Perri cried as she talked. Lauren hugged her.

"Ma, it's okay. Daddy loved you and he wants you to be happy."

"Can somebody make me happy and put some food on the table?" Langston said, walking into Perri's bedroom eating a bowl of cereal.

"Boy, get out of here with that!" Lauren yelled. Perri just covered her face with both hands. As Lauren was leaving the room to chase Langston back down the stairs, Perri stopped her.

"The rings are in the safe for Langston to give his wife."

"Well, they're gonna be in there for a long time. Who's gone marry somebody that walks around the house eating cereal?"

As if it were the most natural thing ever, Perri called Carlton. When he answered, she knew he wasn't at home. The background was too noisy. "Hey Perri."

"Hi. Obviously, you're out."

"At the gym. What's up?"

"I know it's short notice, but can you have dinner?"

"Have plans tonight, but tomorrow I'm all yours."

She smirked slightly but wondered what kind of plans.

"I'll call you tomorrow to work out the details."

Over the next week, Carlton and Perri saw each other three times. The third time, she agreed to let him pick her up rather than meeting him. Lauren was out with her friends, but Langston and Brandon were there. "What are your intentions toward my mama?" Langston asked Carlton, trying his best not to laugh. Brandon was standing beside him with his arms folded, nodding. He was holding in laughter, too.

"I intend to feed her, 'cause as I understand it, you eatin' up everything around here." Neither Langston nor Brandon held their laughter any longer.

Carlton and Perri went to Sheldon's, a very nice restaurant on Lake Norman. He expected them to have a good meal, and the service was always exceptional, but the addition of the jazz saxophonist was the icing on the cake. The performer was a local musician, but he was very talented and played the work of all the great jazz saxophone players, including Kim Waters. He played a medley of his songs, finishing with "Soul Serenade." The audience applauded and then it happened. He started playing "Sweet and Saxy." Perri trembled. Kim Waters became her favorite after Lawrence introduced her to his music. Lawrence had played "Sweet and Saxy" in Hilton Head the first time they made love, and he had played it in the car for her driving home the night before he passed, which was the last time they made love. Perri hoped Carlton couldn't see her face. She was biting her bottom lip to hold back the tears.

It seemed like the song went forever. When he was finally done, Perri excused herself. Once in the ladies' room, she covered her face and cried into a wad of tissue. After a few minutes, she had to go back out. Perri blew her nose, touched up her make-up, and walked back to the table with a smile.

"You ready to leave?" Carlton asked, standing and holding her chair.

"Not unless you are."

"No."

"Can we have another drink?"

He got the waiter's attention and ordered two more drinks. Perri checked her phone to make sure Lauren was home, and the alarm was set.

"Everything okay?"

"Yes, just making sure Lauren is in on time!" Perri smiled.

"Okay, Mama Bear!"

"That I am!"

They stayed a little while longer, and then Carlton told her he was ready to leave. He reached for her hand as they walked to the car. Perri hesitated slightly, but then decided it was okay. They rode home talking about the musician's performance. Perri was a little uneasy, but tried not to show it. She changed the subject twice, but both times they ended up back there; talking about "Sweet and Saxy."

Back at Perri's house, Carlton didn't want to leave, but she hadn't invited him to stay. "Can we sit by the pool for a few minutes? I want to tell you something." Carlton was looking right in her eyes.

She wanted to say no, but didn't.

The only lights on were around the inside upper edge of the pool. Perri pushed a button on the side of the gate, and lights came on at each corner of the fence. The lights were camouflaged by trees, which made the fenced in area exquisite. They took seats side by side, so Carlton turned his chair to face her. Her heart was racing.

"Why did the music make you sad?"

Obviously, she hadn't covered it up well. Her answer wasn't immediate, stalling and swatting at a candle fly. He waited. She was looking at the ground. He leaned forward, but still didn't say anything. Perri moved only her eyes to look up at Carlton. Her voice was just above a whisper. Finally, Perri answered him. "Kim Waters was Lawrence's favorite jazz sax player, and 'Sweet and Saxy' was our song. When I heard it, I got emotional."

"You didn't have to walk away, you could have told me."

Perri looked at him with a blank expression on her face. "Why would I tell you that? That was personal between me and my husband."

"Your late husband."

She wanted to say something, but there wasn't anything to say. He met and held her gaze. Perri wanted to be angry, but there was no point.

"You said you have something to tell me." Perri was hoping to change the subject. He didn't hesitate.

"Perri, I want you in my life. I care about you deeply. Losing a spouse must be horrible, but you can't live there. You have to move on. You are incredible, and you deserve to keep living. You deserve to be loved and to love again." He paused briefly. With his thumbs, he wiped away the tears rolling down her cheeks. He took both her hands in his. "Let me love you. I can't give you all of this…." He looked at the pool, then at the house, and then around in general… "but I can make you happy. Let's find a new song; our song."

Perri shifted in her chair but didn't take her hands out of his. Something needed to be said. She wiped the tears on the right side of her face. He wiped the left side.

"What is your favorite kind of music?" She asked.

"R & B, love songs. I like a Ballad. People like Luther Vandross and I grew up liking Isaac Hayes!"

"Which Luther song would sum up tonight?"

"The Night I Fell in Love."

Perri drew in her breath. His response caught her off guard. He stood up and pulled her into his arms. He held her until she put her arms around him, too. A couple of minutes later, he walked her to the door. They kissed. There were those feelings again. The ones that made her nipples hard and her panties wet.

Perri didn't dream that night because she didn't sleep.

Chapter 25

For several weeks, Perri and Carlton spent a considerable amount of time together. One Friday, he talked her into coming to his place. As the evening progressed, he played a variety of music. When Luther started singing "Here and Now" he took her hand, pulled her off the sofa and they danced. They danced through "So Amazing" and "A House is not a Home." When "So Amazing" came on the second time, Carlton told Perri that was their song. This time as they danced, he caressed her body; he kissed her lips, and her neck. After a while, he guided her to his bedroom. He laid her on the bed; her feet were still on the floor. She kicked off her shoes.

"Are you okay?" he whispered in her ear.

"Yes."

He undressed her slowly, down to her bra and panties. Then he took off his shorts and t-shirt.

"Are you sure?" He wanted her to say she wanted him.

She nodded.

"I can't hear you."

"Yes." Perri didn't want to say much. Physically, the answer was "absolutely." Emotionally, not so sure. To keep from crying, she tried to concentrate on the music playing in the other room. It was the instrumental introduction to "Superstar." Perri closed her eyes and gave in to the moment, to the feelings.

Both completely spent, they lay there just looking at each other. She could talk now.

"You are so amazing!" Carlton smiled and kissed her on the nose. "You wanna call the kids and tell them you'll be home in the morning?"

Perri glanced across the room at a clock. "No, I better not. I haven't ever stayed out all night."

"I'll take you home then."

"Carlton, that's not necessary."

"Perri, it is necessary. First, I don't want you to go. Second, I am not going to make love to you, and then watch you walk out of here and drive across town, like you're just anybody I had in my bed."

He felt a protest, but he put his finger to her lips. "Your choice; stay or I drive you home."

There wasn't a protest. Her response was to just put her legs over his and roll on top of him.

Perri eased out of bed and went to the bathroom and had paid little attention to the music, but now heard it. It was Will Downing. Could she get her clothes and leave without waking Carlton? What he said to her was great, but she needed space. Coming out of the bathroom, Carlton sat on the side of the bed waiting for her. "You going or staying?"

"I'm going. I don't want the kids to know I'm not there."

"Understand." He reached for his boxers.

"But you don't have to take me home. I promise I will be fine." Perri walked over to stand directly in front of him. He kissed her stomach.

"Perri, that's not open for discussion."

"Can we compromise?"

He tilted his head, looked up at her, but didn't respond.

"You follow me, so I will have my car in the morning."

Carlton agreed to the compromise. "But sit down for a minute. Let's talk."

She hesitated, but sat.

"I know you need to process our time together tonight."

"Yes, I do."

"Well, let me tell you this. You are an incredible lover, and while we are great in bed together, we connected on another level tonight." He paused, but Perri didn't respond. He continued, "I have fallen for you, girl!"

Perri just smiled. Carlton decided he had said enough. They were both quiet for a while. Finally, she leaned in and kissed his lips.

"Let's talk tomorrow."

He followed her home. It was almost two o'clock in the morning when they got to her house. He didn't linger. Kissed her goodnight and got back in his car. "Let me know when you get home."

When Perri went in, there was a light on over the kitchen sink. The same light she would leave on when Langston or Lauren were out. Turning it off while using the light on her phone to go upstairs. One of them, maybe both, knew their mom was out late. Her closet light was on so she could see to get into her room. That's what she did for them, too.

Quietly, Perri closed her bedroom door and walked into the sitting area. Her legs were weak. Not from her physical activity, but from her emotions. She laughed when her kids would say, "the struggle is real" but right then, her struggle *was* real. The confusion was real. Everything had two sides; her being totally smitten with Carlton, but still loving Lawrence. Her desire to make love to Carlton again was real, but her husband had been her first and only until tonight. She wanted to shower, but liked the way her underwear and her skin smelled like Carlton.

Perri almost fell into the recliner. What had she done? What would Lawrence think if he knew? With closed eyes, the tears fell. The voice in her head said clearly, "Lawrence is gone, but you're still here." Pacing around the room, Perri weighed the pros and cons of being with Carlton. Of having sex with him, and they weren't in a real relationship, at least not in her mind. Carlton was a good man, a great man, in fact. Her son and daughter liked him a lot, and he liked them. "I wonder why he never married or had children." In the midst of her contemplation, the phone rang. It was Carlton letting her know he was home. They didn't talk long, but he asked if they could see each other "later today?"

"Sure," then realized it was three in the morning.

"Good night, my love."

"Good night."

Saturday morning, Perri was cooking breakfast and talking with Lauren. Langston was outside shooting free throws waiting on his omelet. Perri's phone rang.

"It's Uncle C, I'll get it," Lauren said and answered.

"Hi Uncle C, what's up?"

Carlton was surprised. "I'm alright, what's up with you?"

"I'm good."

"Your Mom busy?"

"She's right here cooking breakfast, but I need to ask you something."

Perri stopped what she was doing, afraid Lauren was going to ask Carlton about her being out late the night before.

"Can you come over and take me driving? I need to practice, and my mother is scared to take me."

"Not true!" Perri answered loud enough for Carlton to hear her.

"I can't get a car until I have a license and I can't get a license until I can drive!"

Carlton was amused that Lauren was having this conversation with him. "Yep, I'm game. I can do that if it's okay with your mom."

"Okay, hold on." Lauren gave Perri the phone and explained the plan.

"Tell Langston to come in," Perri told her and took the phone. "Good morning!" hoping she sounded cheerful. The truth was, she was tired from not much sleep.

"How are you?"

"I'm fine."

"I didn't ask you how you look. I asked how you feel."

"Oh, my goodness, that is such a line!"

They laughed.

"I am calling to see if you could have dinner, but I guess I've been summoned to driver's ed."

"If you don't have time, or don't want to, it's fine."

"I have time and I don't mind at all."

A few hours later, Carlton came over and he and Lauren left so she could drive. Shortly after, Deuce and Brandon came to get Langston. Perri was home alone for about two hours. A nap helped her fatigue from the night before.

About the time they should be back, she heard voices downstairs. It was Lauren and one of her friends coming in with food and Carlton behind them. The instant she saw him, her body reacted, catching his eye just momentarily. Perri walked down the stairs with her hands up like, "where's mine?" Lauren and her friend laughed.

"Ma, we knew you wouldn't want this fast food, so Uncle C will get you something else. And where's Lang, by the way?"

"He's with Deuce and Brandon."

"Good, then we don't have to deal with him. We can watch movies in peace." She and her friend sat down in the breakfast nook.

"Get your bag, let's go," Carlton said as though it were the most natural thing in the world. She didn't respond, just picked up her bag and walked toward the door.

"Lauren Cooper, don't leave this house unless you let me know."

"I got this Ma!"

Carlton opened the car door for Perri. She got in and waited for him to get in. "What just happened in there?"

He laughed. "I think we got dismissed."

"I guess we did." Perri turned toward the window to fasten her seat belt and when she turned back, Carlton was close and kissed her. She blushed. He turned out of the subdivision without saying anything.

"Where are we going?"

"Sit back and enjoy the ride." They drove uptown, parked, and walked to a Japanese restaurant. When they finished eating, they walked through the park around the corner, holding hands.

"Do we need to talk about last night?" he asked.

"No, I'm good."

"Are you sure? So, you don't have any regrets?"

"I don't have any regrets. I am perfectly fine with last night."

After a little while, they walked back to the car. "Do you need to check on Lauren?"

"I don't think so. I'll check my phone." She looked quickly. There were no messages and no missed calls. "Nope, we're good."

As they drove, Carlton told Perri about the two young men he recruited the week before. He had passion in his voice as he talked about his next trips.

"Did you intend to make a career in the Navy when you joined?"

"I didn't have a plan when I joined. I was obligated to three years like all midshipmen in the academy. When the three years were up, I didn't have any reason to get out, so I stayed, and now nineteen years later, I'm still in."

"It has obviously been good for you."

"More than you know!"

They talked a little more, and then she asked a curious question. "Did the service keep you so busy, you decided not to have a family?"

He was quiet for a few seconds. "No, marriage never presented itself, so no children either."

Perri looked over at him. He looked sad. "Was that a question I shouldn't have asked?"

He reached over and took her hand. "You can ask anything you want, anytime. I don't have anything to hide from you."

"You looked sad." She squeezed his hand.

"The one long-term relationship I was in ended and it took me a minute to get over it. She was dealing with some mental health issues. I tried, but I just couldn't make it work. I didn't know from one day to the next who was going to show up."

"What do you mean?"

"One morning, we made love, laid in bed for a while talking, then got up and went to work. About two hours later, her co-worker called me to say I needed to come get her. She had fallen apart, talking to herself and didn't know where she was."

"Did you get her some help?"

"Of course, I tried. But she wouldn't take the medicine they gave her. Because I made her take it, I became the enemy."

Perri looked at his profile as he talked. He was frowning, and that wasn't a usual expression on his face. Talking about this was obviously painful for him.

"I'm sorry. I didn't mean to make you relive an obviously bad time in your life." She was looking at him, and then touched his face.

He smiled a little. "It's fine. I just hadn't thought about all that in a long time."

"Do you ever hear from her?"

"Nope, not in years."

Carlton pulled into his garage. They went inside and spent the next couple of hours in bed.

Chapter 26

Perri and Sharon were walking to the coffee shop on Friday afternoon, and Sharon confided in Perri that she and her boyfriend were discussing marriage. "I'm ready," Sharon told Perri. As they talked, Perri listened intently. Sharon had been widowed years longer, but Perri could not relate on any level to her words. When Perri tuned back in to Sharon, she heard her say, "…and I'm ready to have sex on the regular too!" They both laughed, but Perri didn't comment.

Lauren and Langston went to a friend's birthday party, and Carlton was still out of town on a recruiting trip. Perri was home alone, on a Saturday which rarely occurred. Sitting in her favorite spot on the balcony, with a cup of coffee and a magazine, but not reading, Perri thought about the conversation with Sharon. There was no way she could or would get married again. Lawrence was her one and only husband, the father of her children, and he loved her and nobody else could love her like that. She liked Carlton a lot. They enjoyed each other's company. They had amazing sex "on the regular," but marriage was out of the question. Taking a sip of coffee, Perri silently wished Sharon well.

"What is he doing here?" Perri thought to herself when she pulled into the driveway, coming back from Sunday brunch and running a few errands to see Carlton's SUV. She again thought of the conversation with Sharon. He came to meet her when he heard the garage door go up.

"Hey sweetie." He kissed her forehead.

"Hi," Perri responded rather dryly, looking past Carlton to see who else was there. She could hear Lauren and Langston coming down the stairs, arguing as usual. Langston pushed Lauren out of the way when he saw Perri.

"Maaa!" he said, putting his arms around her and kissing her three times on the cheek, then hugged her tightly.

"I can't breathe." They all laughed.

"Ma, he wants money."

"Money for what?"

"Uncle C is taking us to the baseball game."

Perri looked at Carlton, who just winked at her. Lauren explained the plan. Carlton was taking the two of them, Brandon and one of Lauren's friends. The friends' dad was going too, and they were riding back with him. Perfect plan, except nobody ran it by her.

"When did you two start making decisions without my input?" She stepped out of her shoes and looked from one to the other.

"We talked to Uncle C about it," Lauren answered.

Perri wanted to scream. They were all moving too fast and assuming too much. But she couldn't say anything to the kids, but would deal with Carlton. "For future reference, I need to know what you're doing."

"Okay, Ma!" Langston said.

"Do you want to ride downtown or relax until I get back?" Carlton asked.

Perri wanted to tell him to go and not come back, but they needed to talk. Rather, she needed to talk, and he needed to listen. "I'll ride." Perri changed her clothes, and they left.

On the ride back to Ballantyne, Perri told Carlton he overstepped his boundaries by making plans for her children without her input.

"Babe, they called me. I would never create a situation. They love you, but they miss their dad. They miss having another player on the team. I'm not their dad, they know that and I know it, but I'm honored they want me in their lives." Perri was listening, but was stuck at "they miss their dad. When they called, I didn't think you would object. I apologize."

She didn't know what to say.

Going into the house, Perri and Carlton bumped into each other, and her hips brushed his crotch.

"You did that on purpose," he said, smiling at her.

"I did not."

"I know you want me, girl." He grabbed her and kissed her. His hands traveled up and down her back and butt. He picked her up and carried her to the stairs. "Lead the way. I want you in your bed."

Perri turned around on one foot. "Are you crazy? First you play daddy to my children and now you want to have sex in my husband's bed! No Carlton, no way!"

He was looking at her, but he couldn't believe her screaming at him. They stood and just looked at each other. Then Perri continued in a "loud whisper."

"This is my husband's house; the bed I sleep in is his bed. Lauren and Langston are his children, and I am his wife. You do not have any rights to his children, or to have sex in his bed!"

Carlton laughed. Perri squinted at him.

"Lawrence *is* dead. Your husband *is* dead. Lauren and Langston's father *is* dead. This is your house now. You are his widow, Perri." His voice was even, and at a normal volume. "You had no thought of Lawrence in my bed, on my sofa, or in my shower." No response. "Or did you? So, you were thinking about him when you were laying on top of me. You were seeing him when you were looking into my eyes." Perri still hadn't said anything, but tears were streaming down her face. There was another long period of silence.

Carlton wanted Perri to deny his accusations; to put her arms around him. He wanted her to wrap her legs around him like the last time they were together. But she didn't. He walked away, but stopped at the door. He wanted her to call him to come back, but didn't. "Damn it, Perri!" Still no response from her. He walked out, but sat in his car for a few minutes, still wanting her to fix this. One last look at the door. He backed out of the driveway.

Perri ran upstairs and watched as he drove away. She went to her room, undressed, got in bed, pulled the covers over her head and cried.

Chapter 27

Three weeks passed, and Carlton and Perri did not communicate. He had called her when he got home the night of her meltdown. She didn't answer. He wasn't sure how he felt. He wanted to be angry with her. He was hurt, but not hurt, to the point of giving up on the relationship. But, as time passed, he was becoming numb to the whole situation. He was glad his workload increased. He was back in Pensacola for a week and this week; he was heading to Annapolis. He considered asking to be transferred. The only reason he came to Charlotte in the first place was to be close to Perri. He missed Langston and Lauren, too. They knew he was traveling, so his absence didn't seem so odd to them.

The Monday following the incident with Carlton, Perri called in sick and stayed in bed all day telling Langston and Lauren she had a virus and Tuesday worked from home. Perri missed Carlton, but he needed to understand. Lawrence was her husband, and nobody was making love in that bed but the two of them. If Carlton didn't get that, oh well. It would be good to talk to him. For him to make her laugh. She wanted to kiss him and feel his arms around her; to have him inside her. "But not here. Not in this house, or this room, or this bed."

Perri and Lacey hadn't talked in a couple of days, but Lauren told Lacey her mom was sick. Lacey called to check on her sister, because the "sick" story wasn't working for her. Perri didn't front. She told Lacey the whole truth.

"You need professional help," Lacey told her.

"You don't understand, Lacey," Perri responded to her sister.

"I understand Lawrence is dead. I understand he's not coming back. I understand this man wants to be with you and you're letting your dead husband stand in the way."

"I still love Lawrence!"

"You love Lawrence's memory, and nobody is trying to take that away from you. Consider this; if Lawrence had felt the way you feel after his first wife passed, he would not have married you!" Perri's heart sank. That was her "aha moment."

"I need to fix this, but I don't know how."

"Start by calling to apologize," Lacey told her. "He'll understand. Be honest."

"I'm not sure what the truth is except Lawrence and I were together for over twenty years, and I didn't know how to move on."

"Tell him that, Perri. You don't have to have a script. You'll know what to say when the time comes."

Perri finished her work, cooked dinner, and talked with the kids for a while. When they went to their neutral corners for the evening, she went to her room and called Carlton. The call went straight to voice mail. "Hi Carlton. This is Perri. Please call me." Two hours later, he had not called.

A storm over Washington, D.C. kept Carlton's flight from landing on time. They had circled for almost an hour. When they finally landed and could use the phone, he called the driver to alert him they were on the ground. He saw he had messages, but thought they were in conjunction with the meeting he was headed to. Hours later, when he was settled in his hotel room, he noticed the missed call and voice mail message from Perri. He listened to the message twice to see if he could tell anything from her voice. Langston, Brandon, Trey and Lauren knew he was out of town, so if there was an emergency, he would hear from one of them. As far as they knew, his schedule was why he hadn't been around. He decided he didn't want to talk to Perri, so he didn't return the call. In the middle of the night, he decided he would answer if she called back.

The seasons were changing. It was that time of year when the mornings were cool, and the afternoons were warm. Perri sat outside her bedroom on the balcony having a cup of coffee. She was genuinely sad. Carlton had not called back. It had been two days. The chill made her pull the sweater around her shoulders. Was the shiver from the weather or her mood?

Perri worked remotely that day. The morning went by relatively quickly; there was a good bit of work to do. Shortly after noon, Sharon called to ask one work related question and then told Perri she and her boyfriend shopped for rings over the weekend. When they hung up, Perri went downstairs to fix herself lunch. In the midst, she absentmindedly picked up her phone and called Carlton.

Carlton was walking through the courtyard on the US Naval Academy campus. He was holding the phone in his hand. He looked at the screen when it rang. "Hello."

"Hey."

"Is everything okay, Perri?"

"Yes. I just need to talk to you for a minute."

"For what?" He was emotionless.

"I want to apologize."

"Now is not a good time. I'm in Annapolis and very busy."

"When will you be back?"

"I'll let you know when I get back." Carlton hung up.

The minute he hit the button and disconnected the call, he stopped in his tracks. He had intentionally hurt her feelings. That move was so out of character for him, and he knew she knew it. But he would not call her until he got back. "May not at all."

Langston and Brandon were trying out for fall baseball. Deuce had asked Carlton to help them get ready. They were scheduled to meet on Saturday morning. Carlton forgot about it until he got the text from Brandon. He hadn't called Perri, but chances were she would bring Langston to work out. He would just have to face the music.

Carlton was already at the field when Deuce pulled up with Langston and Brandon. He was disappointed that Perri didn't come. He and Deuce talked for a few minutes, and then he got down to business with the boys. When they were almost finished, Carlton asked if he needed to take them home.

"Naw, Ms. Perri will be here," Brandon answered.

"And guess who's driving?" Langston said.

Before Carlton said anything, Brandon responded to Langston's comment. "Man, that's good. Now we can get a ride 'cause you know Trey is leaving. We just need to talk your mom into getting Laur a car!"

"My mama is so scared and really don't even want her to drive. If my daddy was still here, she would be driving, and have a car! Uncle C, can you talk to my mama about it?" Langston was serious.

"Yeah, I'll talk to her."

"Yes!" Brandon said, pumping his fist and running to the outfield.

They worked out for about thirty more minutes, and then Carlton told them to run a couple of laps. As he pretended to watch, he considered what he would say to Perri. Not about Lauren, but about her call and not calling her back.

Before he could give it any considerable thought, he saw Perri's car coming. Sure enough, Lauren was driving. She got out of the car, but Perri stayed put. Looking at Carlton, he barely glanced her way. He really wanted to run over and grab her, but he couldn't. She'd told him it had to be on her terms. He wasn't sure Perri knew what she wanted, and he just wasn't willing to take the trip to nowhere with her.

Lauren was telling Carlton about driving, and the boys walked over to join the conversation. Perri was still sitting in the car and after a few minutes, got out and stood beside it. The engine was still running. Still looking at Carlton, she asked Lauren, "are you going with Uncle C or me?" The question caught Carlton off guard.

"Ma, Uncle C wants to talk to you," Langston said.

"I'll talk to him later." Perri was still looking at him, but not directing her comments to him.

"Uncle C, if you let Lauren drive home, then you can talk to her," Brandon said.

Carlton didn't like the way this was going, and he didn't like the tension or doing this in front of the kids. He smiled. "Okay Lauren, you can drive!"

Perri got in the car and drove off. Carlton was pissed. He was definitely going to talk to her when he got to her house.

Perri wasn't there when he and the kids arrived, and Carlton couldn't believe it. She was acting out at a major level. He didn't stick around. He told the kids he would see them later. He called her, but no answer.

Hearing the music startled him. He didn't think he left it playing. Then he noticed the flower petals, and then tuned back to the music. It was Luther. The petals went up the stairs. *"What the hell?"* He thought. He walked up slowly, one step at a time. When he reached the landing at the top, he could smell her perfume. He followed the path of flowers strewn down the hall into his bedroom. Perri was standing beside the bed in a purple negligee that he could see straight through. There was a bottle of champagne chilling in the bucket she brought from downstairs, and strawberries on a tray at the foot of the bed. He could see her nipples through the silk. He felt the erection, but he couldn't give in.

"How the hell did you get in here?" When he said it, he remembered he had given her the alarm code and told her where the extra key was.

"I used the key."

"So, seduction is your way of apologizing?" Carlton frowned.

She walked to him and stopped directly in front of him. "I'm sorry. I really am. I thought about everything you said, and you are right. Lawrence is my past."

He didn't comment.

"That marriage is my past. Being with him in that house is my past. I *am* his widow, not his wife." Her voice cracked; she cleared her throat. "And no, I wasn't thinking of him when I was with you."

As if she timed it just right, Luther singing "So Amazing" played. "That's our song Carlton." Perri put her arms around him, and after a few seconds, he gave in and danced with her. When the song ended, she took a flute from the side of the bucket and poured him a glass of champagne, then poured one for herself and held her glass to his lips. He took just a sip. Perri was nervous. Carlton still was quiet. He didn't sing while they were dancing, like he usually did. Perri wasn't sure her plan was working. She wanted him to accept her apology, make love to her, and then they could talk about the future.

"What is all this, Perri? What does this mean?"

"It means you are my future."

He could see the hand holding the glass shake. He wanted to push her down on the bed and crawl all over her, but he had to maintain his composure. "So you're saying if I asked you to marry me, you would say yes?" Carlton's voice was a little firmer than he intended.

Perri took a deep breath. "I'm saying if you asked me to marry you, I would seriously think about it." He started to say something, but she cut him off. "Considering I have two children and their well-being, to add to the discussion."

"Why didn't you make all this happen at your house? I told you I want you in your bed."

"Because of the aforementioned children!" They both laughed.

Perri sat at the foot of the bed, reached for his waistband, and pulled him to her. He finished the champagne in his glass in one gulp and then pulled his shirt over his head. She kissed his stomach, then drew circles with her tongue. Carlton knew he needed to make her stop, get dressed, and go home. He wouldn't believe her until they were together at her house.

They made love for a long time and finished the bottle of champagne. They finally got up and got dressed. Carlton was sitting downstairs on the sofa when she came down.

"We need to talk. Perri, I'm serious…about you, about us, and about knowing you're all in."

"Please give me credit for trying. You have no idea how this feels from my side."

"That's true. But I will not live in his shadow. You need to decide if you want *me*."

"I want *you*."

"Make me believe it… out of the bed."

Perri rested her elbows on her thighs and covered her face with both hands. She was tired; physically and emotionally.

"Carlton, Lawrence's memory isn't going to suddenly disappear because I have sex with you in the bed I had sex with him in. Every time I look at Lauren, I see him. Langston's mannerisms are the same as his. The one thing that drove me nuts about Lawrence, he would make decisions he determined were in my best interest, without talking to me about it. Langston does the same thing! He even does it to Lauren. My house is paid for; my children's education is paid for. Lauren's wedding is even paid for. I don't have to worry about money for the rest of my life. All of that is because of Lawrence. You can accept that and learn to live with it or not. I can only tell you the truth. I can't make you believe it." Neither of them said anything, but they didn't take their eyes off each other. Finally, Perri picked up her purse and walked out.

Carlton walked onto the balcony, but didn't see her. Then he remembered the car was hidden so he would be surprised. He didn't know where she parked. He stood there for a few minutes, thinking about what she did. Was he making an unreasonable demand? What difference did it make that they hadn't been in her bed? Walking back inside, he laid on the sofa, and dozed off thinking about her.

Carlton didn't mean to sleep for so long. He needed to do something. But what? As if the music sent an answer, Carlton realized Luther was singing Superstar in the background. He picked up the remote and paused the music. He knew the playlist by heart. The next song was "The Power of Love" and then their song.

Chapter 28

Carlton drove to Perri's house, only to find Langston there who told him she and Lauren went to a movie. He was meeting some friends at the mall, but told Carlton he was welcome to wait.

Alone in her home for over an hour, it occurred to Carlton he hadn't been upstairs. He took advantage of the opportunity. He looked in Langston's bedroom and then in Lauren's room. Nothing out of the ordinary. Custom made window treatments and comforter sets, built-in bookshelves and desks, abstract art, lots of pictures, dolls and sports equipment.

The extra bedroom was modest. Unlike most people's "extra room" it wasn't the "catch all." He had seen the other extra bedroom downstairs, and it was also neat. The bonus room had exercise equipment, a large television with two gaming consoles, a three story doll house, and remote control cars and a race track. Deuce told Carlton that Perri and the children lived a "charmed life" and he was right. What he noticed throughout the house were the many pictures of Lawrence.

Looking at his watch, Carlton walked down the hall. He stopped at the master bedroom door. He took a breath and stepped inside. The walls were a creamy off white, the bed ensemble, drapes, and even the throw pillows on the love seat were jewel tones. He liked the wide stripes. From where he stood, he could see several pictures. Walking about three feet into the room, he saw a picture of Lawrence; the same one that was on his obituary. He chuckled to himself. "I wonder how the Big Guy would feel watching me make love to his wife."

He stood there. He wanted to feel something, anger, jealousy, desire. But he didn't. Perri was right. It was him. He made all this up in his own head. The situation was what it was. He could keep badgering her and lose her or let it go and work it out.

He couldn't leave. He didn't know the alarm code, and he didn't have a key to lock the door. He also didn't know if Langston told Perri he was there. So, he turned on the television and sat on the sofa. A college football game kept his attention.

"Is that Uncle C's truck?" Lauren asked as they turned into the driveway and slowly pulled into the garage. Perri was puzzled. Langston was supposed to be gone. So, it didn't add up that Carlton would be there. She was tired; done with the back and forth and didn't necessarily want to see him.

When they were finally alone, Perri asked Carlton why he was there. He explained, told her she was right, apologized and admitted he had looked around upstairs and gone into her bedroom.

Perri folded her arms and glared at him. "You had no right…"

Carlton interrupted her. "I didn't have any right. I agree with you. I'm not sure what I thought I was going to accomplish by being in there, but it didn't happen, whatever it was."

Perri didn't understand, but just wanted to move on. He asked her if they could sit outside. She agreed.

Perri was quiet, only answering Carlton's questions. He knew things were critical for them. He told her he had to leave town the first of the week, and would be gone for ten days, and wanted things settled between them before he left. "I will be in Pensacola for a few of those days, if you and the kids want to come down."

She shrugged, "I'll see."

Reaching in his pocket, he took out his phone, tapped the music app and turned up the volume. It was their song. He took her by the hand, pulled her into his arms, and they danced. He could feel her body relax. As the song was ending, he kneeled in front of her. He reached for both hands. He looked directly into her eyes.

She said "yes."

Chapter 29

Lauren slammed the car door. Today was the first day she hated having a driver's license. Her mother had given her a list of errands. A friend had accompanied her on the tasks.

"It's all just too much!"

Her friend laughed. "I think it's kinda sweet!"

Lauren rolled her eyes. Her phone rang. It was her mom… again.

Everything was happening at once. Trey's graduation was Friday, and Perri and Carlton were getting married on Sunday.

Perri was at home waiting on the store to deliver the new bedroom furniture she and Carlton ordered. The decorator came the day before to hang the new drapes and brought the comforter set. Lauren just didn't get why some of that couldn't be done when they got back from their honeymoon. Brandon, Langston, Deuce, and Carlton had moved his furniture the previous weekend. He was out-of-town Monday through Thursday. Trey was going to the beach to meet his friends after the wedding, and Perri and Carlton were leaving Monday to go to Paris for ten days. Langston and Lauren were going back to Pensacola with their grandparents.

Deuce and Bridget were surprised when they found out Perri and Carlton were engaged. Bridget's comment was "at least he's in her age range." Deuce was happy for them in theory, but for obvious reasons, his emotions were all over the place. The kids all took it in stride. Carlton had talked Perri into getting Lauren a car, and that was good for her, Langston, and Brandon. He also talked Perri into letting her go to an after-prom party.

Langston and Lauren talked about the situation among themselves. They liked the idea of Perri and Carlton being married. He was great to them, and it was obvious he adored their mother. They discussed what they thought their dad would think about Perri remarrying and decided he would be fine with it. The ongoing discussion was what to call Carlton. Langston brought it up.

"Uncle C won't work anymore!"

"You're right. What do you think we should call him? Mommy said it's totally up to us."

After a few days and discussing several options, they decided on "Pop."

"So do we tell him, or just start calling him that?" Lauren asked Langston.

"I'ma just start calling him that." Lauren was fine with it.

Perri and Carlton agreed that there would be no wedding talk on Friday at the graduation festivities. It was Trey's day, and it had to be all about him. It was a great time of celebrating for him. Perri had a brief thought of Lawrence.

At noon on Sunday, Carlton and Perri were married. Lauren was Perri's maid of honor, and Langston gave the bride away. Deuce was the best man. It was a beautiful ceremony and reception. The guests were family and a few friends, including Perri's work friend Sharon and her fiancée. The bride and groom danced to their song.

Lacey couldn't imagine what was wrong when her phone displayed Perri's name. She and Carlton were in Paris.

"Hey sis, what's up?"

Perri was whispering, "It just occurred to me I missed my period!"

"Relax, it's probably just stress. You had a lot going on in the last couple of months," Lacey told her.

"No, Lace, that's not it. I think I'm pregnant."

www.ingramcontent.com/pod-product-compliance
Lightning Source LLC
Chambersburg PA
CBHW060859140726

47996CB00001B/43